[spooks]

Confidential

[Acknowledgements]

At Kudos: Stephen Garrett, Jane Featherstone, Simon Crawford Collins, David Wolstencroft, Bharat Nalluri, Jennie Muskett, Nicola Walker, Hugh Simon, Karen Wilson, Faith Penhale, Rory Aitken, Maggi Townley and Lucy Lawson.

At the BBC: Karen Sandford, Jamie Cason, Sue Fell, Caite Petts, Gabriel Glaison, Kate Wheeler and Jac Rayner.

And thanks to everyone who wrote in to the BBCi 'Spooks Expert' column. You guys really kept me on my toes!

All at Contender, but especially Ian Atkins (who provided many hours of invaluable interview material), Michéle Brown, Sasha Morton, Lee Binding, Lydia Drukarz and Wendy Hollas.

The usual suspects – Paul Cornell, Ian Edmond, Gary Gillatt, Rebecca Levene, Steven Moffat, Richie Moosbally, Gary Russell, Rob Stradling, Keith Topping, Gary Wah and Mark Wright. Special mention, as always, for Alexander Graham Bell and Tim Berners Lee, without whom pizza delivery and archive research would be much more difficult.

The h2g2 team – Natalie Johnson, Anna McGovern, Abi Sawyer, Sam Semple, Ashley Stewart-Noble, Mina Ward and Maggy Whitehouse. Thanks also to members of the h2g2 Community, especially Frankie Roberto. Special thanks to Richard Creasey – sir, you're an inspiration.

As ever, thanks and appreciation to Mrs Jones and Miss Riley of St Andrew's Junior School, Mr Cullen and Mr Young of St Edward's College, Mr Trevor Stent and Mr Sandy Gavin of Halewood Comprehensive, and Dr Jackie Miller and Mrs Petula Sawkins of LIHE – thanks for the life lessons and the book recommendations.

I would not have got to the end of this project without the help and encouragement of Paul Condon.

[Contents]

Briefing

MI5 – a world of secrets, intrigue and treachery. A world where you can go anywhere, be whoever you want to be and hopefully save your country from its enemies in the process. But as well as the excitement and danger of working undercover, there's also the routine, the office politics and the general air of insecurity and paranoia that comes with any day job. To us, they're spies, living in the underworld of the British establishment. Among themselves, they're known simply as 'spooks'.

[**spooks**] is, of course, a fictional drama with fictional characters in made-up situations. For the fiction to succeed, though, it must be shrouded in fact. Unlike in *James Bond* or *The Avengers*, this is a world where nobody knows your name. A day in the life of [**spooks**] doesn't begin and end with Martinis, girls and guns. There are no secret bases in hollowed-out volcanoes, no rocket-packs or missile-launching cars and definitely no chance that you can walk away from the day's business physically or mentally unaffected. Here, reality is the key: we get to see the backroom boys and girls who make Bond look good; the hard-working technical crew; the runners who act on MI5's behalf to liaise with members of the public in delicate situations; the clerical staff who work on all the tiny details that make up the bigger picture; and, unfortunately, the petty bureaucrats whose job it is to… well, no-one's quite sure, but so long as they stay out of the way no-one seems to mind them too much.

Yes, this is the less fantastical end of espionage. If you ever found yourself scoffing at the sight of a British intelligence agent blow-drying a cat or inspecting a fake dog turd in the park, then the real-life events that inspired that little event are guaranteed to be ten times weirder. This is not a lifestyle for the squeamish, the lazy, the selfish or the easily distracted. Sometimes your life, or the life of anyone around you, can be put in danger because you miss one tiny detail, whether that be a credit card slip or a clumsily improvised lie that will come back to haunt you.

It's a life that's hard to get into, and even harder to walk away from. That's where I come in. I'm your man on the inside.

The sheer speed of information imparted during one hour-long episode of

[spooks] is such that it's easy to get lost in the drama and miss vital information. The purpose of this book, therefore, is two-fold. First, it serves as a handy aide-memoir for the TV series, with full cast lists, plot synopses and detailed information on the major players, their loved ones, their contacts and their targets. Second, it points to some of the true-life events that helped carve the fictional world of **[spooks]** . Most of the other sections should be self-evident. But elements of the Mission Guide might need a little further explanation:

E p i s o d e

Within the production team, each episode is simply known by its episode number, but to make it easier to distinguish between seasons I've given each episode a three-digit code that tells us which series it's from and its position in that series. So, for example, the second episode of series two is listed as '202'. Where I've described something as 'the second episode', however, this refers to the second episode overall, i.e. episode 102.

W r i t e r / D i r e c t o r / C a s t

The episodes as broadcast did not have cast lists or credits, so here's your full run-down of who played who and who did what (full production credits for each series appear at the end of this book). The cast lists also include, where possible, actors who appeared in scenes that were later deleted for timing purposes.

W h o ' s W h o

It can be quite distracting when you're watching something on TV and an actor or actress appears who you think you recognise but can't quite place. To avoid that happening in **[spooks]** – where every second reveals a piece of vital information – this section provides a few pointers on the career history of the actors involved.

Case Report

The events as they unfold in each episode. As these reports are 'taken directly from MI5 documents', they are, of course, written from MI5's point of view, so some of the reports are very much 'the official story', regardless of the truth as insiders might know it to be.

Security File

Information on key figures and/or targets in each operation. As with the case reports, it should be noted that most of these might well present an official version of events, though it's usually easy to spot these, as the cover story will have been sanctioned 'from above'.

Previous Missions

Should an officer's past history in the Services become relevant to a current operation, we make a note of it here.

Disinformation

MI5 officers often rely on code words or other subterfuge to hide their tracks. Here we look at some of the more creative elements of the Security Service.

Identity Check

Sometimes officers can have four or five different identities active at the same time. Often, the name they are known as in their private life is as fictional as one they might create for a specific operation. This section keeps a close eye on Tom Quinn's team as we see how their private and official lives regularly clash.

Personnel Report Updates

Balancing a personal life with MI5 business can be a tricky juggling act. Many MI5 employees prefer not to reveal their true occupation to even their closest loved ones, while some have chosen to only fraternise with people already part of the Security Service. Much can be gleaned about an officer's state of mind from the effects the job has on his or her private life, so here we spy on the spies to see what they get up to after hours.

Gadgets

Here we can keep a check on the latest in technological trickery, courtesy of Malcolm, Colin and the rest of the backroom boys of Section B.

Quote/Unquote

Some choice cuts from audio surveillance… or just some of the best bits of dialogue.

Notes

Any other observations on the episode – including cultural references and behind-the-scenes information relevant to the episode – are noted here.

Missing in Action

As with every other show, there are instances where scenes are scripted or even filmed that are eventually cut to make the episodes fit their timeslot. In truth, [spooks] is very efficient, with most of what's planned ending up on screen, but here are some of the more interesting casualties of editing.

Expert Witnesses

First-hand evidence from the people in the know.

Most chapters end with a brief essay on a subject, often pertinent, sometimes tangential, to the episode under discussion, either in the form of potted history lessons, info-dumps, behind-the-scenes information or personal responses to the world of [spooks]. With some of these, it's worth pointing out that while the events of [spooks] are always fictional, it's, er, 'spooky' how so many of them reflect – and in some cases predict – the news around us.

Who's Who and What's What?

Part 1
MI5

MI5 – also known as the Security Service or, within the Service itself, simply 'Five' – is the UK's security intelligence agency. It's the role of MI5 to protect national security and 'economic well-being' from terrorism, and to support the law enforcement agencies in detecting and preventing serious crime. They do this by collecting intelligence and disseminating it to the relevant groups, such as the police or armed forces or other intelligence services such as the CIA. They investigate and assess all potential threats to the UK's interests that originate from within the British Isles (including the Channel Islands and the Republic of Ireland) and work alongside others to counter them. MI5 works hand in hand with MI6 – also known as 'the sister service', or 'Six' – who are responsible for investigating threats to national security that originate from overseas.

[Origins of MI5]

Although many attribute the role of the first official spy to Francis Walsingham, who had been the head of the Secret Service under Elizabeth I, the origins of MI5 stem from comparatively more recent times.

The department that would become the Security Service dates back to 1909, when the Committee of Imperial Defence first warned of the dangers of German espionage in British ports. On their recommendation, the 'Secret Service Bureau' was established by two men – Captain Vernon Kell of the South Staffordshire Regiment and Captain Mansfield Cumming of the Royal Navy. They divided their responsibilities up on broadly the same lines that Five and Six operate today, with Kell handling counter-espionage within the British Isles and Cumming looking after overseas threats. The men became known as 'K' and 'C' respectively. Incidentally,

'M' – known to almost everyone as James Bond's boss – did actually exist, though he was never the head of the Service. He was William Melville, a former Metropolitan police superintendent who, as Kell's foot-soldier, raced around the British Isles investigating reports of German spy activity; in effect, he was Kell's first super-spy.

In its first few years of existence, more than 30 spies were uncovered and arrested by the Secret Service Bureau – this despite the fact that, at the time, the Bureau had just ten members of staff, including Kell himself. The Bureau was rapidly mobilised as a branch of the War Office and in January 1916 it became part of a new Directorate of Military Intelligence and was renamed MI5 – with Cumming's team naturally becoming MI6. Military Intelligence already had divisions numbering M1–M4 that were responsible for code breaking, aerial reconnaissance and handling intelligence from Scandinavia and Eastern Europe, tasks which would eventually be dealt with by GCHQ and MI6 (issues such as propaganda, debriefing prisoners of war, telegraph and postal censorship, signals intelligence and weapons analysis were the responsibility of further MI departments). During World War II, MI5's remit was extended to include the co-ordination of government policy concerning 'aliens' and vetting of employees in sensitive areas (which at this time would have included munitions factories) as well as running counter-espionage measures throughout the Empire. By the end of the war, MI5 staff numbers had increased to 850.

During the post-war period, the main threat to security was from Soviet-run spies, and it's this period that was the inspiration for much of the work of John Le Carré. Old-school loyalties were tested by the traitors within the Service: the discovery that senior officers Anthony Blunt, Kim Philby, Guy Burgess and Donald MacLean had all at one time or another been passing secrets to the Soviets did much damage to the stability of the Intelligence Services, leaving behind a trail of paranoia and suspicion as MI5 began to investigate itself as often as outsiders (leading to accusations – later officially disproved – that Sir Roger Hollis, a former Director-General of MI5, had himself been a 'mole').

[Changes]

By the late 1970s, MI5's attention was redirected from counter-espionage work to international and Irish counter-terrorism. The Service's counter-terrorist effort had begun in the late 1960s in response to the growing problem of Palestinian terrorism. During the 1970s and 1980s, the Service also became a key player in combating terrorism alongside other Western security and intelligence services, including the CIA. The Service changed focus significantly with the end of the Cold War in the 1990s and its resources reflected the diminished threat posed by 'subversion'. Additionally, technology became one of their greatest assets, with the increase in CCTV and traffic cameras across the country proving useful in identifying terrorist activity.

No longer the 'private gentleman's club' that many have always imagined it to be, the Security Service has seen many changes in recent years. Not least of these is the greater range of roles open to women, assisted in no small part by the appointment in 1991 of Stella Rimington as the first female Director-General of MI5 (and, incidentally, the first one whose identity was revealed to the public, in a drive for the 'secretive' Security Service to appear more open about its policies). Changes to the Service's role also took place: 1992 saw responsibility for leading the fight against Irish Republican terrorism pass from the Metropolitan Police to the Security Service, and in 1996, the Service's statutory remit was extended further to include supporting the law enforcement agencies in the work against serious crime.

[The Present]

Intelligence services worldwide have been affected irreparably by the Islamic extremist attacks on the World Trade Center and the Pentagon in 2001, the Bali bombing in 2002 and the spate of suicide bombings during the early part of 2003. The fact that this new breed of terrorist seems unconcerned by having to build an escape route into their plan is worrying: it means that threats that previously seemed unlikely now need to be treated as possible, even probable. And tough decisions need to be made. As Stella Rimington notes in her memoirs, before 9–11 it would have been unthinkable of the Security Service to consider mosques legitimate targets, yet now that is exactly what they must do. Yet they also have to strive to maintain notions of civil liberty without risking the country's safety. At the time of writing, the British government is considering a review of the period a terrorist suspect can be legally detained before they need to be released – the proposal is to increase this period to 14 days instead of the current seven. While this might have received strong opposition two years ago, even the most liberal of people can see the need for such questions to be asked.

One significant and positive outcome of 9–11 is that many countries have joined Britain and America in their condemnation of Al Qaeda. Pakistan, Iran and Russia have all expressed their abhorrence over the methods of Osama Bin Laden and his followers, countries that had previously been uncooperative at best with the West yet are now beginning to share their intelligence to prevent a repetition of the carnage of the last couple of years – and, it has to be said, in the hope that they might be able to distance themselves from any connections to those countries deemed central to what George Bush has dubbed the 'Axis of Evil'. The Cold War may be over, but the work of the Security Service remains as important as ever.

Part 2
Origins of
[spooks]

Production company Kudos already had a strong reputation for being innovative on screens both big and small before [spooks] came along. Led by CEO Stephen Garrett and Jane Featherstone, head of drama, the company have been responsible for some of the most challenging entertainment on British television and cinema in recent years. Their satirical *Come On Down and Out* used a controversial game-show format to address the issues of homelessness from a new angle, and their work with impressionist Rory Bremner on the first series of *Rory Bremner... Who Else?* was rewarded with a BAFTA.

Kudos released their first feature film, *Among Giants*, in 1997. It was written by Simon Beaufoy (*The Full Monty*), starred Pete Postlethwaite and Rachel Griffiths, and was directed by Sam Miller. Kudos's second feature film, *Pure* (dir. Gillies MacKinnon, 2002), won the LVT/Manfred Salzgeber Award at the Berlin Film Festival. *By Grand Central Station I Sat Down and Wept* is pencilled for an autumn 2003 shoot, with Mike Figgis in the director's chair.

The International Emmy Award-winning *The Magician's House* was broadcast on BBC1 in 1999, based on William Corlett's classic children's books and starring Ian Richardson and Siân Phillips, with the voices of Stephen Fry and Jennifer Saunders. And in 2000, Kudos brought the highly acclaimed *Psychos* to the screen, a six-part drama for Channel 4 set in a hospital psychiatric wing and written by a first-time writer, David Wolstencroft.

[**spooks**] came about thanks to a number of factors. It began with Stephen Garrett, who was scouting for ideas to capitalise on the company's success with *Psychos*. Despairing of the trend in modern television to set everything in the same 'precinct' environment (mainly police stations and hospitals), Stephen set about trying to find a 'precinct' that was untapped, or at least a concept that hadn't been done to death on television in the last decade or so. It was while browsing through the shelves of a bookshop that he began to pay close attention to the section devoted to John Le Carré's works. Espionage was not a concept that had really been explored much on television in the last 20 years – certainly not since the adaptations of Le Carré's *Tinker, Tailor, Soldier, Spy* and *Smiley's People* in the early 1980s. The more Stephen thought about it, the more a modern approach to the Security Services appealed to him. Of particular interest was the idea of looking at people who lie professionally, something that other shows naturally didn't do; unlike, say, a policeman or a medic, a spy cannot share anecdotes about their day job with loved ones. Their life in effect becomes a series of lies.

After commissioning some initial research into the world of spies in general and MI5 in particular, Stephen approached David Wolstencroft to see if it was an idea he thought he could develop into a series. Entirely coincidentally, David had been developing a similar idea with a view to perhaps selling it as a feature film. Having done a little research into MI5 and MI6, he'd been thinking about a story that stepped away from the usual James Bond/glamorous type and instead featured ordinary people who just happened to be spies. That both Stephen and David were thinking along the same lines from the beginning was taken as a good sign, and a proposal was put together. The proposed show was, it has to be said, very different from the one [**spooks**] eventually became, and though it was offered to a number of British broadcasters, including the BBC, almost every single one of them had a major problem with the idea of a spy show: post-Cold War, with Russia now Britain's ally, they couldn't see who the enemy might be.

[Green Light]

When Jane Featherstone joined Kudos as the series producer, the responsibility fell to her to drive the show and shape its general direction and tone, and her arrival coincided with a fortuitous series of reshuffles within the ranks of some of the broadcasters who had already passed on the show. Kudos now approached Gareth Neame, the new commissioning editor at BBC1, who responded very positively to the idea. This resulted in Kudos receiving a very different brief to their original pitch. Gareth suggested that the series should become more of an intelligent action drama that could still deal with big spy issues. Additionally, one of the options presenting itself was using [spooks] as part of the programming for Saturday nights, traditionally one of the most important nights of the TV week. In recent years, though, research had shown that the home video rental market was working to erode the weekend viewing figures. According to Stephen Garrett, one of the first briefs Kudos received from the controller of BBC1, Lorraine Heggessey, was to 'make television that would stop people renting videos'.

Simon Crawford Collins had by this point been offered the role of producer on the show. Simon had previously worked with Jane on Sex 'n' Death, and both Jane and Stephen were keen to have him on board, though they accepted that as it might take some time before they were officially commissioned, Simon might be forced to accept another project instead. Luckily, the BBC gave the series the green light a couple of days before Simon was due to agree to take on something else. Only then did he learn how 'economical with the truth' Stephen had been as to the certainty that the project would actually go ahead.

Throughout the recruitment process for other key figures in the production, the aim was to find people who understood the concept and could bring something new and edgy to the mix. To work alongside David Wolstencroft (who was still involved in every aspect of the show's development), a number of other writers were interviewed to make up the rest of the writing team. It was with some surprise that the team received a suggestion from an agent to consider Howard Brenton. Howard's reputation as a radical, provocative playwright with a considerable heritage initially made him rather an off-the-wall choice, but his experience and understanding of the material made him an invaluable member of the team.

Simon and Jane also interviewed a series of directors over a couple of months before meeting Bharat Nalluri. He was the first director they met who was able to really capture the pace and essence of speed conveyed in David Wolstencroft's scripts. One privilege of being the first director was that Bharat was responsible for establishing the look of the show as well as working with the producers in casting the lead actors, a process that by all accounts went very smoothly – the team managed to get everyone they'd wanted.

[Music]

The theme and incidental music heard throughout the series was composed by Jennie Muskett, who had previously scored a number of documentaries, including *Baka: The People of the Rainforest* (1987), *The Great White Shark, Lonely Lord of the Sea* (1991) and *The Secret of Life on Earth* (1993), as well as the films *B. Monkey* (dir. Michael Radford, 1998) and *Boxed* (dir. Marion Comer, 2002). *See the interview with Jennie after the chapter on episode 208.*

[Missing Credits]

When David submitted the first script to the producers, he replaced his name on the front page with 'anonymous', simply as a joke to play with the idea of the characters' anonymity within the world he was creating. Little did he realise the effect this would have on the show. During a story conference, Jane Featherstone suggested extending David's joke to the rest of the production team – leave the show without credits to add to the idea that these characters come and go without the people they meet having any idea who they really are.

It was one of the many controversial decisions taken during the creation of [**spooks**] that everyone involved agreed with (as a compromise, the credits would be available on the official BBC website). Likewise, although the scripts for the first series carried working titles, these were dropped in favour of simply numbering the episodes, to make them less theatrical and, again, adding to the overall 'anonymity' idea.

[One Day in September]

The first scripts were near completion and work on the script for episode four was at an advanced stage when, on September 11, 2001, news of the terrible attack on the World Trade Center and the Pentagon first broke. Suddenly, any worries that people might not know who the enemy was went out of the window. The script for episode one was duly amended to take real-life events into account, while the overall effects of this new level of terrorism could be felt right across the production.

[Expert Advice]

During pre-production, the team were lucky enough to be introduced to a real spook by writer Simon Mirren, the third member of the [spooks] writing team. During his extensive research for the series (some of which was used on episodes other than his own), Simon had become acquainted with Nick Day, a former MI5 officer who now runs a corporate intelligence agency called Diligence with his two partners, one ex-CIA, the other a former agent of the KGB. Post Cold War, the men got together to pool their intelligence experience and act as advisors to the corporate sector, providing background checks on potential clients. Nick was hired to help Kudos ensure that where possible the details were as true to life as possible within the confines of a fictional setting. Although Nick didn't give any state secrets away, he was able to help the team get into the mindset of a spook and provide some anecdotal examples of life in the Security Service. The incident with the cat in the very first episode, for example, came from a classic test during MI5 training.

[Promoting the Show]

To promote the show in advance, a series of teaser trailers was created depicting people discussing what their friends or relatives did for a living – for example, children talking competitively about the exciting jobs their family members did and one child sullenly noting that his brother worked in computers, a comment that was juxtaposed with a shot of a cool, dynamic MI5 agent clearly doing something other than boring computer work. Each trailer ended with the tagline for the series: 'MI5, not 9 to 5.'

[Who's Who Behind the Scenes?]

[spooks] has a number of key people who form the core production team in addition to the other writers, directors, editors and production staff that work on an episode-by-episode basis. The creator of [spooks] is David Wolstencroft. Born in Honolulu, Hawaii, David first collaborated with Kudos on *Psychos* (1999), a hard-hitting look into psychiatric care in Britain for which he won the Royal Television Society Award for 'Network Newcomer Behind The Screen'. In addition to creating the series, David is also one of the main writers on the show.

As already mentioned, Stephen Garrett (executive producer for Kudos) was the man who first identified the gap in the market for a spy show and who brought David Wolstencroft on board. He was previously the producer of the feature film *Among Giants* (1998) and executive producer on the International Emmy Award-winning TV series *The Magician's House* (1999–2000) and *Pure* (2002).

Series producer Jane Featherstone's previous productions include *Touching Evil* (1997–8), which starred Robson Green as an officer in a rapid response police force, *Sex 'n' Death* (1999), in which Martin Clunes played a repellent shock-TV host, *Glasgow Kiss* (2000), and *Pure* (2002).

Producer Simon Crawford Collins was the associate producer on *Sex 'n' Death*. Previously he'd been a location manager for such films as *Spice World* (dir. Bob Spiers, 1997) and *An Ideal Husband* (dir. Oliver Parker, 1999).

Gareth Neame, executive producer for the BBC, produced *Truth or Dare* (1996), *The Missing Postman* (1997), *The Woman in White* (1997), *Getting Hurt* (1998), *All the King's Men* (1999), *Happy Birthday Shakespeare* (2000) and *Take a Girl Like You* (2000). As head of drama commissioning at the BBC, he has served as executive producer on shows such as *Clocking Off* (2000), *Hearts and Bones* (2000), *Red Cap* (2001), *Green-Eyed Monster* (2001), *Rescue Me* (2002), *Murder* (2002) and *Trust* (2003).

Part 3
The Characters

Tom Quinn

Tom Quinn is a senior case officer in Section B (Counter-Terrorism) at Thames House. He has been identified as one of MI5's brightest officers, a gifted leader and razor-sharp thinker. Under Harry Pearce, he oversees a team of counter-terrorist agents that includes Zoe Reynolds and Danny Hunter. Tom was recruited to MI5 by Peter Salter,

a former senior officer who Tom now runs as an agent.

At some time in the past, Tom confessed to his then-girlfriend that he worked for MI5. When the girlfriend (thinking Tom was joking) informed all of her friends, Tom ended the relationship. Since then, he has been reticent about entering into a long-term relationship. However, in 2002, Tom began seeing restaurateur Ellie Simm, who was unaware of his real occupation or identity (when they met, Tom was working undercover as 'Matthew Archer', who Ellie believed him to be). Tom submitted her for MI5 vetting before he revealed his true self.

Zoe Reynolds

Zoe Reynolds, a case officer in Section B, completed her training for MI5 in 1997. She is intelligent and self-possessed beyond her 26 years, and a firm favourite with her team leader, Tom Quinn. Whether it's winning the trust of a potential informant or going undercover as a terrorist target, Tom knows Zoe is up to any task. If she had to admit it, she sometimes finds her assignments terrifying – but she'd never let it show. Working for MI5 is all that Zoe has ever wanted and she means to make it to the top. When she first arrived at Section B, it was clear she was slightly overawed by Tessa Phillips and her 'acolytes', a feeling she has found hard to shift. Though clearly a very attractive woman, her

concerns over her career and its effect on her personal life mean she is very cautious about forming emotional attachments outside of the job.

Danny Hunter

Danny is another case officer in Section B. Enthusiastic and eager to do well, his freshness means he is sometimes slightly out of step with some of the older hands like Tom, Harry and Malcolm. Nevertheless, he had the highest ratings of anyone to come through the training centre in recent years. He's a talented surveillance expert with a natural

aptitude for computers and technology. Danny's finally living his MI5 dream and is very impatient to prove himself. He finds Zoe's 'golden girl' status hard to handle, but deep down he's in awe of her and it's thrown him. Additionally, he has a suspicion that part of the reason he got the job was to help the department with their ethnic minority quota.

One thing that did come up in training was Danny's initial reaction to the powers his new job would apparently bring him. Though there's no great cause for concern, it might be worth keeping an eye on him to see if he can resist experimenting with them.

Harry Pearce

The head of the Counter-Terrorism Department, overseeing teams run by Tom Quinn and Tessa Phillips, Harry Pearce was headhunted by the Security Service after an impressive early career in the army. Harry's wealth of experience means he is highly respected by the teams of case officers he oversees, even if sometimes he comes across as a bit

'old-school MI5' (the Governor of the Bank of England is an old school friend of his). As one of MI5's most senior officers, he must be a consummate diplomat and manage the regular interferences of MI6, the police, the foreign office and even the FBI and CIA. Despite his bluff manner, Harry is extremely wise and is not afraid to take advice from his subordinates on the rare occasion that he's stuck for ideas.

Tessa Phillips

Tessa runs Section K of Counter-Terrorism, reporting to Harry Pearce. Although she is equal in rank to Tom Quinn, she has made it quite clear that she felt passed over when Harry Pearce was given the job of division head instead of her. However, while Tom seems to be forging a path up the MI5 ranks, Tessa is apparently content to

maintain her current position for the time being. In MI5, the only way to make decent money is to hit a top position, but after more than 20 years in the service, Tessa seems happy to stay in a 'hands-on' but less scrutinised role. Her slick, no-nonsense manner is something that has gained her as many critics as it has fans. But more often than not, it's her extensive (and often expensive) list of contacts that gains her kudos around the department.

Helen Flynn

Helen recently qualified to work as an administrative support clerk, shared between all of Harry Pearce's teams. Her efficiency and enthusiasm for the role is matched only by her willingness to deliver that little bit extra every time. Helen has admitted to Zoe Reynolds that she only took the admin post to get her foot in the door; more than anything, she really wants to be a fully fledged agent and, knowing of the tradition of utilising clerical staff in emergencies, she saw this as her best chance. In the meantime, she keeps her ears to the ground and learns as much as she can from watching the professionals at work. Her hard work hasn't gone unnoticed.

Ruth Evershed

An academic, Ruth has always harboured desires to become a spy, and when she is seconded to Five from GCHQ she cannot conceal her delight. Despite the fact that her enthusiasm, even for the most deadly of cases, can sometimes seem misplaced, her skills as a research analyst prove to be an essential addition to the team when providing them with background information on each case. However, the ease with which she made the move from GCHQ has already set alarm bells ringing with a number of people in Section B, including its boss, Harry Pearce. Can Ruth really be as good as she seems?

Sam Buxton

Fresh out of training, Sam feels that she has got something to prove among the more senior members of the Grid, and is keen to get herself noticed, a tactic that certainly works with the male members of staff. Confident, bright, and extremely capable, she is immediately put into the field on an operation with Zoe, but her determination can at times cloud her judgement, and it's at those moments that her inexperience and naivety is most evident.

Malcolm Wynn-Jones

Malcolm is an experienced MI5 officer, having been in the organisation for over 20 years. Brought in from the cold, he now works from the Grid rather than from the field. By the book and extremely fastidious, he takes great pride and care in his work. An old-school spy, cut from a different cloth than the younger members of the team, he may be regarded as an old-timer, but he certainly knows how to get results. He is invariably detailed for surveillance work, though more often than not because he's the only person they can send out to fetch drinks and sandwiches who won't moan about it… much. A solitary man, some staff members have observed that he took a shine to

Zoe the moment he first saw her, but his shyness – and, in fairness, self-awareness – has prevented him from ever telling her how he feels.

Colin Wells (pictured right)

An MI5 operative and computer expert, Colin is MI5's technological eyes and ears. If you want to get round some of the world's most sophisticated operating systems or you need a room bugged and secured then Colin has the know-how. To some extent, Colin is intimidated by the dynamism of Tom and Danny but he more than makes up for this with his expertise in accessing all areas.

Christine Dale

CIA officer Christine Dale is ambitious, intelligent and very much aware of her own attractiveness. She knows just what it takes to make an entrance and how to leave a lasting impression. She's also conscious that to survive in what has always been a 'man's world', she needs to be tougher, harder and more ruthless than anyone she comes into contact with. As the CIA liaison with MI5, she comes across as viewing British affairs as trivial in relation to her own country – and her own career. Her contact at Section B is Tom Quinn, with whom she enjoys a relationship that is as fractious as it is flirtatious.

Ellie Simm

Ellie Simm is a chef and owner of a restaurant in Brixton, south London. She has an eight-year-old daughter called Maisie from her ex-husband, Mark Hodd, currently based in the Gulf, who she hasn't seen in four years. Mark left her shortly before she discovered she was pregnant and she briefly considered a termination but now feels she could never have gone through with it. Although initial vetting has revealed that Ellie took part in a 'Women Reclaim the Streets' march in 1992, there are no indications that she has ever belonged to any known political pressure groups and is believed to pose no threat to Tom Quinn's position within MI5.

Dr Vicky Westbrook

When Danny gets badly beaten up by a gang of youths (episode 201), he is rushed to hospital where Dr Westbrook treats him in the emergency ward. A class act with looks to kill and a bedside manner to die for, it's easy to see why she sets pulses racing. The only thing is, it's not Danny's pulse she's interested in, it's Tom's…

Carlo Franceschini

Zoe Reynolds first meets Carlo in a pub and enjoys a quiet drink with him while waiting for Danny to join her. But as time goes on, she finds herself strangely drawn to this charming Italian banker. But there's much about Carlo that Zoe really needs to know (see episodes 201-204).

Part 4
The Regular
Cast

Matthew Macfadyen (Tom Quinn)

A self-confessed John Le-Carré-style spy buff, Matthew Macfadyen initially had a difficult time juggling his character's different identities, especially as one of them just happened to share the same first name as himself: 'During the scene one guy turns to me and asks, "So, Matthew, what do you do?" That's my real name, of course, and it completely threw me. I was Matthew playing Tom playing Matthew. I couldn't get my head round it at all. I was all over the place!'

Born in Glasgow, Matthew spent much of his early life travelling thanks to his father's job with an oil company, which took the family to the Far East and Brazil. After leaving school in 1990, he was accepted into RADA (where he became friends with television presenter and *Merseybeat* actress Josie D'Arby), graduating in 1995. From there he spent three years wowing theatre critics. In 1999, he was nominated for the *Sunday Times*/Royal National Theatre Ian Charleson Award for young actors in classical theatre for his performances as Charles Surface in *The School for Scandal* and as Benedick in Cheek By Jowl's *Much Ado About Nothing*. Coincidentally, Matthew's **[spooks]** co-star David Oyelowo was the winner of the award that year.

Since his TV debut as Hareton Earnshaw in LWT's 1998 production of *Wuthering Heights* (dir. David Skynner), Matthew Macfadyen has managed to collate a credible body of work. He played Private Alan James in the Bosnian war drama *Warriors* (dir. Peter Kosminsky, 1999), for which he was nominated for a Royal Television Society Best Actor Award, and in 2000 he appeared in *Murder*

Rooms (dir. Paul Seed) and the feature film *Maybe Baby* (dir. Ben Elton). The following year came the films *Enigma* (dir. Michael Apted) and *The Reckoning* (dir. Paul McGuigan), and the TV dramas *Perfect Strangers* (written and directed by Stephen Poliakoff) and Andrew Davies's adaptation of Anthony Trollope's *The Way We Live Now* (dir. David Yates). In between series one and two of [s p o o k s], Matthew completed *The Project*, a BBC drama about New Labour's rise to power and their historic 1997 election victory, which reunited him with director Peter Kosminsky.

Keeley Hawes (Zoe Reynolds)

Keeley Hawes always knew she wanted to be an actress – or at least, she knew she wanted to attend the school over the road from her childhood home. It was the famous Sylvia Young Theatre School. Thanks to a grant, her mother was able to get her enrolled there and from the age of nine she studied alongside Emma 'Baby Spice' Bunton, Denise Van Outen and Dani Behr. While still at school, Keeley was scouted by a model agency, though after a number of catalogue and teen magazine jobs – and a brief stint as a fashion assistant on *Cosmo* – she won her first major acting role, in Dennis Potter's last play for television, *Karaoke* (1996).

1998 saw the release of the long-awaited but ultimately disappointing big-screen version of *The Avengers* (dir. Jeremiah S. Chechik), in which Keeley was one of the few saving graces. Fortunately she also got to play Lizzie Hexam in the BBC production of Dickens' *Our Mutual Friend*, alongside Anna Friel and Paul McGann. The same year she starred as a young version of the British celluloid sex symbol Diana Dors in *The Blonde Bombshell*. Next came the film *The Last September* (dir. Deborah Warner, 1999) and the BBC adaptation of Elizabeth Gaskell's *Wives and Daughters*. Among all these other projects, she found time for a special production of her own, her son, Miles. Not that his birth has stopped her working. As well as [s p o o k s], Keeley has worked with Christopher Eccleston in ITV's modern-day *Othello*, Martin Clunes in *A is for Acid*, and Stephen Tompkinson in *Lucky Jim*. But it was the part of lesbian music-hall entertainer Kitty Butler in the BBC production of *Tipping the Velvet* that really catapulted Keeley into the A-list, helped in no small part by the controversy surrounding the show's erotic content, a controversy stoked up by the tabloids, who, as we all know, love a good bit of girl-on-girl action.

David Oyelowo (Danny Hunter)

David was born in Oxford to Nigerian parents. Since graduating from the London Academy of Music and Dramatic Art (LAMDA) in 1998, his work with the RSC has made him one of Britain's most impressive young stage actors. He joined the Royal Shakespeare Company in 1999, appearing in *Volpone*, *Oroonoko* and *Antony and Cleopatra*. In 2000, he made history when he became the first black actor to portray an English monarch for the Royal Shakespeare Company, playing the title role in Michael Boyd's production of *Henry VI*, a role that won him the 2001 Ian Charleson Award for outstanding performance by a young actor in a classical theatre role.

His success on stage helped him make the break into screen acting, first with Tiger Aspect's *Dog Eat Dog* (dir. Moody Shoaibi, 2001), in which he co-starred with Gary Kemp and Alan Davies, then with *Tomorrow La Scala!* (dir. Francesca Joseph, 2002), in which an opera company puts on a production of Stephen Sondheim's *Sweeney Todd* in a maximum security prison. Like his [spooks] character, David is keen to avoid a career shaped by his ethnic background. His biggest ambition is to play a lead role on mainstream TV in which skin colour is totally irrelevant, something, he points out, that has yet to happen to any black actor in Britain. 'I'm doing OK so far at avoiding pigeon-holes. Breaking the mould doesn't come better than playing a black king of England!'

He has been married for five years to Jessica, an actress he met when he was 16, with whom he now has a young son, Asha.

Peter Firth (Harry Pearce)

Born in 1953 in Bradford, Yorkshire, Peter Firth has been a familiar face in British acting since 1970 when, as a 16-year-old, he won the role of Scooper in the children's madcap comedy series *Here Come the Double Deckers*, alongside a cast that also included Brinsley Forde (later the lead singer and guitarist with British reggae band Aswad) and Melvyn *'It Ain't Half Hot Mum'* Hayes (as the token adult in the cast). In 1977, Peter took on a role that gained him the title of the year's most promising newcomer – the psychologically damaged Alan Strang in Peter Shaffer's play *Equus*, for which he received a Tony Award nomination and won the Theatre World Award and the Plays and Players Award for best young actor. Recreating the role in Sidney Lumet's acclaimed film version (which co-starred [spooks] actress Jenny Agutter), Peter won the Golden Globe for best supporting actor and the *Evening Standard* British Film Award for most promising newcomer, as well as an Academy Award nomination.

Fans of science fiction might remember him as the time-travelling star of the Play for Today '*The Flipside of Dominick Hide*' (1980) and its sequel, '*Another Flip for Dominick*' (1982). Other TV appearances include the 1986 BBC production of Jane Austen's *Northanger Abbey*, period drama *And the Beat Goes On* (1996), which cast him alongside Jenny Agutter once again, and the American drama-comedy *That's Life* (2000) in which he appeared for two seasons. He has also continued to work in the theatre in numerous productions including Bill Bryden's *Romeo and Juliet* and *Spring Awakening*, both at the National Theatre, and Peter Hall's *Amadeus* on Broadway.

But it is in the realm of films that Peter has been most visible throughout his career. His many roles include: Angel Clare in the tragic *Tess* (1979), Roman Polanski's version of Thomas Hardy's *Tess of the d'Urbervilles*; a Russian sailor who falls in love with a Liverpudlian girl in Frank Clarke's *Letter to Brezhnev* (dir. Chris Bernard, 1985); another Russian naval officer in *The Hunt for Red October* (dir. John McTiernan, 1990) with Sean Connery and Sam Neill; a doctor in Richard Attenborough's *Shadowlands* (1993); and a British-American naval captain in *Amistad* (dir. Steven Spielberg, 1997). At the end of the 1990s, Peter and his family moved to L.A., where he appeared in *Mighty Joe Young* (dir. Ron Underwood, 1998), *Chill Factor* (dir. Hugh Johnson, 1999), with Cuba Gooding Jr, and the jingoistic World War II blockbuster, *Pearl Harbor* (dir. Michael Bay, 2001), in which he had the small role of the Captain of the USS *West Virginia*. Peter returned to the UK with his family shortly before undertaking the first series of [**spooks**].

Jenny Agutter (Tessa Phillips)

For British viewers at least, Jenny Agutter will forever be linked to *The Railway Children* (Lionel Jeffries, 1970), in which she starred as Bobbie Waterbury, the red-bloomer-waving eldest child of a troubled family. It was a part that she had already played in a 1967 BBC TV series, and in 2001 she returned to the story again, this time as the mother, in a further adaptation for ITV of E. Nesbitt's classic novel.

Her film career continued with *Walkabout* (dir. Nicolas Roeg, 1971), which was set in the Australian outback. After a brief stint with Peter Hall at the

National Theatre, Jenny decided to move to the USA to work in films. Within a few weeks she landed the female lead in the futuristic *Logan's Run* (dir. Michael Anderson, 1976) with Michael York and Peter Ustinov. A year later she co-starred in *Equus*, which saw her character romp naked in the hay with Peter Firth, and in 1981, she played Alex, girlfriend to David in *An American Werewolf in London* (dir. John Landis). While in the States, she was able to exploit the American love of a bit of class by being the Brit-for-hire in shows such as *The Six Million Dollar Man*, *Magnum, P.I.*, *The Twilight Zone* revival, *Murder, She Wrote*, *The Equalizer* and *TECX*.

In 1990, Jenny married Swiss hotelier Johan Tham, with whom she later had a son, Jonathan. After 17 years in L.A., she returned to the UK in the mid-1990s and went on to appear in *The Buccaneers* and star alongside Peter Firth once again in *And the Beat Goes On*, as well as guesting in shows as diverse as *Red Dwarf*, *Heartbeat* and *Bramwell*.

Lisa Faulkner (Helen Flynn)

Lisa Faulkner was undoubtedly the best known of the younger [**spooks**] actors – which was precisely why she was cast, as the production crew knew exactly the impact her dramatic early exit would have (see episode 102).

Unlike many of her contemporaries, Lisa didn't attend drama school, but acting was something she felt drawn towards. The death of her mother when Lisa was just 16 motivated her to achieve her dream. Her first screen appearance was as a minor character in the controversial film *The Lover* (dir. Jean-Jacques Annaud, 1991). In 1995 she made her breakthrough, starring in *Dangerfield* as Alison Dangerfield, and the following year she played the daughter of her [**spooks**] co-stars Peter Firth and Jenny Agutter in *And the Beat Goes On*. With dreadlocks, piercings and a psychotic long-lost father, she underwent a massive transformation as idealistic eco-campaigner Louise in Channel 4's *Brookside* from 1998–9. She then moved from Britain's most deadly close to its most notorious hospital for a three-year stint at *Holby City* (she'd already been there a few years earlier, as a patient in *Holby*'s sister show, *Casualty*). It was her portrayal of speed-snorting doctor Victoria Merrick that really switched the 'lad-mag' audience on to Lisa (she came 16th in *FHM*'s recent 'Top 100 Sexiest Women' poll), making her departure from the show all the more shocking (her character suffered a fatal stab wound). In between her increasingly high-profile TV work, Lisa's also completed two further feature films, *The Scarlet Tunic* (dir. Stuart St. Paul, 1998), an adaptation of a Thomas Hardy short story, and *The Baby Juice Express* (dir. Michael Hurst, 2001), a 'sperm donor heist movie'.

Since her headline-grabbing final episode of [**spooks**], Lisa has starred alongside former Spice Girl Melanie Brown in the drama-comedy *Burn It*, one of the major shows for BBC3's 2003 (re)launch.

Esther Hall (Ellie Simm)

Esther Hall's first taste of fame came when she played a sex-mad 'northern oddball' in an episode of BBC2's *The Cops*. She was Romey Sullivan, one half of a lesbian couple, in two series of Russell Davies's uncompromising *Queer as Folk* (1999), and Katie in *Men Only* (2001), both for Channel 4. Other TV appearances include *Always and Everyone*, *Clocking Off*, *Fat Friends* and, as Rachel Finn, the love interest between Joe Duttine and Martin Kemp in *Serious and Organised*. Between seasons of [**spooks**] she completed work on *Blue Dove* with her *Cops* co-star Paul Nicholls, and in 2003 she starred in a major ITV adaptation of D.H. Lawrence's *Sons and Lovers* with Sarah Lancashire and Hugo Speer.

Megan Dodds (Christine Dale)

Graduate of the famous Juilliard School, Megan made her Broadway debut in *The School for Scandal* at the Lyceum Theatre, New York. She has appeared in a number of films and TV productions, including *Ever After* (dir. Andy Tennant, 1998), *Urbania* (dir. Jon Shear, 2000) and the TV show *Sword of Honour* (2001) for Channel 4, and made her West End debut in Ben Elton's *Popcorn*. Although she appears in just the first episode of series one, Megan becomes a member of the regular cast for series two.

Shauna Macdonald (Sam Buxton)

Shauna Macdonald (Sam) played Heather in an episode of the Sherlock Holmes/Conan Doyle series *Murder Rooms* (2000). Her film work includes *The Debt Collector* (dir. Anthony Neilson, 1999) opposite Billy Connolly, *Daybreak* (dir.

Bernard Rudden, 1999) and *Late Night Shopping* (dir. Saul Metzstein, 2001). She has been a regular performer at the Royal Scottish Academy for the last four years, most recently as Emma Goldman in *Assassins*.

Nicola Walker (Ruth Evershed)

Graduate of the Cambridge Footlights, Nicola Walker played one half of the folk duo at the first wedding in *Four Weddings and a Funeral* (dir. Richard Curtis, 1994). On television, she co-starred alongside David Bamber in the sitcom *Chalk*, played D.I. Susan Taylor in three series of *Touching Evil* and starred in the apocalyptic mini-series *The Last Train* (1998). Her stage work includes *Sexual Perversity in Chicago* at the Crucible Theatre, Sheffield, *Free* at the Royal National Theatre and *Dead Eye Boy* at the Hampstead Theatre. She can also be seen in the feature film *Shiner* (dir. John Irvin, 2000), which stars Michael Caine and Martin Landau.

Hugh Simon (Malcolm Wynn-Jones)

Hugh Simon's CV includes appearances in the mini-series *Selling Hitler* (1991), *Lovejoy*, *Dangerfield*, *The Bill*, the Reeves and Mortimore revival of *Randall & Hopkirk (Deceased)*, the BBC2 dot.com drama *Attachments*, Colin Bird QC in *North Square*, and two episodes of the third series of *Cold Feet* as John Thomson's gay landlord. He also played Winston Churchill in Channel 4's mini-series about the life of right-wing politician *Mosley* (1998).

Rory Macgregor (Colin Wells)

Rory appeared in episode three of the first series, but he becomes part of the regular cast from the beginning of series two. Having appeared in supporting roles in *Lexx*, *Hollyoaks*, *Bad Girls* and *My Family*, he made his feature film debut with the flatulent family comedy *Thunderpants* (dir. Peter Hewitt, 2002). In 2003, he'll appear in the *Smack the Pony* movie *Gladiatress* (dir. Brian Grant, 2003) and Richard Curtis's *Love Actually* (2003), which also stars Liam Neeson, Martine McCutcheon, Rowan Atkinson and *24*'s Elisha Cuthbert.

Natasha Little (Dr Vicky Westbrook)

Natasha was born in Liverpool in 1970. Her early years were spent in the Middle East where her father set up immunisation clinics for the World Health Organisation and her mother taught at an English-speaking school. After appearing in a school production of the musical *Chicago*, she was hooked, and from there went to the Guildhall School of Music and Drama. She appeared in a number of stage productions before winning the role of Jenny in ITV's long-running firefighting drama *London's Burning*. Best known for playing Rachel in the legal drama *This Life*, Natasha's other TV work includes the BBC adaptation of William Makepeace Thackeray's *Vanity Fair* (as Becky Sharp) and *Love in the 21st Century* for Channel 4, while her feature films include *Greenfingers* (dir. Joel Hershman, 2000) and *Kevin & Perry Go Large* (dir. Ed Bye, 2000). In 2003, she appeared in the critically acclaimed *The Vagina Monologues* at the Arts Theatre in London's West End.

Enzo Cilenti (Carlo Franceschini)

Enzo Cilenti played Antonio Bellini in the TV series *Trial & Retribution II*, and can be seen in the feature films *Wonderland* (dir. Michael Winterbottom, 1999), *Late Night Shopping* (dir. Saul Metztein, 2001) and *24 Hour Party People* (dir. Michael Winterbottom, 2002).

Part 5
Glossary

As with any organisation, there's plenty of lingo, jargon and insider terminology to take in during [spooks]. Here are just a few of the basics (you'll find references to others in the Episode section as and when they appear in the series).

Agent

Someone who sits within, or has contact with, a targeted organisation. Not MI5 staff – each agent is run by an officer. Some agents are paid, others are motivated by moral duty. MI5 aims to recruit and maintain agents for as long as possible. Some may be actively involved in an operation, others may be watching and waiting to be of use.

Backstop

A person who can vouch for your legend if a target starts asking questions. For example, someone living in a house your alias purports to have lived in or someone who pretends to be an old college friend.

Brush contact

Another means of passing information. An agent and officer arrange to 'meet' at a busy location (often a rush-hour tube or train, or a pub). The agent will exit, leaving the message behind for the officer to pick up or vice versa.

Buggers and Burglars

MI5 slang for CMOs – officers who are experts in covert methods of entry, i.e. breaking into buildings and planting bugs.

COBRA

COBRA stands for 'Cabinet Office Briefing Room A'. COBRA meetings are held in Downing Street, within Cabinet Office buildings, in times of national emergency. Senior MI5 and MI6 officers are usually part of the briefing team in such circumstances.

Dead-letter drop

Sometimes it may be too dangerous for an agent to meet an officer, and a dead-letter drop is used to pass messages. This could be under a stone in a park or in a hollow in a tree. A system of signals will be used, like chalk marks on walls, lampposts or bus stops, to indicate there is a message waiting for retrieval. Messages are invariably written in code or invisible ink.

Five

MI5, officially known as the Security Service. MI5 deals with security risks that originate within the British Isles, the Republic of Ireland or the Channel Islands.

Flagging

A security level, colour-coded to indicate the degree of secrecy. Yellow flag is for restricted information; red flag is for top-level eyes only.

GCHQ

'Government Communications Headquarters', responsible for collating information and disseminating it to the relevant departments.

'Going native'

Slang for an officer going so far underground on an operation, they start genuinely living their alias's life. For example, an officer working on a drugs sting who picks up a habit of his/her own.

The Grid

The nerve centre of MI5 counter-terrorist operations and Section B's home within Thames House. Entry to the Grid is via the 'Pods', a set of unusual revolving security doors.

Jammer

A special piece of equipment used to jam electro-magnetic signals in a public area – especially useful for blocking signals to mobile phones.

KGB

'Komitet Gosudarstvennoy Bezopasnosti' – the Committee of State Security for the former USSR. The KGB was gradually disbanded in the 1990s and replaced by a number of other organisations. Many former KGB agents moved into security consultancy across the globe.

Legend

The detailed history and background of an alias identity: where he/she was born and educated, employment and relationship history etc. Usually legends will be designed to be difficult to verify – aliases are often born in countries with no official birth records system or have worked in companies that have gone into liquidation.

Lockdown

The securing of an area, preventing anyone from entering or leaving.

Millbank

Labour Party headquarters in central London.

MOD

Ministry of Defence.

'Off-piste'

Used to describe someone who is improvising outside of their prepared legend or mission briefing.

Registry

The place where all files are kept on investigations past and present. The people who staff the Registry were traditionally women (though this has changed in recent years), and they had to rule their records with rods of iron (hence the common term 'Registry Queen').

Safe house

A building, usually run-of-the-mill domestic accommodation, used by officers to meet agents. Each safe house will have a system of signals to indicate whether it is clear to enter. For example, an ornament in the window facing right indicates it is unsafe, while facing left gives the all-clear.

Six

MI6, the Secret Intelligence Service. Or if being referred to by someone within MI6, the 'sister service', which deals with security risks that originate abroad.

Spook

MI5 slang for an operational officer.

Thames House

MI5 headquarters on the north bank of the Thames, a short walk from the slightly more modern-looking MI6 building at Vauxhall Cross.

Watcher

An MI5 officer who specialises in surveillance.

Whitehall

A part of London that contains the main government offices. Whenever people refer to Whitehall it's generally to moan about their restrictive bureaucracy.

Series One (2002) Six episodes

[Regular Cast]

Matthew Macfadyen (Tom Quinn)

Keeley Hawes (Zoe Reynolds)

David Oyelowo (Danny Hunter)

Peter Firth (Harry Pearce)

Jenny Agutter (Tessa Phillips)

Esther Hall (Ellie Simm)

Heather Cave (Maisie Simm)

Hugh Simon (Malcolm Wynn-Jones)

Graeme Mearns (Jed Kelley)

Episode 101

First Broadcast (BBC1): May 13 2002

Written by **David Wolstencroft**
Directed by **Bharat Nalluri**

[Cast]

Lisa Faulkner (Helen Flynn), **Lisa Eichhorn** (Mary Kane), **Megan Dodds** (Christine Dale), **Ken Bones** (Keith Burns), **Adam Kotz** (Dr Mike Lynott), **Karen Westwood** (Dr Karen Lynott), **Alexandra Robinson** (Sarah Lynott), **Anni Rademacher** (Claire Lynott), **Rachel Power** (Rachel), **Paul Haigh** (Rob), **Derek Riddell** (Steven), **Nick Lamont** ('John' from the 'Gas Board'), **Matt Delamere** ('Ringo' from the 'Gas Board'), **Kerry Rolfe** ('Osprey'), **Louise Ludgate** (Female PR), **Oliver Fox** (Clive), **Tara Moran** (Guest 1), **Stephen Hudson** (Hack), **Royce Mills** (Toby McInnes), **George Eggay** (Male Nurse), **Kay Noone** (Elderly Woman), **William Buckhurst** (Disposal Expert), **Sam Redford** (Landlord), **Meredith Braun** (US TV Reporter), **Jon Huyton** ('Foxtrot'), **Corinne Skinner Carter** (Danny's Mum*), **Ewan David Alman** (Bruno, Danny's Brother*).
* scenes excised

[Who's Who]

Director Bharat Nalluri was raised in Newcastle and used his father's Super 8 camera to make his own films. He later got the chance to do the real thing with the British thrillers *Downtime* (1997) and *Killing Time* (1998). He moved to the USA to direct *The Crow: Salvation* (2000), the third in the Crow series, in America, and returned to the UK to make *Cyclops* for Tiger Aspect in 2001. He was the second-unit director on *Resident Evil* (dir. Paul W.S. Anderson, 2002). As the first director to be hired for [**spooks**], it was Bharat who set the tone and style for the series, and he worked closely with editor Colin Green on the fast editing and split-screen technique. A veteran of pop-music promos (including the multi-award-winning video for Peter Gabriel's 'Sledgehammer'), Colin was also one of the editors on satirical puppet show *Spitting Image* for many years. His filmography includes the TV adaptation of *Animal Farm* (dir. John Stephenson, 1999), the mini-series *Jake's Progress* (1995) and *Merlin* (1998), and the feature film *Mike Bassett: Football Manager* (dir. Steve Barron, 2001) among others.

Lisa Eichhorn (Mary Kane) made her screen debut opposite Richard Gere in the WWII film *Yanks* (dir. John Schlesinger, 1979), though the bulk of her subsequent career has been spent on stage in London, New York and Los Angeles. She can be seen in the remake of *The Vanishing* (dir. George Sluizer, 1993) as Jeff Bridges' wife and in *The Talented Mr Ripley* (dir. Anthony Minghella, 1999).

Derek Riddell (Steven) plays Rab in the Channel 4 comedy *The Book Group*, while other credits include *Strathblair*, *Clocking Off* and *The Project* with Matthew Macfadyen. Royce Mills (Toby McInnes) is a familiar face from British comedies, though it's his voice that's well known internationally, having played the dreaded Daleks in a few episodes of *Doctor Who*.

[Case Report]

A consignment of explosives and detonators, sourced by Irish Loyalists in Londonderry, entered Liverpool docks at around 2.30am, Tuesday morning. It took just over two hours for Agent 'Osprey' to contact Danny Hunter and get the information to him. Initially, Osprey believed that the 20 explosives and detonators were pipe bombs, though she later learned that only five were pipe bombs – the rest were Semtex, possibly activated by remote via a mobile phone signal.

The first of these devices was detonated under the car of Karen Lynott, killing her instantly and wounding her youngest daughter, Sarah. Karen was a family planning doctor, as is her husband Michael, who revealed to Tom that he had been receiving anonymous death threats from anti-abortion campaigners but had decided not to inform his wife. It was this that first gave the Section B

[M a r y   K a n e]

Aged 15, Mary Kane went into hospital with appendicitis and came out with a terminated pregnancy. The doctor who performed the termination, Dr Harrison, became Kane's first target when she became a pro-life terrorist 25 years later. Mary Kane was, until her arrest, a leading figure in the Defenders of the Innocents. She has been on the run for some time, and indeed was convicted in her absence for the Absalom clinic bombing. Her husband, Paul Kane, was, at the time, on death row for the shooting of an abortion clinic doctor in Sarasota, Florida, USA. She is believed to be big on anniversaries, as many of her acts of terrorism have coincided with dates personal to her (her actions in the UK were timed to coincide with her husband's execution in Florida).

Kane was invited to the UK by a growing pro-life organisation who run the 'Call to Justice' website. She managed to escape from the USA and enter the UK via France under a false passport. At the time of this case, she'd been hiding out in a cottage somewhere on the Wirral Peninsula, Merseyside, for no more than six weeks.

While in the UK, she had been having a sexual relationship with a man called Steven who was a member of the Merseyside group, and is believed to be the father of Kane's unborn child.

Connected to a number of small-scale groups in the UK, she was planning to join another anti-abortion group in Dundee before MI5 apprehended her and handed her over to the CIA.

team the clue that the bomb had been detonated by an extremist pro-life terrorist group – a group still in possession of 19 other weapons of potential mass destruction.

With the help of Keith Burns of Special Branch, a cover story was placed with the local press that an undiscovered World War II bomb had gone off, denying the pro-lifers the publicity they sought. Meanwhile, an A-B-C foot surveillance operation revealed the involvement of Mary Kane, a known anti-abortion terrorist whose husband was on death row in Florida state penitentiary for the Absalom bombing (see Security File). Kane was traced back to a cottage in The Wirral, Merseyside, and a warrant was issued to allow Zoe Reynolds and her Liverpool team to install surveillance equipment in the property without Kane's knowledge. Though very little was gained by this, they did learn the identity of one of her potential new recruits, Rachel, whose husband Rob had already been identified as the man who helped Kane bomb Karen Lynott's car.

Zoe posed as a pro-life supporter and befriended Rachel, and then by claiming that Zoe's pregnant friend had been rushed to hospital, Zoe was able to bring Rachel in contact with Tom Quinn. Tom showed her the effects of Mary Kane's work – young Sarah Lynott, who was still in intensive care at St Mary's Hospital, Liverpool (Sarah subsequently died). Distressed by the experience, Rachel called her husband and from there Danny learned of Kane's next target, Dr Diane Sullivan, another family planning doctor, based in St John's Wood, London. Meanwhile, Mary Kane left Merseyside and relocated to a B&B in Shoreditch, east London. As Kane's husband was due to be executed that Saturday, it was clear when she intended to kill Sullivan.

At this point in the operation, instructions came to Harry Pearce that complicated matters further. The Americans were demanding that, on her arrest, Mary Kane was to be extradited to Florida. To buy us more time, Harry refused to sign the extradition warrant due to potential policy conflict, citing the standard government policy that the UK does not favour sending individuals to countries where they might subsequently die (and Florida, of course, supports the death penalty). Christine Dale, CIA liaison in London, warned that any attempt to hinder the acquisition and extradition of Mary Kane could result in a serious diplomatic uproar. They wanted Kane back in Florida in time to see her husband executed. Additional concern was raised by Toby McInnes of the Foreign Office. A British company called Athol Pharmaceuticals were in the process of licensing a contraceptive called Mendocryn to companies in the USA, a licence that could be worth as much as £3 billion to British industry. In short, it was essential that Harry's team found Mary Kane alive and that they got as much information out of her as they could before she was in turn handed over to Christine Dale.

Dr Diane Sullivan was placed safely out of harm's way before being interviewed so that a detailed weekly schedule could be compiled of all her movements. Zoe stepped in and posed as Sullivan, with the back-up of a team of bomb disposal experts, led by Danny Hunter. As they followed Kane, Kane followed 'Sullivan' to Borough Market, which runs alongside London Bridge station. Received intelligence suggested that Kane's bomb contained enough explosive to turn the entire area into 'Ground Zero'.

Danny's team were equipped with a signal jammer for Kane's remote device (which, as suspected, was activated by a mobile phone signal), but, typically, the jammer could only operate in bursts of 30 seconds at a time. The team waited until Kane placed her devices under Sullivan's car and then Tom intercepted her before she could detonate and confiscated the mobile phone intended to send the detonation signal. From there she was taken to a safe house and

interrogated by Tom. While Kane had been in Merseyside, her rubbish bins were searched and a pregnancy test kit was found. Tom revealed to Kane that he knew she was pregnant by a man other than her husband. He promised her that her co-operation would ensure she was extradited to a state without the death penalty in order to save her unborn child. It was a promise he knew he was in no position to keep, but it nevertheless persuaded Kane to reveal the locations of her network of supporters and, equally important, the whereabouts of the remaining explosive devices.

Once Kane's information was verified, she was handed over to Christine Dale and taken back to Florida to witness the execution of her husband. Mary Kane is now being held on death row until after the birth of her child.

[Previous Missions]

Tom – acting as 'Matthew Archer' – was trying to make contact with a potential new recruit for 'The Shaw Project' and knew he regularly ate at a restaurant in Brixton, south London. After 20 meals there, 'Matthew' finally made contact, but by then he'd struck up a relationship with the restaurant's chef and co-owner, Ellie Simm.

Prior to this, Zoe Reynolds hasn't had a major surveillance operation since she left training five years ago.

[Identity Check]

'Matthew Archer' is a civil servant who works in IT across several government departments. He was born on 04/08/69, his driving licence is registered to 26 Chantry Road, near Earls Court, and he shops at BHS, West Ealing. It's no wonder Ellie noted Matthew's presence in her restaurant if his receipt is anything to go by – salmon starter (£8.50), veal main course (£16.75) and a glass of rosé wine that cost him £4.50. And he didn't tip!

When using the 'Dickson Murray' cover, Danny poses as Chris Patterson, aka N5. Zoe's team in Liverpool includes a 'John', a 'Ringo' and a 'Paul'. Jed answers one of the phones at the Grid on behalf of 'Susan' at 'Greengage Catering'.

[Disinformation]

The property currently being handled by 'Dickson Murray Estate Agents' is a safe house used by Danny to make contact with one of his agents, known as Osprey. The tour guide at Thames House, having informed a party of journalists that the Service is about openness now, tells them that the door to the Grid is just the 'coffee room'.

On Tom's suggestion, a story is fed to the press about a World War II bomb as a cover for the investigation into the attack on Karen Lynott's car.

Zoe's bugging team pose as 'the Gas Board', complete with official ID. One of her team is equipped with a small gas canister to convince neighbours of the gas leak.

[Personnel Records Update]

Tom Quinn has now officially registered his relationship with restaurateur Ellie Simm for vetting. Though he retains the use of his own home, he regularly stays over at Ellie's and has done for some time. (Ellie's daughter Maisie seems perfectly comfortable with the situation.)

Danny Hunter has just moved out of his mother's house to an apartment that would appear to be beyond his means. It looks likely that he will be subletting a room to Helen Flynn from clerical. Meanwhile, Zoe Reynolds is still looking for new accommodation: she has caught her landlord in her room uninvited on a number of occasions (apart from the disturbance this is causing to Zoe's sleep, it could also be a cause for concern from a security point of view). Malcolm Wynn-Jones has offered her use of his camp-bed, though it's generally felt around the office that this might be more a pretext than a genuine offer.

[Gadgets]

We see Zoe's all-purpose lock-picker which helps her gain access to Mary Kane's cottage. Danny has a jammer that blocks Kane's mobile-phone-activated remote for the bombs.

Harry reveals to Tom that he didn't tell his wife his real occupation until they had signed the marriage register: 'I like to have things on paper.'

Mary Kane justifies her actions to her new recruit Rachel: 'Imagine a man with a gun. You'd be scared, so would I. But if you saw him walk into a playground and point that gun at a child, how scared would you be then? And what if you saw him pull the trigger and shoot one child, one then another, would you still be scared, or would you stop thinking about yourself and just try with every fibre of your being to stop him before he killed the whole school? Of course you would. I know your fear, Rachel, but always remember who we're fighting for and who we're trying to stop.'

Helen, as Toby McInnes enters the Grid: 'Creature of the night, two o'clock.'
Danny: 'Ooh, Foreign Office – get out the garlic.'

Harry: 'I signed up here because I knew who the enemy was and I wanted to fight them. These days the enemy don't even have a flag.'

[Missing in Action]

The scene in which Mary explains her philosophy to Rachel was scripted to include an exchange where Rachel's children ask if they can play on the PlayStation, and Mary tells them they can only play driving games (clearly violence is something she only expects them to be exposed to once they grow up).

Another scene was dropped where Zoe finds her landlord waiting for her in her bedroom (which is why she is so eager to find somewhere else to live), as was an early scene showing Zoe bonding with her Liverpool 'Gas Board' team, and enduring a bad joke courtesy of 'Paul'. Two scenes were filmed involving Danny that were cut for timing purposes: one, at Danny's family home, revealed that his mother is aware to some extent of what he does for a living and that he has a DJing brother called Bruno (see the section on 'The Interactive Episode'); the other saw him reveal to Zoe that he

[Notes]

The exterior and foyer of Thames House — MI5 Central HQ — are in reality the Freemasons Hall, Great Queen Street, London, home of the United Grand Lodge of England (the governing body of Freemasonry in England, Wales and the Channel Islands). The real Thames House can be found in Millbank, just opposite Lambeth Bridge.

The opening scene with the car bomb exploding is quite a clever shot for British TV, in that it uses lighting across the refuse collector's face to just suggest the explosion — a trick we might expect from a low-budget drama that can't afford to do the stunt for real — only to reveal almost casually the wreckage of the car still flipping over in the background as the camera rotates into position.

The script for this episode was already completed by the time of September 11 2001, but was rewritten slightly to take the attacks on the World Trade Center and Pentagon into account.

Danny advises Zoe to use a surveillance tactic called A-B-C, where three operatives tail a suspect at different positions — one close by (A), one a little way back but close enough to step in should A's situation make it difficult to continue without being discovered (B), and one following from across the street (C) in case the suspect crosses the road. A fourth operative, often an MI5 officer, is in position to take photographs of the suspect.

got a girl pregnant while at school, which is why he is so touchy over the subject of abortion. In this scene, we also learn that Zoe was once given the job of handling the material collated from phone conversations between 'Andrew and Fergie', which she claims left her feeling sorry for them.

[Expert Witnesses]

Series creator David Wolstencroft: 'With [s p o o k s], I really wanted to break the speed limit and to learn a lesson from the Americans in terms of the pace of the scripts.'

Matthew Macfadyen (Tom): 'Real-life spooks are playing the long game. It can take six months or more to recruit an agent you think is ripe for turning. It must take incredible patience.'

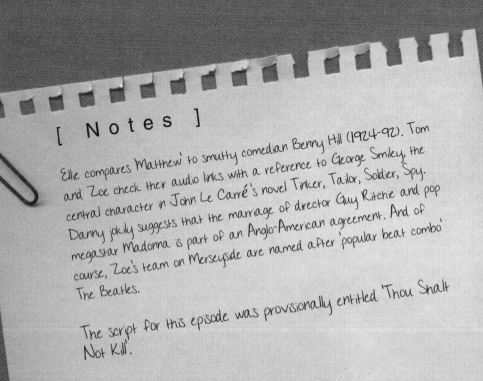

[Notes]

Ellie compares 'Matthew' to smutty comedian Benny Hill (1924-92). Tom and Zoe check their audio links with a reference to George Smiley, the central character in John Le Carré's novel Tinker, Tailor, Soldier, Spy. Danny jokily suggests that the marriage of director Guy Ritchie and pop megastar Madonna is part of an Anglo-American agreement. And of course, Zoe's team on Merseyside are named after 'popular beat combo' The Beatles.

The script for this episode was provisionally entitled 'Thou Shalt Not Kill'.

Lisa Faulkner (Helen): 'I was so over-excited at my audition. I spent the whole meeting asking if spies still did things like leave newspapers on tubes with messages in the crossword... I'd love to just do the "out in the field" work. When we filmed that side of things, I was running on adrenaline all day. It was such a buzz.'

Hugh Simon (Malcolm): 'The producers talked about the fact that Malcolm has a crush on Zoe right from the start. When I auditioned for the part, that was the section they asked me to read, where Malcolm very ham-fistedly says, "I've got a camp-bed in my flat," which isn't what Zoe's after at all, but that's poor old Malcolm's idea of playing court to her. I think he admires her from afar, but never in the world would he have the nerve to ever make an approach – but he'd be content to nurse a silent, secret crush on her.'

Pro-life Terrorism

2003 marks the 30th anniversary of a historic decision on the part of the United States of America's Supreme Court to legalise abortions.

But those who opposed the Supreme Court ruling have not ceased in their battle to have it overthrown, and as recently as 2001, the anti-abortion campaign in America was bolstered by support of arguably the best kind – the incoming President of the United States, George W. Bush. Less than a week after taking office, Bush signed an executive order which deprived international agencies of federal funding to support women seeking an abortion. The move, which was a direct reversal of the previous Clinton administration's policy on the matter, was also timed to coincide with the anniversary of the Supreme Court's controversial 'Roe vs. Wade' decision which legalised abortion 28 years earlier. Significantly, Bush has been quoted as saying that he believes the Supreme Court, in legalising abortion, had 'overstepped the Constitution'.

While most campaigners are happy to work through political means, or by organising peaceful demonstrations and leaflet picketing, as with most pressure groups there are some extremists for whom a peaceful route just isn't enough. One of the most common forms of protest open to 'pro-lifers' used to be the picketing of abortion clinics, with the protestors hoping to persuade pregnant women not to have abortions. The picketing of hospitals was, however, made illegal in 1984.
One month after Bush took office, American anti-abortion activists won the right to continue publishing the names and addresses of abortion doctors on the internet, thanks to a ruling from a federal appeals court in San Francisco which invoked the First Amendment that guarantees free speech. In response, doctors on the list took to wearing bullet-proof vests

and living under police protection. They recalled only too clearly how, in 1998, Dr Barnett Slepian, a 52-year-old obstetrician, was shot by a sniper at his home in Amherst, near Buffalo. The New York doctor had carried out legal abortions at a women's clinic in Buffalo and also had a private medical practice. His name had appeared on an anti-abortion website as one of a number of doctors who, the site claimed, were guilty of murder because of their participation in abortions. Soon after his death, Dr Slepian's name was crossed out on the site. James Kopp, an activist suspected of being behind the killing of Dr Slepian, appeared on the FBI's Ten Most Wanted list for two years until his eventual arrest in 2001. Kopp, who had been arrested several times for his anti-abortion activities, was also wanted in Canada and the US in connection with at least four other attacks on abortion doctors. Having been traced to Ireland, where he had been working in a Dublin hospital, he was eventually tracked down to Dinan, France, where he was arrested and extradited to the USA. In May 2003, Kopp was sentenced to 25-years-to-life behind bars.

In 1996, almost a third of all abortion clinics reported violent attacks, such as bombings, arson and vandalism. The year after saw US abortion clinics report 17 very serious attacks. One clinic, in Greensboro, North Carolina, was burned down after an arson attack and forced to close. At another hospital in Atlanta, Georgia, protestors set off two bombs.

Although these were isolated incidents, and not condoned by the mainstream pro-life movement, they occurred at a time of mounting violence against abortion clinics. In 1992 there were 194 violent incidents reported at hospitals around the US, and in 1993 there were at least 329 attacks. As a result of the violence, many doctors and hospitals are now not prepared to perform abortions, making it increasingly difficult for many women to exercise what they see as their constitutional right.

But could this happen in the UK? Well, it hasn't so far. As in the USA, pro-life organisations continue to lobby parliament and try to promote awareness of their concerns. One such group, the UK Life League, have distributed leaflets that depicted graphic images of aborted foetuses with the headline: 'RIP. In memory of the six million unborn British babies murdered by abortion since 1967.' The similarly named Life group tried to have a party political broadcast transmitted during the 2002 General Election, but when their intended material was submitted to the main broadcasters, it was rejected: it too depicted images of foetuses which were felt to be too disturbing to be beamed into the homes of

British families. One concern of British pro-choice campaigners is that if their opponents are denied a voice in mainstream media, it could conceivably drive some extreme elements towards harder action to ensure they're heard.

The number of abortions performed in the US is, however, falling, from 1.6 million a year in the late 1980s to 1.4 million a year in the mid-1990s. Many pro-choice campaigners are certain this is because women have been frightened by the extreme militancy of a few hard-line 'pro-lifers'. Pro-life campaigners, however, argue that the real violence is the 1.5 million abortions performed every year. ■

Episode 102

First Broadcast (BBC1): May 20 2002

Written by **David Wolstencroft**
Directed by **Bharat Nalluri**

[Cast]

Lisa Faulkner (Helen Flynn), **Kevin McNally** (Robert Osborne), **Debra Stephenson** (Claire Osborne), **Daniel Chenery** (Sammy Osborne), **Shane Attwooll** (Brian Lyndon), **Tom Goodman-Hill** ('Nick Thomas' / Kieran Harvey), **Jasper Jacob** (Bill Watson), **Rod Hallett** (Andrew Dorland), **Lucy Allen** (Burglar One), **Dominic Kinnaird** (Burglar Two), **Jonathan Lomas** (Burglar Three), **Tonya Kerins** (Runner), **Rory Macgregor** (Colin Wells, the Technician), **Eleanor McReady** (Rosie), **Tehmina Sacranie** (Operator*), **Julian Wadham** (Derek), **Stephen Omer** (Vicar*).

* scenes excised

[Who's Who]

Kevin McNally (Robert Osborne) shot to fame with the BBC series *Diana* (1983) as John Leigh, though he'd had (very) small roles in *Poldark* (1975), *I, Claudius* (1976) and the film *The Long Good Friday* (in a blink-and-you'll-miss-him scene as Paul Freeman's bit of rough – he has exactly the same amount of dialogue as Pierce Brosnan… none!). Since then he's had a guest role in *Doctor Who* and small roles in *Cry Freedom* (dir. Richard Attenborough, 1987) and *Entrapment* (dir. Jon Amiel, 1999), co-starred alongside Minnie Driver and Mary McCormack in *High Heels and Low Lives* (dir. Mel Smith, 2001) and played the ship's captain in Channel 4's *Shackleton*.

Debra Stephenson (Claire Osborne) is best known for playing Shell Dockley in the ITV prison drama *Bad Girls*. Shane Attwooll (Brian Lyndon) played Gareth Davies in ITV's *Nuts and Bolts*. Tom Goodman-Hill ('Nick Thomas') played Ray in the award-winning comedy *The Office* and had a small role at the end of the BBC's dino-drama *The Lost World*. Julian Wadham (Derek) played Prime Minister William Pitt in the film *The Madness of King George* (dir. Nicholas Hytner, 1994) and has a small part in the unwelcome prequel to *The Exorcist* (dir. Paul Schrader, scheduled for release in 2003).

[Case Report]

Attempts to obtain intelligence via surveillance on believed ultra right-wing leader Robert Osborne (see Security File below) had so far been unsuccessful. Osborne's acute awareness of MI5's interest in him was such that his house was equipped with high-level security equipment that Section B's teams had been unable to penetrate.

Intelligence did however manage to learn that Osborne had a violent temper, and that his wife, Claire, had found herself on the receiving end. Any woman under that kind of pressure could of course be vulnerable for recruitment. A runner was already in place, handling two contacts posing as computer tutors at a class at Chadbridge Community College, Romford. Claire Osborne attended these classes, and the contacts were instructed to befriend her. Unfortunately, vetting had not picked up on the runner's alcoholism. After she had an RTA involving a minicab while five times over the limit, Harry suggested that Tom step in, and Helen Flynn was recruited from the clerical pool to pose as Tom's wife to aid his cover for 'Operation Greensleeves'.

Installed as the teachers, Tom and Helen wasted no time in befriending Claire Osborne. When Claire had her handbag stolen by a black youth at a shopping centre (in reality an MI5 contact), Tom and Helen were on hand to recover the bag and comfort Claire; when Claire's car broke down, Tom was able to fix the problem (which, of course he'd caused in the first place). Despite (or perhaps because of) a fairly unfriendly first meeting with Claire's husband one evening, Tom and Helen managed to receive an invitation from Claire to join her and her husband for dinner. Though she had rehearsed their joint back-stories meticulously, Osborne managed to catch Helen out by addressing Tom as her 'boyfriend' rather than husband. Helen

[Robert Osborne]

CLOSED

Osborne is believed to be either behind or in some way involved with a huge extreme racist organisation mounting a full-scale race war in the UK. With Osborne's reputation for paranoia, an infiltrator is out of the question. He has a wife, Claire, who shows signs of domestic violence, and a son, Sammy. He was in the army – reaching the rank of Corporal – but was kicked out shortly after his first posting to Cyprus.

Osborne runs a successful waste disposal business in Essex which, it is suspected, is used to fund a nationwide network of race violence somehow linked to Bill Watson, an independent MP for Chigwell. Other known contacts of Osborne include: Brian Lyndon (who, intelligence revealed, has a liking for curry and sex chatlines); Nick Thomas (a would-be campaigner for Osborne's cause); and 'Bora' – one of a number of men under investigation from Customs for trafficking illegal immigrants into the UK. Organisation on this scale could clearly be a threat to national security.

FILE UPDATE

After his wife left him, Osborne was killed in a car accident under suspicious circumstances. Case files were passed to Scotland Yard for further investigation.

REPORT APPROVED BY H. PEARCE, MI5

[Claire Osborne]

Claire Osborne subscribes to a number of specialist computing magazines, which was interpreted by intelligence as a desire on her part to advance herself in the hope it might provide her with a better chance of leaving her husband. Although she outwardly supported her husband's racist stance, it was believed this was more down to insecurity on her part than a real belief. Her husband paid £10,000 for Claire's breast enlargements.

FILE UPDATE

Having been recruited by Tom Quinn to assist in the collation of information about her husband's activities, Claire Osborne was later assisted to leave her husband and start a new life abroad with her son. She was last seen at Gatwick Airport travelling under the name 'Sykes'.

managed to improvise a way out of a difficult situation, but as they later discovered, the damage was already done.

Simultaneously, a cargo of illegal immigrants from Chechnya was intercepted by HM Customs. The traffickers panicked and threw the illegals overboard, all of whom drowned; their bodies were later washed ashore in Kent. Tessa Phillips, who was handling the case, suspected that the traffickers would now change their routes, and the long operation to catch them would have to be mounted again from scratch. As Tessa was already shorthanded, Harry authorised a loan of Zoe to Tessa's team which resulted in one of Zoe's contacts in Ostend informing her that the traffickers were using old heroin routes. Inspecting surveillance photographs of a meeting with a man known as 'Bora', Zoe identified one of the other men at the meeting as Robert Osborne. Piecing together information that Tom recovered from 'Operation Greensleeves', the connection was clear – Osborne was assisting in the trafficking of illegal immigrants who would end up overcrowding the UK's holding centres and choking the system. Once his followers had stirred up a number of race riots, Osborne would then encourage his friend Bill Watson (MP for Chigwell) to raise the issue of asylum seekers in the House of Commons. Sadly, though Tessa's agents were eventually able to track down the new routes, by then Robert Osborne had become aware that his plan had been exposed; all evidence suggested it was he who once again gave the order for the immigrants to be thrown overboard. Tessa Phillips was at the time watching a live feed from the scene where the few survivors had been brought ashore, and her report on the matter makes for distressing reading.

After extensive investigations into his background, it was discovered that Osborne's contact Nick Thomas was actually a freelance undercover journalist called Kieran Harvey. Harvey was working for an independent radio producer in Soho and had been recording his conversations with Osborne with a digital recorder hidden inside a pen. Tom was informed of the discovery and when he finally met with 'Thomas' he confronted him with the truth and forced him to hand over any information he had already collated. At this point, Harvey revealed he was ready to leave Osborne anyway; he'd acquired enough information for his report and had planned to go into editing for a few months.

Convinced she had gained Claire Osborne's trust, Helen told her she knew about Robert's abusive temperament. Helen promised to introduce Claire to 'someone' who could help her to escape her husband. Tom met Claire at an agreed location and revealed only that he works for a 'government department'. He assured her that he and Helen had only gone to such lengths because they wanted to help her, and that they knew she could tell them what Robert was up to. As a sweetener, he also offered her £600 a week. After giving the matter a little thought, she agreed to give him what he wanted.

Tom and Helen prepared to pull out, but Osborne had grown too suspicious of them; he sent his right-hand man Brian Lyndon to kidnap them both at gunpoint.

Tom and Helen were taken to a kitchen adjoining the staff canteen at Osborne's plant – along with the dead body of Kieran Harvey. When Osborne arrived with his wife in tow, a severely beaten Tom tried to protest their innocence, but Osborne revealed that he knew Tom was lying, thanks in part to Helen's lie about her 'boyfriend' that had given them away, although he had been aware someone was trying to infiltrate him for months. Holding Helen next to a vat of boiling cooking oil, he then demanded information on the extent of MI5 penetration of all far-right groups, including the names of all sources and the people running them. To force Tom to talk, Osborne plunged Helen's hand into the deep-fat fryer. Tom tried to convince him that Brian Lyndon was behind a betrayal of his boss to buy them both time, but Osborne refused to believe him; he pushed Helen face-first into the oil before shooting her dead.

The events from this point are a little confused. Tom believes that it was Claire Osborne who threw a cigarette into the oil, causing it to flare up. He took advantage of the distraction and escaped. Once he was certain he had evaded Osborne and Lyndon, he managed to locate a public callbox from where he called in to the Grid. He was guided to the nearest safe house where Zoe found him an hour later.

Once Tom's information on Osborne had been collated, Harry Pearce had planned to sanction the arrest of Robert Osborne, but this was blocked at government level. Harry was informed that the government view was that Osborne should be left alone as they believed he could be used as a remote pawn to move

[Notes]

Tom's tips to avoid getting drunk: eat well beforehand (cheese is recommended as it lines the stomach with fats), and during the meal only wet your lips with your drink so you can stave off the effects for longer.

In the final scenes, Bill Watson receives photos of the dead refugees with the words 'Happy with your wash?' on the back, in reference to a soap powder advertising campaign from the 1990s.

Entirely coincidentally, the first transmission of this episode was followed by an item on the evening news about changes to British asylum regulations.

Tom and Helen use a code system to call in to the Grid – AKA 'Sunnycabs' – at midnight each night. If they call in late, each minute should be assumed to be a notification of their current level of risk: one minute late means a minor problem; five or more minutes late suggests something serious has happened; an additional code – 'the cat's in the van' – indicates an urgent problem. Tom receives a message written in invisible ink on a subscription card slipped into a copy of History Today which was delivered to the nearest newsagent the same morning.

[Notes]

Early on, the storyline for this episode was originally planned as the season finale with another character entirely as Osborne's victim, but during development the episode was brought forward. After the team met with Lisa Faulkner (who was auditioning for another role), the decision was made to increase the role played by Helen Flynn and rewrite this episode to include Helen and give her a shocking exit.

The script for this episode was provisionally entitled 'Looking After Our Own'.

[Quote/Unquote]

Robert Osbourne: 'This time last year no-one knew what a Muslim was. Now everyone's looking at people in the street. "Where's he from? What's he doing?" They've started to see things they've never noticed before: asylum seekers clogging up the hospitals; shop assistants who can't speak English; black media corrupting our children... Everyone's crying out for a voice of reason. Someone to make them realise that they're not alone, they're not on the extreme, that they are the majority, that it's their country and it's alright to get angry!'

Danny: 'Tell me something I don't know.'
MI5 Officer: 'I'm banging your sister.'

the right further right and the left more to the centre. This would then make it easier for them to pass a bill that allows them to control immigration.

Though Harry's team was forbidden to intervene by Whitehall, it was with no small amount of guilty relief that they heard of the death of Robert Osborne in a car accident. All accusations of MI5 involvement in Osborne's death have been handled personally by Harry Pearce who, naturally, has denied any responsibility on the part of MI5.

[Disinformation]

Tom and Helen posed as husband-and-wife computer tutors Steven (D.O.B. 22/08/67) and Susan Wilkes (D.O.B. 17/05/72) of 32 Abbey Crescent, Romford, Essex, where they've lived for a few months. Prior to that they lived on Mervyn Road (a contact had already been installed in case Osborne checked up on them). They met in Brighton (where Susan had lived since the age of three) in a shop that sold ornaments and they'd argued over a turtle that they both wanted. They have been married for three years and have a middling credit rating. After Osborne caught Helen off-guard, she told him she had been having an affair as part of their 'open' marriage. (See also Personnel Records Update below.)

'Matthew' told Ellie that he was being sent away on a fact-finding tour of the USA and Japan.

[Identity Check]

Tom narrowly avoided paying for a meal at Ellie's restaurant with his real credit card.

[Personnel Records Update]

Helen Flynn's body was recovered from Osborne's plant with the help of Special Branch. The severe nature of her wounds from the hot oil was such that she had to be formally identified by dental records. A cover story was prepared to state that she had died in a car accident, which helped to explain why the funeral had to be 'closed casket'.

A number of the Section B team have noticed that Danny Hunter seems to be spending a lot of money on new clothes. His new leather jacket must have set him back a few hundred pounds alone. Just before 'Operation Greensleeves', Helen revealed to Tom that, as Danny's flatmate, she'd observed that he takes an inordinate amount of time to get ready each morning.

During the operation, after the eventful dinner with Osborne and his wife, Helen made advances towards Tom. Though he politely brushed them off as an effect of the alcohol she had drunk, it was also clear that Helen did have a slight crush on him, which made dealing with her death all the more difficult for him.

At school, Maisie Simm was asked to draw a picture of her family; it pleased Tom/'Matthew' to see that she'd drawn him in too (even if she misspelt his name 'Mattew' and drew his nose too big). Tom had already realised that Ellie was not particularly happy living above her restaurant, so the tragic conclusion to this operation convinced him to invite both Ellie and Maisie to move in with him.

Harry has openly expressed his dislike for Derek, from Millbank, on a number of occasions (usually to the effect that he believes him to be a 'little shit').

[Gadgets]

Osborne's house has all the latest in security alarms, but MI5 have the latest in equipment that can bypass them all... for a time. Kieran Harvey has a basic recording device hidden inside his pen.

[Missing in Action]

A voice-over was recorded for the scenes of Helen's funeral in which the vicar (actor Stephen Omer) revealed the cover story for Helen's life – that she worked as a cleric at the Department of Environment – and for her death – that she died in a tragic car accident.

[Expert Witnesses]

Debra Stephenson, on Claire Osborne: 'She's not a bad woman, but she is quite selfish. She wants what is best for her and her son and for a while that means turning a blind eye to her horrible husband's dodgy dealings. She only agrees to help Tom and Helen for her own sake, not for moral reasons. Until then, she just goes along with whatever gets her the nice house and glamorous clothes. She's a classic "Yummy Mummy".'

Lisa Faulkner: 'I had a bit of a love-hate relationship with Helen. She's a bit of a hero-worshipper. She's desperate to be good mates with Zoe and she even makes a really cringey move on her boss Tom. Plus she has to deal with another senior officer, Tessa, being a total cow, talking down to her like a bog-standard secretary. I couldn't deal with that every day.'

Director Bharat Nalluri: 'We deliberately cast Lisa Faulkner in the role, a very well-known face; certainly out of the young cast she's probably the most well-known TV face in Britain at the time so you expect it even less that we were going to kill her off at the end of episode two. The way her character was built up you really cared for her. We always saw her as the one that would drag people in because everyone else was very spooky and methodical in their procedure – they're trained spies. With Lisa's character, she was the fresh new one, the audience in a way. The audience really reacted because they saw themselves.'

Violence on TV

Although [**s p o o k s**] was signposted from the very beginning as a hard-hitting drama, the conclusion to episode two – which saw Helen brutally tortured with a deep-fat fryer before being shot in the head - – still came as a major shock to many viewers. It could be argued that the main reason for the stunned response to this sequence was less to do with the actual violent content (which, after all, was more implied through clever editing than actually shown) and more to do with an audience unprepared for shock endings in British drama. As viewers, we have become so used to being spoonfed with easy-to-watch soap operas and magazine covers blurting out the resolution to every major storyline that the fact that a production company can keep such an ending a complete surprise is almost a miracle in itself.

In an article for the *Observer* published some weeks after the initial broadcast, executive producer for [**s p o o k s**], Stephen Garrett, found himself explaining the decision to kill off a popular character in such a seemingly 'gratuitous' way:

Everyone knows that lead characters have got to come back next week. Heroes don't die, in fact they barely ever even get hurt. Violence takes place in a fantasy world in which blows to the head with iron bars leave small bruises rather than crushed skulls, gunshot wounds leave neat abrasions in conveniently fleshy parts of the anatomy rather than eviscerating their victims, and fights that would hospitalise Tyson are walked away from with barely a mark.

It is this kind of cartoon violence that is insidious, numbing and ultimately corrupting. This is the violence that children can copy – because it looks such fun. To create, on the other hand, a sense of genuine threat, to stimulate in the imagination of the viewer vivid pictures of the consequences of evil, is to take an audience seriously.

The production team had clearly thought this through; as far as they were concerned, the episode had shown a responsible attitude to the dramatisation of everyday violence in the lives of these fictional characters. However, not all viewers agreed…

In Britain, all broadcasters receive guidance from a statutory body called the

Broadcasting Standards Council. The Council has no powers of censorship of its own, though it does set the codes of conduct that all broadcasters are expected to reflect in their editorial policy, and considers and adjudicates on complaints from viewers on matters of fairness or decency. It is not, however, a harshly over-zealous organisation: it does not seek to inhibit creativity, and its findings are based on the context of any material, as well as the reasonable expectations of an average viewer when approaching the material either for the first time or on repeated viewing. Indeed, on average it tends to uphold only 20 per cent of all complaints, which has, on occasion, left it open to attack from lobbyists such as the late Mary Whitehouse – former leader of the Viewers' and Listeners' Association – for being too accepting of some of modern broadcasting's 'permissiveness'.

The biggest indication of a programme's intended audience is its time slot. Anything transmitted before the 9pm 'watershed' should be suitable for a family audience, while anything after that time is at parents' discretion, though some programmes might not be suitable for a younger audience. The broadcaster must be aware that anything broadcast immediately after 9pm might still be attracting a younger audience and it shouldn't just assume all the kiddies are safely tucked up in bed.

The unexpected departure of Helen in episode two of [spooks] led to 154 viewers complaining to the BSC. Most of the complaints were, naturally, regarding the violence, though others mentioned concerns over depicting torture for entertainment, possibilities of imitation, the fact that the victim was a young female, that there had not been sufficient warning to the audience prior to transmission and, bizarrely, that the final scenes depicting Osborne's death in a tunnel were in some way a visual reference to the death of Princess Diana.

Invited to comment on the criticisms, the BBC naturally apologised for any distress caused by the segment, but went on to note:

..this had been a serious piece of television drama, an episode in a series which aimed to show the kind of threat which might be faced by agents engaged in the fight against terrorism, broadly defined. It had been broadcast after the watershed and preceded by a warning that it contained upsetting scenes.

Some of the people who complained had drawn the BSC's attention to the lack of preparation for the level of violence the episode would contain. Certainly it had not been hinted at in the trailers that the BBC had run over the previous week, and during an interview on Radio One on the afternoon of the transmission, actress Lisa Faulkner had given no indication that her character was about to be killed off – in the interests of preserving the surprise. However, the BBC did precede the episode with a warning that it might be distressing for some viewers, and in their statement to the BSC, they also pointed to the context of the piece – that Osborne had clearly been identified as a violent man, and that, actually, most of the action from the scene had not been depicted at all. The character's scalded face was not shown, and it was 'the viewers' imaginations that filled in the details of the perpetrator's viciousness'.

Significantly, one of the concessions the BBC did make was that the character of Helen had been set up as if she were a regular character, so her death came as a massive shock. However, the audience had been prepared to some extent, as the course of events was attributed to Helen's mistake in 'going off-piste' during her discussions with Osborne.

The episode itself was viewed by the full Commission of the BSC, taking into account the BBC's statement. They agreed that the scene in context was necessary for the ongoing story of the series, and that the likelihood of 'copycat' behaviour was slim. They also rejected the concerns over the similarity between Princess Diana's death and that of Robert Osborne. They did, however, express concern over the level of warning at the beginning of the programme, which they felt should have been more 'specific, clear and unambiguous'. This was the only aspect of the complaints to be upheld.

Violence on television has been a major concern to British TV viewers almost from the moment the medium first arrived in our homes. After all, it beams directly into our living rooms (usually) and appeals massively to children. Its power can be seen both in the cost of advertising on television and in the amount of money that's been raised by charity telethons over the years (both the corporate and charity worlds at least agree on the power of television to be able to reach its audience). Yet, as Stephen Garrett suggests, it's not really acts of violence that we should be worried about, it's that violence could ever be depicted without showing the consequences – an accusation that is unlikely to ever be directed at [**spooks**]. ■

Episode 103

First Broadcast (BBC1): May 27 2002

Written by **Simon Mirren**
Directed by **Rob Bailey**

[C a s t]

Christopher Fulford (Johnny Marks), **Katie Jones** (Leyla), **Karzan Krekar** (Serka),
Ray Panthaki (Chalak), **Oliver Haden** (Sonay), **Kevork Malikyan** (Ozan Cosar),
Fisun Burgess (Selin Cosar), **Donald Pirie** (PC Steven Bowers), **Ralph Ineson** (Sam
Walker), **Steve Garti** (Stan, Tom's Informer), **Rory Macgregor** (Colin Wells, the
Technician), **Jeremy Bulloch** (Roger Welks), **Beth Vyse** (Tara Welks).

[W h o ' s   W h o]

Scriptwriter Simon Mirren has worked on the BBC's long-running medical drama
Casualty and the series *Waking the Dead* and scripted the feature film *Greenwich
Mean Time* (dir. John Strickland, 1999).

The cast list for this episode is blessed with a number of actors whose faces will
be familiar to viewers, though their names might not be. Christopher Fulford
(Johnny Marks) has appeared in almost every British cop show since *Juliet Bravo*.
He played Napoleon in the mini-series *Scarlet and Black* (1993), had a supporting
role in *Prime Suspect 4* (1995), and a lead role in the drama *The Last Train* (1999).
More recently, he appeared in the Sylvester Stallone actioner *D-Tox* (dir. Jim
Gillespie, 2002) and the BBC period drama *Servants*.

Oliver Haden (Sonay) was a regular in the short-lived soap *London Bridge*, and
in 2001, he appeared in the feature film *The Point Men* (dir. John Glen), opposite

Christopher Lambert and Vincent Regan. Ralph Ineson (Sam Walker) played Finchy in the mockumentory comedy *The Office* and Luke Mullen in Kay Mellor's *Playing the Field*. Ray Panthaki (Chalak Bakuri) can be seen playing Private Bedford in the apocalyptic thriller *28 Days Later...* (dir. Danny Boyle, 2002). Steve Garti (Stan) played PC Colin Jellicoe in the BBC series *The Cops* and pops up regularly in advertisements (including the McDonald's 'hospital dash' ads).

Jeremy Bulloch (Roger Welks) holds the distinction of having played one of the coolest characters in cinema history – the original Boba Fett in *The Empire Strikes Back* (dir. Irvin Kershner, 1980) and *Return of the Jedi* (dir. Richard Marquand, 1983). He was also a semi-regular in the ITV series *Robin of Sherwood*.

[Case Report]

Posing as a PR executive called 'Emily', Zoe befriended a Turkish travel agent called Sonay. Sonay invited her to a drinks party in a function room at the State Consulate of Turkey, which coincided neatly with MI5's annual check of its surveillance devices there. Zoe was briefed on where to find MI5's bugging devices and instructed to use the cover of the party as a means to gain entry. Matters were complicated slightly when Sonay revealed that he'd told the Attaché General, Ozan Cosar, that 'Emily' was his wife, and that they were expecting their first child (knowing that Cosar was a family man, he hoped this would impress him enough to help Sonay benefit from Turkey's bid for the next Olympics).

Meanwhile, although officially on leave to celebrate his birthday, Tom arranged to meet one of his contacts, Stan, who told him that he'd been approached by four British Northern Ireland ex-military men with a view to buying an arsenal of weapons, including SD-Hecklers and short-stock AK47s.

Soon after the drinks party began, the function room was stormed by eight people wearing masks. These were later identified as a party of five Kurdish freedom fighters and three men led by former British soldier Sam Walker. The attackers assaulted the officer on guard outside the state consulate (PC Steven Bowers) and the security guards inside and then headed straight for the party, indicating they knew exactly where to go. As the attackers entered the ballroom and began pushing the guests up against the wall, Zoe slipped her video-linked mobile phone into the breast pocket of Sonay's jacket, which provided the Grid team with an immediate

[John William Marks]

CLOSED

Born 30/03/57 in Blackheath, London. His father was English-Irish, his mother was Irish. Trained in survival skills, weapons and counter-surveillance, he was also fluent in Arabic and Urdu, with a good command of French and Spanish. Whilst in MI5's service he was employed by Northern Ireland Militant Groups (1981 – 83) and Kurdish Liberators (1984 – 87) in areas around Syria, Iran and Iraq. He was first observed passing on classified information to members of the Iraqi army in 1979. For ten years he procured information and sold it to the highest bidder, in which time he became sympathetic with a Kurdish mountain tribe who helped him move through the mountains from country to country. Having betrayed British intelligence and that of the Arab states, he moved on to the Irish but was killed by a car bomb in 1987. His remains were formally identified by Harry Pearce.

FILE REOPENED JUNE 2002

Johnny Marks did not die in 1987 – it was Johnny's brother who Harry identified. After acquiring the names and addresses of 3,000 active agents around the world, Marks used this information to secure his freedom. Only once he had escaped did we learn that he had already handed the data disk containing this information over to Tessa Phillips. He is still at large and should be approached with caution.

Known contacts prior to the Turkish Embassy siege include Sam Walker (35), and two men known only as Victor and Levi, all ex-military.

visual feed into the room and informed us that the terrorists were equipped with explosives. The Kurds secured the room as their leader – identified as Leyla Bakuri – called out for Ozan Cosar by name. At that point one of the other terrorists began smashing all the mobile phones in the room; eventually Zoe's feed was lost.

Piecing together the footage from Zoe's phone and that from security cameras outside the state consulate, Harry Pearce noticed that the Kurds were not afraid to reveal their faces, suggesting they were determined to see this through regardless of the consequences. The three other men, however, remained masked by balaclavas, which Harry believed meant that they were dependent on another way out. Once Tom had arrived at the Grid and shared his new information, it became clear that three of the men who had stormed the function room were almost certainly from the same group that Tom's contact had spoken of.

The three masked men left the room, ostensibly to secure the building, while the Kurds tied a distressed Ozan Cosar to a chair. They strapped dynamite to his back and placed him on the function room's balcony. By this point, Danny's team had surrounded the area and tried to insert a thermal imaging camera through a hole in the wall to the ballroom. Its vision was blocked by the anti-surveillance curtains the Kurds had hoisted against the interior walls, but the surveillance teams did manage to get a sound feed installed. It was thanks to this that the team outside were able to discover much of what went on in the first hour of the siege. Unfortunately, the Kurds eventually found Zoe's bag of surveillance tools, which she'd thrown under a table the moment the Kurds first burst in. When they threatened the life of PC Bowers, Zoe was forced to reveal that the tools were hers. At first she claimed the tools were a present for her husband, 'for fun', but the terrified Sonay broke down and confessed that Zoe was not his wife. Her cover story blown, Zoe told her captors that she worked for the Secret Service, although she continued to maintain her 'Emily' identity.

Tessa Phillips examined security footage of the three masked men before they entered the state consulate. With them, she identified a fourth man – former MI5 officer Johnny Marks. She shared her suspicions with Harry, who was incredulous as he had personally identified Johnny's dead body after a car bombing in Northern Ireland 15 years ago. Harry had known that Johnny Marks and Tessa had been romantically involved, but only at this point did he realise that the State Consulate of Turkey was located five doors down from the Cranborne Bank, a private obscure bank used to make payments to MI5 agents around the world. To protect the agent, the bank uses swift-codes that allow MI5 to credit or debit an agent's account without revealing his or her location. Previously, only three people knew the location of the bank: Harry, Roger Welks (the manager of the bank) and the Director of MI5. Now Harry realised that Marks must also know of the bank's existence. Marks had tracked down Roger Welks and kidnapped his daughter. He then forced Welks to hand over the access codes. Not only could Marks now clear the funds of the bank (funds which run into millions), he could also uncover the identity and location of each and every undercover Five and Six agent across the world. The siege was therefore a cover for Marks's own enterprise. As Marks had not been seen actively taking part in the siege, it made sense to assume that he must be communicating with his team from afar and that he was holding Welks's daughter while his men transferred the funds into his account and transmitted the swift-codes to his mobile laptop.

With the SAS in place outside the state consulate, a police negotiator made contact with the hostage-takers. Leyla revealed the demands of the Freedom Fighters – the release of her parents, Pejan and Zana Bakuri, as well as two other political prisoners. She insisted that she would only negotiate with the person in charge of 'Emily'. Tom stepped in and assured Leyla that he was trying to present her options to the Turkish government. Meanwhile, Colin Wells, one of Section B's technical crew, was able to source footage of Kurdish prisoners being released, which was then fed through cable direct to the function room, while

Tom himself delivered medicine for Osar, which was collected at the front door by Zoe, still held at gunpoint by Chalak Bakuri.

Danny's team were unable to gain access to the bank, which suggested that Marks's men would also have no alternative escape route, but Tessa found a map of the underground war-room

passages that run underneath all the buildings in that area, including the bank.

Using the map Tessa found, Danny's team made their way into the bank and captured Marks's men, but not before they had transmitted all the information to Marks. The function room was stormed by the SAS and Tom managed to pull Zoe through the front door. He took a bullet to the side before marksmen shot Chalak Bakuri (he was later pronounced dead at the scene). The building was evacuated and Leyla and her team were arrested. Roger Welks's daughter was found safe and well, but Johnny Marks escaped…

Tessa returned home to find Marks waiting for her. She begged him not to sell the names of the agents. Harry arrived at Tessa's apartment to arrest Marks, but the former officer persuaded Harry to let him go in exchange for the 3,000 agents' names and addresses. Harry agreed, unaware that Marks had already left the disk with Tessa.

[Identity Check]

Tom is forced to maintain his identity of 'Matthew' by telling Maisie that he has been called back into work to fix one of the main relay circuits, a problem that, he claims, is his own fault. Zoe poses as 'Emily Arlington' (D.O.B. 14/04/68), a PR consultant. According to her driving licence she lives in Monmouth Street, NW5. Her favourite football team is Manchester United (though her support is largely influenced by star player David Beckham).

[Personnel Records Update]

Helen Flynn's record revealed that she was born on 22/06/75 and died on 29/05/02. She collected the toys from McDonald's happy meals for her godson. Danny cleared her desk out at Section B, weeding out her personal effects from any 'sensitive' material. Danny is a Crystal Palace supporter.

Tessa reveals to Harry that when Johnny Marks was alive, as well as being his runner, she'd also been his lover. She had become pregnant by him (a baby girl), though the shock of his death caused her to miscarry at five months.

This operation takes place on the same day as Tom's birthday.

[Gadgets]

Zoe's little bag of tricks includes lock-picking equipment and a mobile phone that contains a video camera linked directly to the Grid.

[Missing in Action]

A scene was filmed but not used in which Danny helps Zoe run through her briefing for infiltrating the embassy (this was replaced with the much more concise shot of Zoe getting ready with the voice-over of Tom's briefing). Danny then heads off to see Helen's mum with her effects, a job he's been putting off as it would make everything 'final'.

An additional scene was filmed with Ellie and Maisie preparing for a birthday party for 'Matthew', in which Tom realises all too late that he's sent Ellie flowers with a card signed 'with love from Tom'; fortunately, Ellie assumes it's a reference to the Tom Jones CD he borrowed from her (the first scene of the script showed Tom jogging while singing along to Jones's 'Sex Bomb'!). The scene also reveals that 'Matthew' has told Ellie he's training for a marathon, just another example of his 'deceitful ways'.

[Expert Witnesses]

Keeley Hawes: 'A spy has to be brilliant at improvising and picking up on other people's behaviour, but unlike acting, your life depends on it and I'm sure some MI5 officers become compulsive liars!'

Series producer, Jane Featherstone: 'Zoe has that fantastic ability to tune in to another human being. The ex-spies we spoke to said that women officers are generally better than men at reading people because they can do that chameleon-like thing of imitating and mimicking others.'

International Terrorism

On Bank Holiday Monday, April 5 1980, I witnessed my first counter-terrorism operation. For the previous six days, 26 people, including a police officer, had been held at gunpoint by six armed terrorists at the Iranian Embassy in Princes Gate, London. Although I'd had a vague idea that something was going on, I wasn't really sure what it was. I had no idea that the terrorists were Arabs funded by Iraq to embarrass the Iranians and demand autonomy for an oil-rich region in southern Iran known as Khuzestan. All I knew that Monday evening was *Coronation Street* had been cancelled and something very frightening was being shown on live TV. I was nine years old and very, very scared.

I was convinced that whatever was happening 200 miles away in London would result in another war (despite my mother's assurances to the contrary). But almost as soon as it had begun, it was over: an explosion inside the embassy flowered smoke clouds out of a window and black-clad SAS figures somersaulted over the balcony and disappeared into the grey fog

and began taking out the terrorists one by one. Looking back through records of the time, the whole thing took just 11 minutes.

Though the SAS suddenly became every schoolboy's heroes that day, one of the main reasons the siege ended so dramatically was the intelligence the men received about the situation. Since the late 1960s, MI5 had seen a rise in what became known as 'international terrorism', with groups like 'Black September', a Palestinian terrorist organisation led by 'Carlos the Jackal', who targeted Israeli athletes at the 1972 Olympics. Whereas traditionally the Security Service's targets were Soviet-backed groups intent on stealing state secrets and trading information, these new enemies were different. For one thing, they didn't strike quietly like the Russians. They had no intention of returning to a target more than once. They struck fast and hard to focus the world's media on their cause, and were more than willing to kill to achieve their aims. The gentlemanly act of spying swiftly became a thing of the past. Even the process of collating information on terrorists was more difficult, more fraught with danger: agents can't casually befriend a terrorist if they operate only in family-run cells of two or three; anyone who does manage to successfully infiltrate a terrorist group won't be able to extricate themselves from the situation easily; and should the Security Services act on information provided by an infiltrator, the terrorists could easily work out which of their number was a traitor and dispose of the problem.

As former head of MI5 Stella Rimington notes in her autobiography, terrorism didn't begin with September 11, and, sadly, nor will it end there; terrorism has proven too effective in getting the world's attention. As the first and then second plane struck the World Trade Center, I was once again transfixed by the horror of terrorism brought so clearly into focus by television and now the internet. My mind briefly flickered back to the events my nine-year-old self had witnessed. It says a lot for young Maisie Simm in this episode that she can sit through the live broadcast of a siege and not seem particularly distressed. Perhaps our children have become desensitised to images of violence and terror, or perhaps they now accept this as just another part of life. ■

Episode 104

First Broadcast (BBC1): June 4 2002

Written by **Howard Brenton**
Directed by **Rob Bailey**

[Cast]

Anthony Head (Peter Salter), **Bronwen Davies** (Andrea Chambers), **Jukka Hiltunen** (Horst), **Hugh Laurie** (Jools Siviter), **Jules Werner** (Istvan Vogel), **Patrick Kennedy** (Radio Operator), **Robert Finan** (Geoff Catty, 'Penguin Man'), **Christopher Jupe** (Waiter), **Matthew Thomas** (Demonstrator), **Freddie Stuart** (Ted, the Drunk Man), **Gurdial Sira** (Mr Patel, the Shopkeeper), **Gabriel Crosse** (Policeman), **Sarah Goodchild** (Sue, Cheeky Girl 1 at Staff Training), **Joanne Baxter** (Cheeky Girl 2 at Staff Training), **Richard Armitage** (Armed Police Officer), **Peter Pedrero** (Riot Policeman).

[Who's Who]

A prolific and frequently controversial playwright, scriptwriter Howard Brenton has worked with both fringe and leading theatre companies since the late 1960s. His stage plays include *The Churchill Play*, *Romans in Britain*, *Christie in Love*, *Brassneck*, *The Saliva Milkshake* and *Iranian Nights*. He also wrote the 1986 TV series *Dead Head*, which starred Denis Lawson as a minor criminal on the run from government security agents.

Anthony Head (Peter Salter) might still be better known to most British viewers as 'that bloke off the coffee ads', but since 1995, when he joined the cast of short-lived sci-fi series *VR.5*, he's been carving a career for himself in the United States –

notably in the hugely successful *Buffy the Vampire Slayer*. Taking a rest from *Buffy* in 2002 gave him the chance to return to the UK for a variety of different projects, including playing the villain in a series of *Doctor Who* audio plays, starring alongside Nigel Havers in the mini-series *Manchild* and, of course, playing troubled super-spy Peter Salter in [**spooks**] . He is often credited as 'Anthony Stewart Head'.

Hugh Laurie (Jools Siviter) is best known for his comedy partnership with Stephen Fry, having worked alongside him on *A Bit of Fry and Laurie*, various roles in *Blackadder*, *Jeeves and Wooster* and the feature film *Peter's Friends* (Kenneth Branagh, 1992). He's also appeared, solo, as Cruella De Vil's henchman Jasper in the live-action remake of *101 Dalmatians* (dir. Stephen Kerek, 1996), adoptive father in *Stuart Little* (dir. Rob Minkoff, 1999/2002) and prospective father Sam in *Maybe Baby* (dir. Ben Elton, 2000), which also featured Matthew Macfadyen.

If you pay attention to adverts, you might recognise Bronwen Davies (Andrea Chambers) from commercials for Toyota Corolla, Levi's shaped denim and Blockbuster home video.

[Case Report]

During a surveillance operation on a demonstration against the globalisation of trade, Zoe and Danny identified one of the protestors as Peter Salter, a senior agent in MI5 currently being run by Tom Quinn. Concerned that they might have stumbled into the path of another investigation, they gave instructions to their police contacts to release him and his accomplice (Andrea Chambers – see Security File). When they later informed Harry of their discovery, he tactfully urged them to decide that they were mistaken – if it were known that Peter Salter had been on that riot

without authorisation it would have put them all in a very difficult situation.

Though Tom was still on sick leave after being shot during the consulate siege, Danny realised that he would want to be briefed about Salter's activities, as Salter was, ostensibly, still listed as one of Tom's agents. Tom immediately came to Thames House and challenged Harry about being kept in the dark about Salter, forcing Harry to explain that it was because Salter was involved in a special op involving MI6 – specifically Jools Siviter (the animosity between Tom and Jools is of course well known).

Harry arranged for himself and Tom to be briefed at MI6 by Siviter. Siviter, however, led Harry and Tom away from Six to a safe house in Vauxhall where one of his teams had a nearby flat under surveillance (apparently, Six has had that address bugged for some time as it had at one point been the home of a known anarchist). Entirely coincidentally, Andrea Chambers had led Peter Salter to that address and the pair had set up home there. In among audio footage of Salter and Chambers' lovemaking, Six had been able to record their conversations, which was how they learned that Salter had acquired a 'dead ground' map showing the locations of every CCTV camera in every government building, military installation and communications location in the country; the map also revealed areas the CCTVs don't cover. At this point, however, MI6 lost contact – it seemed Salter had discovered the bugs and was 'cleaning' the flat systematically.

Peter Salter managed to escape and installed Andrea at a B&B in Camden. He then arranged to meet Tom at North Greenwich station. There he claimed to be employing a very complex cover in order to penetrate the anarchist cell, but when Tom voiced his concern over how 'off-piste' things were going, Salter confessed that he'd fallen in love with Andrea. Tom had no choice but to pull his former mentor off the operation, giving him until the next morning to extricate himself and, if possible, Andrea.

To make sure certain things went to plan, Tom posted Zoe and Danny in a car outside the Camden B&B, but Salter had obviously detected their presence; as they tried to maintain surveillance, Danny and Zoe were interrupted by police officers investigating a complaint about a couple having sex in view of children. As Danny tried in vain to convince the officer that he had blundered into a delicate MI5 operation, their targets managed to make their escape. Intelligence later found Salter's clothes and mobile phone dumped in a street bin, which suggested that whoever helped him escape had forced him to strip to avoid any chance of him being bugged.

[Peter William Salter]

CLOSED

Born 11/05/54 in Chelmsford, Essex, an only child. Salter's father was a non-commissioned officer in the 23rd Middlesex Rifles (he was killed by a bomb in Famagusta, Cyprus, in 1958). Salter's mother worked as a cleaner, but after her husband's death she campaigned for increases in army widows' pension rights (the fact that she already had a security file suggests she really got up the noses of someone at the MOD). She died in 2000.

Salter won a scholarship to St Edmund's Hall, Chelmsford (leaving with 11 O-Levels, four A-Levels, three S-Levels), then went to Oxford (achieving a first-class degree in maths and philosophy), where he was a Rugby Blue and active member of the Floodlight theatre group. Recruited at Oxford to GCHQ. Did his basic training at Cernwith Rifle Range, Wales. Highly experienced in advanced computer code breaking. Earned black belts in jujitsu and karate. Volunteered for MI5 service in 1977, commended for bravery after Operation 'Burnt Field' in Belfast 1978. Seconded to MI6 1985–89, and returned to MI5 in 1992. He was responsible for recruiting Tom Quinn.

Although by the end of his career, Salter was being run as an agent by Tom Quinn, for the last few months of his life he had been brought in by Harry Pearce on a joint operation with MI6 to handle a Foreign National (MI6 were prima mobile). It was during this operation that he helped to infiltrate and expose an anarchist terrorist cell, and prevent an air traffic disaster that would have certainly killed the President of the United States. His death after a subsequent breakdown and suicide due to the effects of terrorist brainwashing techniques was a terrible loss to the Security Services.

REPORT APPROVED BY J. SIVITER, MI6

The next time Salter was heard of was at the Geo-topology Research Unit at Medway University Ordnance Survey. He'd led a small team of anarchists in a break-in. Salter was arrested by police but the rest of his team escaped. He was quickly brought in to Thames House (Tom having briefed the Grid staff to treat him with the respect a returning hero deserves). Harry appointed Tom quiz-master (much to the annoyance of Jools Siviter).

During the debriefing, Salter seemed disorientated, which he put down to tinnitus, an after-effect of the stun grenade the police used in his arrest. He claimed that the raid on the university had been an attempt to steal hard drives which would be sold on to raise funds for the anarchist group. He also claimed that he had been picked up by the anarchists not far from where Zoe and Danny had lost sight of him, and had been blindfolded and taken to a rural location that he believed to be East Anglia. However, there was something in Salter's manner that alerted Tom to the possibility that his former mentor had lied. Simple guesswork led him to deduce that Salter had in fact been taken to Wales (which is on the opposite side of the country to where Salter was trying to direct him). Salter's deception therefore cast a shadow across his claim to be working deep undercover; indeed, it was highly likely that he was in fact working with the anarchists because he genuinely believed in their cause.

It became apparent to Tom that Salter would require deeper debriefing; his priorities appeared skewed and he was talking of disillusionment with his role, with the Service and with society in general. When Salter requested a toilet break, Tom accompanied him to the nearest bathroom. There, Salter punched him in the throat to wind him. As Tom struggled to breathe, he watched helplessly as Salter removed Tom's belt, created a makeshift noose and hanged himself. By the time help arrived, Salter was pronounced dead.

Piecing together the little that could be gleaned from Salter's interviews, the remaining anarchists were rounded up and their leader marked for deportation. But then Danny Hunter realised that Salter's expedition to the university was not an opportunist robbery after all. Salter had managed to hack into the mainframe for UK Air Traffic Control – and they only had four hours to find out what damage he'd done before the President of the United States flew into the UK. Danny's quick thinking enabled us to notify the President's aides; his flight was rerouted to Paris and a disaster was averted.

[Andrea Chambers]

Andrea Chambers (25), no higher education, former sushi-bar co-owner (funded by her mother). The bar failed and she became an it-girl around town. She then spent a weekend on a Yorkshire commune and became an anarchist soon after. Peter Salter made contact with her, seduced her and maintained a relationship with her for two months solely to obtain information about Istvan Vogel – known associate of a German called 'Horst', a former German Secret Service agent who defected. It was Horst who loaned her the use of a flat in Vauxhall, unaware that it was heavily bugged by MI6. Possible connection to Robert Louis Mannox and Mark Develow of 'Green Action', who were also present at the rally where Peter Salter was first identified.

REPORT APPROVED BY J. SIVITER, MI6

[Istvan Vogel]

Istvan Vogel used to work for the Dusseldorfer Bank before he 'got religion' and became an anarchist, co-ordinating 'The World Order' responsible for anti-American protests around the world (he protested against Bush in Genoa). He has vowed to 'scorch the earth and not leave a bank or stock exchange standing'. When Salter first made contact with him, Vogel's plan had been to occupy The Mall to prevent Bush from driving to dinner with the Queen before blowing up the gas main and setting it alight. The explosion would have been bigger than Vogel's one in Stockholm. However, Peter Salter persuaded him to follow another course instead, which led directly to Vogel's arrest and subsequent extradition.

REPORT APPROVED BY J. SIVITER, MI6

[Disinformation]

Although Danny has been tapping into the CCI database and adjusting his credit rating since 'Operation Greensleeves' (see episode 102), it is only now that Harry Pearce reveals he has known about it all the time. In an attempt to prevent Jools Siviter from finding out about this (and possibly sacrificing Danny's career just to score a point against Harry), Danny is encouraged to confess all and as a punishment is made to help with office staff training for as long as Harry sees fit.

Tom jokes with Ellie that the gunshot wound he received outside the State Consulate of Turkey is the result of an accident with an industrial-strength stapler. When Danny phones Tom, he refers to Thames House as 'The Fox on the Hill'.

[Identity Check]

For the purposes of the surveillance operation on the anarchist rally, Zoe is 'X-Ray Red' while her agent with the penguin hat, Geoff Catty, is 'Tango X', and Zoe's police contact is 'Delta Blue'. Meanwhile, Zoe discovers that not all pseudonyms are authorised when Tessa reveals to her that one of her sources, an anarchist called 'Billy Turner', is a 'phantom agent' – he's a name Tessa has made up so she can pocket the money supposedly meant for funding her contacts. But now that Zoe knows about him, she's decided to kill him off. If nothing else, it explains how she can afford such an expensive apartment... and how she can afford to give Zoe £10,000 in an attempt to buy her silence and persuade her to tell Harry that 'Billy' simply didn't show up as arranged.

[Personnel Records Update]

Having discussed all the options with his colleagues, Tom decides to confess all to Ellie, including his job, his real name and the fact that the tax demands he receives as 'Matthew Archer' are sent from a special office in the Inland Revenue that prevents him from being traced. On Ellie's insistence, he also explains the need for his deception to Maisie.

As a rule, Tom never discusses how Peter Salter recruited him to the Security Services.

Tom tries to explain his occupation to Ellie: 'It's a job with an office. There's a canteen, there's a pension. It's not out of the ordinary.'
Ellie: 'You just got shot!'
Tom: 'Well, there are perks...'

Danny, expecting a severe roasting: 'That it?'
Harry: 'What do you want? My tongue down your throat?'

Jools Siviter: 'Always gives a bit of a frisson, don't you find, going amongst the plebs talking of high state secrets?'

Peter Salter, to Andrea Chambers: 'I'm the thing a Security Service fears the most; the spy who goes through traitor's gate willingly, and embraces everything he's been trained to destroy.'

[Notes]

Harry makes a biblical reference when he cryptically asks Tom, 'How shall we lay down our burdens? (Specifically it's from Matthew, 11:28-30, almost certainly a dig at the persona Tom's been hiding behind in his relationship with Ellie.) Salter quotes Shakespeare's Coriolanus ('There is a world elsewhere', Act III, Scene III) and Hamlet ('Good night, ladies, good night', Act IV Scene V).

Ellie sarcastically suggests to Tom she should change her name to 'Pussy Galore', the character Honor Blackman played in the James Bond movie Goldfinger (dir. Guy Hamilton, 1964).

This episode was broadcast on a Tuesday as the usual Monday slot was occupied by the televised celebrations for the Queen's Golden Jubilee.

The script for this episode was provisionally entitled 'Traitor's Gate'.

[Gadgets]

A small matter of a 'dead ground' map proves very handy in bypassing the country's security cameras. Zoe's binoculars are pretty top-of-the-range.

[Missing in Action]

A tiny scene between Tessa and Zoe was cut: in the ladies' bathroom, Tessa gloats about Salter being lost, and Vauxhall Cross going 'potty'. This explains Harry's later comment to Tessa where he says he'll brief her on what she hasn't already learned 'in the ladies…'

[Expert Witnesses]

Anthony Head (Peter Salter): 'I was sent the script and turned to see what sort of dialogue – Y'know, you turn to see the first speech you can find, and there was this staggeringly beautiful speech about disillusionment, and I thought, My God, this writer knows what he's talking about, and then looked at the front cover and there was Howard's name. Howard Brenton is one of our great political voices from the 70s, 80s onwards, used to write a lot of wonderful plays. I worked with him at the National in a play called *Dance on the Death* that he translated. I actually went into the interview going, "This is written by Howard Brenton!" I was bowled over. It was a lovely, lovely piece and I'm very proud of it.'

Esther Hall (Ellie Simm): 'Imagine moving in with the man you love and then discover you don't even know his real name? It's the ultimate betrayal. Suddenly you're in a relationship with a complete stranger. You discover your partner has always been acting in some way, that he's always been at an emotional distance. If someone's lied that much, how can there ever be any trust in your relationship again? In [**spooks**], Ellie is the person the audience can identify with. You can't help thinking: What if that was me? What if I got involved with an MI5 officer? It makes you realise that your life would change for ever.'

Episode 105

First Broadcast (BBC1): June 10 2002

Written by **Howard Brenton**
Directed by **Andy Wilson**

[Cast]

David Calder (Sergei Lermov), **Tim Pigott-Smith** (Hampton Wilder), **Nicholas Farrell** (Richard Maynard), **Hugh Laurie** (Jools Siviter), **Steve Weston** (Senior Prison Officer), **Jonathan Jones** (Male Reporter), **Amanda Drew** (Female Reporter), **Naoko Mori** (Annette), **Mark Dexter** (Mark Hodd), **Mark Long** (Derelict Man), **Joan Blackham** (Woman at the Opera), **Aleksandar Mikic** (Young Man), **Christopher Wells** (Hardy, the Heavy), **George Khan** (Sheikh Rasul).

[Who's Who]

Director Andy Wilson worked on Granada TV's superb *Cracker* (episode 'To Say I Love You'), *An Evening with Gary Lineker* (1994), *Bad Boy Blues* (1995), *Playing God* (1997), *Psychos* (1999) for Kudos, *Gormenghast* (2000), and *Lenny Blue* (2002).

Tim Pigott-Smith (Hampton Wilder) first came to public notice as the sadistic Captain Merrick in Channel 4's *The Jewel in the Crown* (1984). Other prominent roles include *The Chief* (where he took over from Martin Shaw), *The Vice* and the film *Bloody Sunday* (dir. Paul Greengrass, 2002). Nicholas Farrell (Richard Maynard) was also in both *The Jewel in the Crown* – as Teddy Bingham – and *Bloody Sunday*, and can also be seen in the mini-series *Hold the Dream* (1986), *Lipstick on Your Collar* (1993), *The Riff Raff Element* (1993), *To Play the King* (1994), *Sex, Chips &*

Rock 'n' Roll (1999) and *The Jury* (2002).

One of Britain's best-kept secrets, David Calder (Sergei Lermov)'s first major role in a TV series was as Detective Inspector Resnick in Lynda La Plante's *Widows* (1983/5). He starred in the pedestrian-but-worthy *Star Cops* (1987) and historical medical drama *Bramwell* (1995), and played Metropolitan Police Chief Sir Paul Condon in the controversial true-life mini-series *The Murder of Stephen Lawrence* (1999). He also had a small-but-significant role in the James Bond film *The World is Not Enough* (dir. Michael Apted, 1999).

Mark Dexter (Mark Hodd) played Prince Albert in the Jack-the-Ripper thriller *From Hell* (dirs. Albert Hughes/Allen Hughes, 2001).

[Case Report]

Hampton Wilder, the former MP who had been imprisoned for embezzlement in 1993, had contacted MI5 saying that on his release from prison he needed to discuss a matter of national security. On the day of his release, Danny picked Wilder up from HM Prison Edgefield and drove him to Thames House. The first thing that struck the team as odd was Wilder's apparent conversion to Christianity. The second was his assertion that the information he had could result in the fall of the government. He revealed to Harry that, during his time in prison, he had written his memoirs, a very full and frank exposé of a number of scandals that had been hushed up, including an allegation that the Prime Minister's friend Richard Maynard was as implicated in the illegal sale of arms to Iraq as Wilder himself was. He had planned to arrange for the book's publication in Europe on his release, but just five weeks earlier, he 'found' Jesus. Repenting for his vengeful former self, he decided to destroy the manuscript. He'd hidden it under a rose bed in the prison, but when he went to retrieve it, it had gone.

Tessa expressed the opinion that Wilder was lying and that the memoirs had never actually existed, but as Harry pointed out, they didn't have to: even the suggestion that they might exist would be enough to do significant damage to the government. But to see how Richard Maynard might react to the allegations, Harry decided to invite him to a routine Ministry of Defence briefing and suggested Tessa might observe his reactions. At the briefing, Harry showed pictures of Sergei Lermov (see Security File below) to Maynard. The Minister showed no sign of prior awareness of the arms trading, though he did freely admit to having once met Lermov. Tessa offered to give Maynard a tour of Thames House, during which she asked him directly if there was any truth in Wilder's accusations. Maynard protested his innocence.

At the same time, Tom approached Lermov, who reluctantly corroborated Wilder's accusation and named Maynard as his contact in the Ministry of Defence. Tom was suspicious of Lermov's manner, which suggested to him that Lermov felt he was protected by someone in higher authority. Having discussed this with Harry, the two men realised that Jools Siviter had to be involved somehow. Tom and Harry interrupted Siviter at the opera, where Jools casually revealed that he had been in possession of the memoirs all along; MI6 had placed an agent inside Edgefield prison, so Wilder's memoirs were dug up and removed almost as soon as Wilder had buried them. He confirmed that Wilder's allegations were almost certainly a case of slander, motivated by revenge, as Maynard had been the one who had informed MI6 about Wilder in the first place.

The following morning, a team of speed-readers were briefed to read the document and find anything that might discredit or verify it. At the same time, Tom met with Maynard, who repeated his innocence and confirmed that it was he who had informed MI6 of Wilder's business practices. Despite proof of Maynard's innocence, however, by the next morning the tabloids had learned of the accusations and published a story alleging that Maynard had been involved in a 'Desert Orgy'. Within hours, Richard Maynard resigned.

Harry visited Jools Siviter at his club. Siviter admitted to having been responsible for the leak. With his knowledge of foreign policy, it looked increasingly likely that Maynard was being groomed to take over as Foreign Secretary. As MI6 knew that he was in fact a CIA agent, they could not allow Maynard to take such an influential position, so the memoirs presented them with the perfect route to get rid of him. While Harry deprived Jools of half a

[Hampton Wilder]

EXTRACT

In 1993, Hampton Wilder visited the Middle East as a gesture of goodwill to secure an agreement over some legitimate small arms. He was accompanied by Richard Maynard, a member of the Commons Committee there to scrutinise arms procurement. However, Wilder was also involved in illegal arms trading, arranging for the sale of anti-tank weapons to Sheikh Rasul, a member of the royal family of the Confederated Gulf States. Worried that Maynard might notify the authorities about his transactions, Wilder arranged for him to be photographed alongside both the Sheikh and his 'Mr Fixit', former KGB agent Sergei Lermov. He then invited Maynard to join him in his enterprise, but on their return to the UK, Maynard notified MI6 immediately and Wilder was arrested.

Although Wilder was tried and imprisoned later that year, it was for the lesser crime of embezzlement, the result of a deal with the government to prevent him from being prosecuted for treason.

[Mark Hodd]

Hodd has been working in the Gulf for the last two years, having left his ex-partner, Ellie Simm, and their child behind. Known contacts include a police officer, Sergeant Brian Malhorn at Metropolitan Central, now suspended after attempting to pass information about Tom Quinn onto Hodd.

FILE OPENED AT REQUEST
OF TOM QUINN

[Sergei Lermov]

CLOSED

Sergei Lermov, former Cultural Attaché at the Russian Embassy and ex-KGB agent who had worked for Sheikh Rasul. He returned to London from Amsterdam three days prior to Wilder's release. After the end of the Cold War, Lermov travelled around the world, eventually settling in London to work for 'Hope for Chechnya', a charity that tries to get food and medicine to a part of the world that, it was suspected, was being used as a cover for arms dealing. He was also a known spy, feeding information about Chechnyan contacts back to the Sluzhba Vneshney Razvedi – the Russian Foreign Intelligence Service. The only reason he was allowed to remain in the UK was because he was the middleman in a gun-running cartel operating out of the Confederated Gulf States.

After Lermov was found with a dead boy in his room at the Hotel Ukraine, Moscow, Jools Siviter managed to save him from his KGB masters and help him escape to the West. From that point on, and unbeknown to MI6, Siviter ran Lermov as a double agent. But during the 'Rose Bed Memoirs' scandal, Lermov was found dead. Despite some effort on the part of his killer to make it look like a mugging gone wrong, the stab wound directly beneath his heart indicated that this was a calculated assassination, possibly by order of his former KGB colleagues.

[Quote/Unquote]

Wilder: 'This might come as a surprise to you, but prison is full of thieves.'

Tessa (on Wilder): 'There's a sense of... evil about him.'
Harry: 'MI5 doesn't do evil, just treachery, treason and Armageddon.'

Tessa (to Richard Maynard): 'A bonk in the MI5 building – it's got to be worth some air miles.'

Jools Siviter: 'It's been a very, very long night. The death of an agent and possibly one of the worst productions of Wagner I have ever seen. Dear God! The Valkyrie were all dressed in scuba gear.'

Zoe (discussing Danny's friend): 'Throw her out.'
Danny: 'But I like her.'
Zoe: 'Then throw her out nicely.'

bottle of excellent brandy, Tom called on Wilder, who confessed that his memoirs were all lies. The only truth to come from the whole business was that Wilder genuinely had been 'born again' and was distraught at the misery his lies had caused; as a punishment for his former wickedness, he had been literally whipping himself for weeks...

[Disinformation]

...or rather disorientation, as Harry puts some of his recent training in 'psych ops' (psychological operations) into practice during his interview with Hampton Wilder. We also see Tom speaking to a tramp who may or may not be an undercover agent. Oh, and then there's the small matter of a memoir that... well, might not be completely the truth.

[Identity Check]

When Danny's 'ladyfriend' Annette drops by unexpectedly, Zoe quickly learns that Danny met her under the guise of 'Celestine', a dealer in an exchange room in the city. He introduces Zoe as 'Sally', his cleaner (see Episode 204), whose cat 'Claws' has just died. At the Grid, Tom answers a call as 'Rodney'.

As he introduces himself to Ellie's ex, Mark, Tom automatically jumps into his 'Matthew Archer' persona, only for Maisie to address him as Tom.

[Personnel Records Update]

Tom is taken by surprise when he is introduced to Ellie's former partner, Mark Hodd, who has returned from the Gulf and decided to pay a visit on his daughter, Maisie. After a fairly fractious first meeting with Tom, Mark tries to use a contact in the police to get information on him via his car registration, which triggers a security alert. Frightened off after being pulled in by MI5 officers, Hodd leaves the UK for the Gulf without saying goodbye to Ellie or Maisie. Ellie blames Tom for this and decides to move out of Tom's apartment. Having already relinquished the lease on her old flat, Ellie is forced to stay in a flat owned by her friend, Di.

Tessa has had an on-off affair with Dick Maynard for some years. After she learns of his resignation from the cabinet, she confesses to him that she told the Russians that Lermov had betrayed them, and so in effect signed Lermov's death warrant. He tells her that he has obtained a post at Harvard and is about to leave for the USA. She remains ignorant of his connections to the CIA.

Zoe finally confides in Danny about Tessa's phantom agents and the bribe she gave Zoe to stay quiet.

[Missing in Action]

In the first interview with Wilder, as scripted, Harry supplies Wilder with another quote from his favourite gospel, Matthew (7:20), while Wilder compares Tessa Phillips with the heroine from Thomas Hardy's *Tess of the d'Urbervilles*.

[Expert Witnesses]

Hugh Laurie (Jools Siviter): 'It wouldn't surprise me if our spies were in it for the excitement they'd seen on TV shows and films. I thought [Barry Foster in *The Sweeney*] was one of the greatest performances I'd ever seen on TV, and it was a great thrill for me to play a similar character in **[spooks]**. I based everything about Jools' manner and tone on him. I just nicked his whole thing shamelessly.'

Matthew Macfadyen: 'MI6 is more establishment than MI5, which really rankles Tom. As far as he's concerned, plummy accents might be alright in an embassy in Moscow, but you can't have someone like Jools running agents in England. He really resents Jools' air of superiority.'

[Notes]

Jools Siviter is interrupted during a performance of Wagner's Ring of the Nibelung.

The script for this episode was provisionally titled 'The Rose Bed Memoirs'.

As Danny checks all of his security devices set to protect his vodka from Zoe, we get to see a number of basic tricks used by spies to detect whether their things have been tampered with: there's a sliver of sellotape on the light switch; a light dusting of fine powder on the carpet to reveal trespassers; a hair balanced along the top of his drawer; a magazine has been placed on top of his clothes, lined up to match the pattern on his jumper; and there's still an unopened seal on his bottle of vodka. Despite all these precautions, Zoe still manages to siphon all of Danny's vodka into a teapot and refill the vodka bottle with cold tea. Likewise, Danny has found the money that Tessa gave to Zoe (which she'd hidden behind a plug socket in her room), but has left it there.

Spycatcher

The events in this episode draw clear parallels to the lives of real-life politicians Jeffrey Archer and Jonathan Aitken.

Both were prominent members of the Conservative Party before they were sent to prison for their respective offences, and while in prison, Archer published his diaries. But it's the response to even the threat of the existence of Hampton Wilder's book that is this episode's closest link to real-life events. For in 1987, MI5 became a target for media attention after one of its former senior officers, Peter Wright, decided to publish his own memoirs and in turn break with traditions as old as the 'secret' Security Services themselves.

Wright's *Spycatcher* is by far the most famous and certainly the most notorious book on the subject of British intelligence, not just because of the secrets it revealed, or because of any scandals it might allude to, but simply because of the fact that it was the book the British government went to extraordinary lengths to ban.

Prior to the late 1980s and *Spycatcher*'s eventual publication, the British public might well have been aware of the existence of MI5 and MI6, but they didn't really know what they got up to; the average person had just a vague idea that their work might be only slightly less dramatic than the exploits of James Bond or Bodie and Doyle from *The Professionals* (who, in any event, worked for the fictitious CI5, but that's another matter). But in 1985 newspapers and TV reports tried their best to get round government restrictions to report on a historic court case being held in Australia where the British government were fighting to block the publication of this autobiography by Peter Wright, who had been with the Security Services since the mid 1950s and had retired in 1976 at the level of Assistant Director-General of MI5.

Dissatisfied with his miserly pension and unable to find decent work in the UK,

Wright had emigrated with his wife to Australia before settling in Tasmania to become a farmer. He had already been involved in one exposé of MI5 when, in 1983, he had helped journalist Chapman Pincher write *Their Trade is Treachery*, which told of the battles against subversives in post-war Britain. But his own magnum opus would be a different affair, detailing his long-held belief that Roger Hollis, former Director-General of MI5, had in fact been a Russian spy. It would also reveal that all foreign conferences held in London during the 1950s and 1960s had been bugged by MI5. More importantly, though – and certainly of most concern for MI5 – the book would claim that there had been a major cover-up regarding an attempt by 30 MI5 officers to besmear the name of Harold Wilson (and in turn the Labour Party) by 'proving' that the former Prime Minister had links to subversive Communists controlled by the KGB. By alleging that MI5 had gone outside of its remit by apparently conspiring to overthrow a democratically elected leader, Wright sent the British establishment reeling. Such a claim could potentially undermine the Security Services irreparably and leave Britain at greater risk from subversive activity.

The real story of *Spycatcher* began in September 1985, when the British Attorney General instigated an injunction in New South Wales, Australia, to prevent Wright's publishers, Heinemann, from releasing the book. Back home in Britain, the summer of the following year saw both the *Observer* and *Guardian* publish articles that were based on material from Wright's book and aired his allegations for the first time. Again, the Attorney General managed to obtain injunctions on both papers. The case in Australia continued for nearly two years, with Cabinet Secretary Sir Robert Armstrong sent as Britain's chief witness to discredit Wright's claims and argue for the book's withdrawal. Armstrong was, in fairness, an outsider to the affairs of MI5 with no first-hand experience of the cases Wright had written about. As such he relied heavily on reports hurriedly compiled for him by teams of people back in the UK. Exploiting the lesser formality of Australian courts of law, Peter Wright's lawyer, Malcolm Turnbull, took every opportunity to make the British government's representative look as foolish as possible. He decimated Sir Robert's testimony and famously coerced Armstrong into admitting he had been 'economical with the truth', an understated but cutting term that has since entered the English language.

Ultimately, the British lost their case and in March 1987 the judge found in favour of Wright and Heinemann. Having been victorious in Australia, Wright's publisher decided to release the book in America. Despite remaining illegal in Britain, the widespread availability of the book made it relatively easy for eager British readers to obtain copies (indeed, one such copy was obtained by Labour MP Tony Benn, who got round the Conservatives' ban on the book by reading extracts of it at Speaker's Corner in Hyde Park). Meanwhile, having publicly lost face already, the Conservative government continued to restrict the British press. When the *Independent* printed extracts from *Spycatcher* in 1987, the government sued the paper for contempt of court, citing the existence of the previous injunctions. The case was thrown out of court when it was pointed out that as the book had already reached half of the known world, it was fair to describe its revelations as being already in the public domain. Finally, in 1991, all 24 judges of the European Court of Human Rights unanimously found the British government's restriction of the press to be in breach of the European Convention on Human Rights.

Peter Wright later confessed in a 1988 interview for the BBC's *Panorama* that his account of the Wilson affair had indeed been 'unreliable'. When Stella Rimington was Director-General of MI5, she instigated an investigation into the allegations, indicating that there was no evidence of such a conspiracy. But the damage has been done. As Rimington notes, had the government not focused such attention on *Spycatcher* in the first place, few people would have bothered to have read such a 'disappointingly dull' book.

Peter Wright died in April 1995, but his legacy lives on. Having successfully published his own version of events, he paved the way for other MI5 officers to do the same (which had, of course, been the real fear all along). When Stella Rimington herself decided that, as the first female DG of MI5, her autobiography would be in the public interest, it was denounced by senior civil servant Sir Stephen Lander as 'a moral betrayal', despite Rimington's care to ensure every page of the book had been vetted by MI5 and the government. At the same time, Richard Tomlinson, who had served in MI6 for four years in the early 1990s, found his own book, *The Big Breach*, under the spotlight when it was alleged that it was being published with the assistance of Russian intelligence agents who offered him a £35,000 deal (Tomlinson denied the allegation). And in 2002, former MI5 officer David Shayler was found guilty of breaching the Official Secrets Act for copying documents that he believed were in the public interest and handing them to a newspaper.

Ultimately, though, the real legacy of Peter Wright's autobiography is the level of openness and accountability that the Security Service was all too eager to accept. The Security Service Act of 1989 gave MI5 (and, in a later amendment, MI6 and GCHQ) a statutory foothold and a clear legal basis for operation for the first time.

But then, having been shamed into admitting that they had (in Wright's words) 'bugged and burgled [their] way across London at the State's behest, while pompous bowler-hatted civil servants in Whitehall pretended to look the other way,' there really was no other course of action open to them. ∎

Episode 106

First Broadcast (BBC1): June 4 2002

Written by **David Wolstencroft & Howard Brenton**
Directed by **Andy Wilson**

[Cast]

Joel Trill (Operator), **Linda Marlowe** ('Jodie'/Madge the Housekeeper), **Lorcan Cranitch** (Patrick McCann), **Dinah Stabb** (Rosie, the Registry Queen), **John Owens** (Old Geezer), **Alastair Parker** (Policeman), **Roger Hammond** (DG), **Shivani Ghai** (New MI5 Recruit*), **Barbara Keogh** (Old Woman in the Cottage*).
* Scenes excised.

[Who's Who]

Lorcan Cranitch (Patrick McCann) shocked audiences as the troubled D.S. Jimmy Beck in the groundbreaking police drama series *Cracker* (1993–95) before moving to *Ballykissangel* to play Sean Dillon. More recently, he played father to *EastEnders* fave Patsy Palmer in *McCready and Daughter* (2001).

Linda Marlowe (the housekeeper at the safe house) appeared as the self-serving Esther Freeman in Lynda La Plante's sequel to *Widows*, *She's Out*. Dinah Stabb played Mrs Fagunwa, mother of the main murder victim in *Prime Suspect 2*, though she's possibly more familiar to older viewers as the daughter in the British Telecom *'It's Good To Talk'* ads with Bob Hoskins.

[Case Report]

Concerned by the possible risk posed to his new family, and with the hope that it might convince Ellie to move back in with him, Tom Quinn, with the assistance of Danny Hunter, had his house fitted with the latest in security protection, including security glass and a bomb-proof door.

Patrick McCann, a known IRA commander, contacted Section B by walking straight up to an MI5 safe house, ringing the doorbell and bullying the housekeeper into letting him in. Through CCTV cameras at the house, he informed us that he wanted to speak to a senior MI5 officer urgently with regard to information on terrorists from a group known as Asabiyah, the existence of which was believed to be known to only a very few security personnel worldwide.

Harry summoned an emergency meeting, with Tessa Phillips, Tom Quinn, Danny Hunter and Zoe Reynolds in attendance. Harry was dead set against dealing with McCann under any circumstances, but the rest of the team felt they couldn't afford not to. Tom contacted McCann via a mobile phone SIM-card that had been left with the housekeeper and arranged a meeting. Fully aware that the first thing McCann would do is search for wires, Tom insisted he go in completely unbugged.

In a remote rural location, Tom met with McCann, who revealed that he was working in secret against his own side. He claimed that his group had been raising funds, working as 'management consultants' in Colombia and Somalia. Two of their team went to the Sudan to advise a group there about some anti-tank weapons they had recently acquired. The Irishmen discovered that the group were in possession of a detailed aerial map of Sefton B Nuclear Power Station with a view to making it a target for terrorism. The effect of an explosion at this location would, of course, make Ireland uninhabitable and devastate much of the mainland. By the time McCann's branch chief realised his mistake in dealing with these people, members of Asabiyah were already on their way. McCann still had men working on the inside of Asabiyah, perfectly positioned to acquire information – which he was offering to MI5 in return for a blind eye being turned to their activities for 36 hours. He gave Tom another SIM-card for his phone that would only be operational for nine minutes that evening. McCann's sense of urgency alerted Tom to the fact that the planned Asabiyah attack on Sefton B would be sooner than he'd first realised.

Back at Thames House, Tom learned that Harry had secretly had him followed and had placed a trail on McCann. He refused to take the Irishman at his word and stressed that the information McCann was offering was contaminated and therefore unreliable. Tom felt compelled to go over Harry's head; he gained permission from the Director-General of MI5 to overrule his superior and agree to McCann's terms. Unfortunately, at that point information came in about an Irish splinter group's plan to hit Broad Street tube station with a bomb in rush hour the next morning. Simultaneously, the MOD reported the loss of five pounds of Semtex explosive from an armed shipment in Newcastle. Harry ordered that Tom's deal with McCann must be ignored and that defusing the bomb at Broad Street was to become their priority.

Tom told Zoe to work a fake decoy op to make it look to Harry like they were going to stop the bomb, when in fact they were actually working to evacuate the station due to a 'damaged roof' but allowing the bomb to go off for McCann's benefit. Meanwhile, Danny was told to find out everything he could about the Asabiyah terrorists' weapon. At 7.30am, the device was detonated with minor structural damage to the station and no casualties.

Though Harry was angry with Tom for leading his team in the deception, he recognised that the situation could have ended up much worse. But when Danny managed to identify the Asabiyah weapon as a 'Light Forces Anti-Tank Guided Weapons System' (or 'L-FAT-G.W.S'), Harry began to take McCann's information seriously. He allowed Tom to meet with McCann in another remote

location. McCann was furious that MI5 had gone against their agreement, but nevertheless he presented Tom with a laptop that contained all the information he needed, as promised. Tom was able to transmit that information directly to Danny. The Asabiyah terrorists were located by Special Ops before they could do any damage at

Sefton B and 'disincentivised'… terminally.

Having averted disaster, Danny advised Tom to take the rest of the day off. Tom returned home to spend the day with his girlfriend and her daughter, who had just moved back in with him. He stored the laptop in a filing cabinet, completely unaware at this point that the computer had been rigged by McCann's branch chief with a slab of C4 explosive…

[Disinformation]

Aside from the 'damaged roof' ruse employed to allow McCann's bomb to go off without incurring casualties, this episode sees a number of interesting instances of disinformation across the board, starting with the housekeeper of one of MI5's safe houses, who calls the Grid and claims to be from the 'Sovereign Guest House' wanting a credit card check on Patrick McCann; the request is met with a security briefing from his file. Then there's the matter of a report of foot and mouth outbreak in Holywell, near Sefton B, which is placed with news agencies to allow a buffer zone and police roadblocks to be set up around the power plant.

Next up is Tessa, who is once again called upon by Harry to supply a well-placed source with Muslim connections who might be able to shed more light on Asabiyah's intentions. Realising that Tessa's source was in all likelihood worthless, Zoe finally confessed to Harry that Tessa had tried to buy her off to protect her phantom agents…

[Identity Check]

Although the housekeeper in the first scene is identified in the script as 'Madge', she calls into the Grid under the name of 'Jodie'. McCann refers to the housekeeper's boss as 'the landlord' (see episode 210). For the purposes of dealing with Patrick McCann, Tom's codename is Davy Crockett.

[Previous Missions]

Harry has reason not to trust the IRA. In 1978, he was stationed in Ireland along with his best friend, Bill Crombie. Looking for an IRA brigade commander, the two entered a known rebel pub. Harry left, but Bill stayed. He was thrown into the boot of a car, tortured and mutilated with a blowtorch. His dead body was dumped two weeks later. The brigade leader they were hunting, and the man responsible for Bill's death, was Patrick McCann.

It's suggested that the idea of closing down Broad Street station to minimise a major terrorist incident was a method also used during a similar threat to Heathrow airport's tunnels in 1994.

[Personnel Report Update]

Once Harry has been made aware of Tessa's deception, he has no choice but to dismiss her. Tessa tries to blackmail Harry, warning him that she's aware that he had actually witnessed his old friend being kidnapped by McCann and despite being armed had done nothing to save him because he'd been afraid. Harry allows Tessa to think she has the upper hand before summoning security to escort her off the premises to a nearby safe house.

Tom, meanwhile, manages to persuade Ellie to move back in with him thanks to the security devices Danny installed at Tom's house. But due to a spot of cake mixture that Maisie accidentally smeared on the security swipe card, Tom finds himself locked outside the house just as McCann phones to tell him about the bomb in the laptop. With time running out, Tom calls Danny to talk Ellie through the disarming process. But when Ellie is unable to follow Danny's instructions, all she can do is hug her daughter tightly and watch as Tom helplessly looks at them through the living-room window. All the time, the seconds are ticking away…

[Gadgets]

On Tom's request, Danny installs a complete security system at Tom's house, including bomb-proof steel doors with central-locking windows (front and rear

[Patrick McCann]

McCann joined the IRA in 1974, aged 16. His fierce loyalty and cruel
spirit ensured he rose quickly through the ranks as an active service
leader, and was personally responsible for the torture and murder of
over 20 RUC soldiers and two security operatives. He continues to serve
as a section commander in an IRA splinter group which, in recent years,
has worked as freelance consultants in Colombia, Somalia and the Sudan...

[Sefton B Nuclear Power Station]

Sefton B consists of four main reactors and two reprocessing plants,
Britain's main plutonium stockpile. Area D421 houses 20 tanks of liquid
high-level radioactive waste. Breaching just one of the tanks would
release a cloud 45 times as deadly as that of Chernobyl. Each of the main
tanks is reinforced with three metres of concrete. Normally more than
half of the tanks are empty, but with the recent glut of increased capacity
even the standby tanks are full.

However, two of the intermediate-level tanks have walls of concrete that
are just one metre thick, which is why they are in the process of being
refurbished, with particular attention being paid to the roof.

ground and first floors, and roof access), window bars, hinge-locks for entry doors...
and a universal swipe card that locks everything up nice and tight. Whether you
want it to or not...

[Missing in Action]

There were a fair few scenes cut for this one as they didn't really help to advance
the plot, although they did give insights into a few of the characters. A series of
small scenes depict Jed – the Grid's technical guy usually left to man the phones –
training an attractive new recruit and trying to impress her by making a joke about
the fact that Harry regularly picks up a bunch of flowers but tries to carry them so
no-one will notice. In the script, Jed speculates that Harry's having an affair with a
low-ranking woman in the MOD despite being married with a kid. When Harry later
explains curtly that the flowers are for his friend's grave, Jed feels suitably
admonished (this embarrassing incident might explain Jed's absence in series two).

Another scene sees Danny and Zoe in their apartment preparing to meet Ellie and
Maisie for the first time. Zoe mocks Danny for practising his 'welcoming' grin, which
turns out more like that of a 'village idiot'. It soon becomes obvious that the two are
nervous as Tom has briefed them as part of his campaign to win Ellie over and get her
and Maisie to move back in with him. The scene would have also explained why Ellie
didn't just move back to her old flat above the restaurant ('my leasehold's a little
tenuous').

One last scene would have come after Tom was released by McCann with the
laptop. He runs across fields until he finds an old cottage where an old woman (who
would have been played by Barbara Keogh, Dot's friend Lilly from *EastEnders*) lets
him use her phone to transmit the laptop's contents to Danny.

[Expert Witnesses]

Lorcan Cranitch, on McCann's first meeting with Tom: 'I'm told this is a
normal procedure for MI5 when they meet certain targets. It's to prove that no-one
is wired to recording equipment. We got dressed to film the rest of the scene, but we
were lucky to do that. In real life they would hold their entire conversation naked!'

[Asabiyah]

Asabiyah is an ultra-extremist splinter group from Al Qaeda based in the Sudan. They consist of some of Bin Laden's fervent followers and have been yellow-tagged, but MPs, most of Downing Street and the Foreign Office have been left uninformed of its existence to prevent leaks. They were believed to be responsible for two embassy bombings in 2000. They work in pairs, family units such as brothers who don't write anything down and so remain impenetrable. One CIA proxy agent got close but his cover was blown (what remained of his genitals were posted to the American Embassy in Paris). To date they have not shown interest in the UK; their efforts have been aimed mainly at India and Indonesia.

Peter Firth: 'Tessa annoys Harry intensely – and he doesn't trust her. But we're having great fun with it. I feel I know Jenny [Agutter] as a best friend even though over 30 years we've barely seen each other.'

[Quote/Unquote]

Patrick McCann: 'If they do what I think they're going to do, then most of Ireland's uninhabitable for the next 200 years. Not to mention everything north of Bristol... not that we'd miss Wales.'

The Director-General (speaking to Tom Quinn during his medical examination): 'It's finger-up-my-prostate time, so I'd be grateful if you'd leave.'

Harry: 'It's never over. We may dance with the devil, Zoe, but it's always to his tune.'

[Notes]

At this time, Tom's mobile number was 07700900002 (the number's since been discontinued).

The name of the terrorist group 'Asabiyah' is an Arabic word used to represent a group feeling of loyalty — even a supreme loyalty — to one's family, faith or way of life.

The script for this episode was provisionally titled 'Mean, Dirty, Nasty'.

On June 20 2002, two days after this episode was broadcast, a debate was held in the House of Commons on the subject of 'Energy Towards 2050' in which John Whittingdale OBE, Member of Parliament for Maldon + East Chelmsford, mentioned [spooks], noting that the story of that week (some of which had been filmed in his constituency) drew attention to the concerns of many regarding 'the safety and security of nuclear power'.

The IRA in Colombia

In this episode, McCann's group is not actually named. But in the real world, the episode has coincidental parallels with the IRA, who, like McCann's group, have been known to campaign for funds outside of the UK. Indeed, they have appealed for support ever since they were first assembled from such disparate groups as the Russian Soviets, Nazi Germany, members of the Spanish Eta and, playing on feelings of 'patriotism', the Irish-American community of the USA. But as the Northern Ireland peace process continues, many members of the republican terrorism groups are finding it harder to earn money, for their campaign and themselves.

In the summer of 2001, three Irishmen were arrested in Bogotá, Colombia, on suspicion of being terrorists after they had spent over a month in the Colombian jungle with the Revolutionary Armed Forces of Colombia (FARC), a Marxist guerrilla force funded in part by the drugs trade. Initially, it was thought the men might have been negotiating to buy weapons. However, after more detailed investigations, the Colombian authorities revealed that the men were being held on suspicion of training FARC rebels in IRA bomb-making techniques. IRA training manuals and maps were found and submitted as evidence against the men by Colombian police.

The three alleged terrorists had been travelling under the names 'Edward Joseph Campbell', 'John Joseph Kelly' and 'David Bracken' (David Bracken's also the name of an assassin in Frederick Forsyth's *The Day of the Jackal*), though they were later positively identified as James Monaghan, Martin McCauley and Niall Connolly. Monaghan was a veteran of the IRA; in 1973 he developed the IRA's first mortar and was believed to have had a hand in the evolution of IRA remote-controlled devices for land-mines and bombs. McCauley too had been a part of the Provisional IRA for some time. Like Monaghan, he had been involved in designing mortars, rockets and bombs for use against British targets, and during the 1980s he'd served a prison sentence for arms possession. Connolly, the only one of the three who could speak

Spanish, had been a Sinn Fein representative in Cuba.

FARC has been fighting a war in the jungles of Colombia for decades and had effectively taken control of over a third of the country in this time. But just two months before the Irishmen were caught, nearly 120 people were killed when a church roof collapsed after a mortar attack that bore all the hallmarks of the IRA. A United States senate report published some months after the event stated that the urban bombing campaign in Colombia strongly suggested the FARC guerrillas were putting into practice methods they'd learned from IRA terrorists. Prior to this, FARC cells were more likely to use much cruder techniques such as 'donkey bombs' – literally donkeys weighed down with explosives and steered into position.

Intelligence sources led the Colombian authorities to believe that the representatives of the IRA would provide training in return for cash that FARC had raised through its production of cocaine. But the real issue here was that the IRA were now in desperate need of the money – arguably they were the one 'industry' that was hardest hit by the Good Friday Agreement. All of a sudden, there were a lot of trained IRA terrorists facing 'unemployment' in a world where their skills were highly sought by others.

What's ironic is that FARC is officially seen as the American government's most pressing problem in Latin America (over $1.3 billion has been committed to fighting a war on drugs – and specifically FARC – in Colombia); the Irish-American community in the USA has, historically, been the IRA's biggest source of funding. That the IRA had now allied itself with the American government's 'public enemy number one' did not sit well with its supporters, many of whom felt the IRA was biting the hand that feeds it. If the US Department of State in Washington decided to freeze the assets of the Provisional IRA – as they had already done to the 'Real IRA' splinter group in May 2001 – it could have denied the group of over $5 million in funds.

Monaghan, McCauley and Connolly deny any involvement with FARC, claiming they had gone to Colombia merely to observe the peace process between the former President Andres Pastrana and the FARC rebels. Arguing that they have already been found guilty by the world's media, the men have refused to enter the court in Colombia and face trial. At the time of writing, the case has been adjourned by the judge until June 2003. ■

The Interactive Episode

Available exclusively via BBCi: April 23 – June 18 2002

[Cast]

David Oyelowo (Danny Hunter), **Fraser McAlpine** (Nick Sever), **Vivienne Vellacott** (Faith Allam – face only), **Briony McRoberts** (Faith Allam – voice), **Sophie Humes** (Club Patron), **Kiki Kendrick** (Tina), **Paul Loades** (Nick Moran), **Jason Durran** (Bruno Hunter – face), **Jimmy Akingbola** (Bruno Hunter – voice), **Jamie Cason** (Mikhail Zabolotsky – face), **Tim Treloar** (Mikhail Zabolotsky – voice), **Ewan Bailey** (MI5 spymaster – James Richardson), **Kenny Blythe** (Male Bioterrorist).

[Case Report]

Bruno Hunter, Danny's brother, had been working as a DJ at the Skylight club for some time thanks to the 'influence' of Nick Sever, a local gangster. But when Sever began calling in favours and coercing Bruno into working for him, Bruno reluctantly told his brother that he'd got himself into a tricky situation. Bruno didn't know that Danny worked for MI5 (Danny had always led him to believe he worked 'in the city'), and Danny knew that he couldn't use MI5 resources for personal reasons. Without consulting Tom, Danny began using the New Recruits team, a network of civilian contacts experienced in using the internet for in-depth research and surveillance. Thanks to one of Nick Sever's tattoos, the Recruits discovered that Sever was part of an extremist group known as 'Tribe', set up by an enigmatic figure called Oliver Mansal. Registry files suggested that Tribe were involved in drugs trafficking, but Danny was concerned that they might be into something more. The most pressing problem, however, was that Tribe had officially disbanded years ago.

Tribe had been under investigation by a journalist, Grace King. King went missing some time ago, but the Recruits managed to trace her answering service and learn that she had met with Nick Sever at his flat three months ago. The police were informed, Sever's flat was searched and the discovery of a quantity of drugs was sufficient for him to be arrested.

Other members of Tribe were suspicious of Bruno after Sever's arrest. Insistent that Bruno had to make reparations, they instructed him to baby-sit Mikhail Zabolotsky, a Russian scientist linked to the arms trade and neo-Nazis who had recently arrived at Heathrow. Thanks to information on an exploitable design flaw in the case discovered by the Recruits, Danny was able to pass on a default combination to Zabolotsky's briefcase, which contained paperwork for various chemicals and contact details for a Peter Grady.

Bruno escorted Mikhail to an appointment but then went to ground.

[Quote / Unquote]

Danny (on a phone message): 'I've found the device but I need you to break the code! I have the numbers Faith keyed in – three, four, six. Text me the correct sequence to turn this thing off... We've got 30 minutes. Get on with it!'

Meanwhile, Danny's Recruits discovered that the chemicals listed in Zabolotsky's briefcase were the ingredients for a deadly bioweapon. After a man matching Zabolotsky's description was pulled from the Thames, Bruno resurfaced and told Danny that Zabolotsky had met a man later identified as Scott Moran. The name in Zabolotsky's case, Peter Grady, was the alias of MI6 officer James Hopkinson, and Mikhail was his agent. At their last meeting, Mikhail had been attempting to get money from Hopkinson (who organised the cover-up to protect his other agents) when Mikhail was found stabbed in the river, apparently killed by Moran (though later information suggested this was all part of a cover-up initiated at MI6's request). When Moran was positively identified as a Tribe member, the CIA provided vital information on both Tribe and Oliver Mansal.

According to intelligence received by the CIA, Tribe were against the intermingling of races. With the anniversary of their founder Mansal's death fast approaching, Danny found a prospective inside contact in Tribe from Grace King's files, a woman called Tina. She'd uncovered a terrorist action headed by Faith Alam, who planned to run Tribe with a new agenda – to destroy organised religion, which she saw as the cause of the world's conflicts. Her plan was to release deadly spores created from the chemicals listed in Zabolotsky's case with places of worship as her target.

Further information from the CIA revealed that Faith planned to escape to Birmingham by train and then fly to Boston. As it happened, Faith's planned escape route via Broad Street station was blocked due to the temporary closure of the London station as part of an entirely separate MI5 operation (see episode 106). Faith was subsequently traced to Birmingham via a car-hire firm and arrested. Having identified one of the targets as the Middle London Mosque, a device there was defused and removed. Two other devices were located in London, one in a cathedral and one in a synagogue.

Danny called the mobile numbers of his recruits to tell them he'd found the remote timer Faith had set to detonate the devices – and it was already counting down. As the bomb squad were already tied up at the cathedral, he was relying on the Recruits to message him the code to disarm the timer and stop the devices going off. With the code revealed as 66 (NO) 463 (GOD), disaster was once more averted and the mission accomplished.

By order of the DG of MI5, all of the Recruit's access websites were sealed, outside access to the MI5 intranet was restricted, password details altered and telephone numbers changed. All DNS entries for websites involved in this case were then redirected to point somewhere harmless on the BBC.

[Expert Witnesses]

Series producer Jane Featherstone: 'The interactive side added a fascinating new dimension. The audience had a unique window on to the world we'd created and through it they engaged with the characters and their stories on a much deeper level. What's wonderful was the way the TV series and the website were so interwoven. They sent the audience on a very unusual journey.'

Jamie Cason, editor, Drama and Entertainment Online: 'The appeal was that [spooks] was all about ordinary people leading extraordinary lives – in effect leading double lives – to the extent that their own families didn't know what they did for a living. So the idea behind [spooks] Interactive was allowing members of the audience to experience this in some way, to allow them to pick up on clues, interact with the characters and in effect "become" spies.'

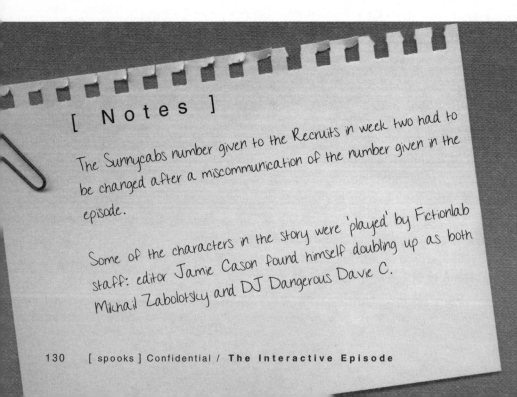

[Notes]

The Sunnycabs number given to the Recruits in week two had to be changed after a miscommunication of the number given in the episode.

Some of the characters in the story were 'played' by Fictionlab staff: editor Jamie Cason found himself doubling up as both Mikhail Zabolotsky and DJ Dangerous Davie C.

The making of [spooks] Interactive

In the autumn of 2001, Fictionlab, BBCi's online drama team, presented their concept for a new interactive experience – provisionally called 'Spies' – to other divisions within the BBC.

Inspired by the intricate online support for Steven Spielberg's film *AI*, Piers Beckley of Fictionlab had created 'Spies' to allow members of the audience to take part in and, more importantly, interact with a dramatic story across a variety of media, including (initially) radio, webspace and mobile phone. It would enable viewers/listeners to get to know the characters outside of the proposed weekly instalments and hopefully encourage them to pay more attention to little details in the hope that they might lead them to a clue about the ongoing mystery. Sitting in on the presentation was Gareth Neame, head of drama commissioning at the BBC. By this time, Gareth had of course commissioned [spooks], which focused on similar themes and settings to the 'Spies' concept. Soon after, Gareth approached Fictionlab with a view to adapting 'Spies' as an online version of his new drama.

[spooks] Interactive represented a major departure for the Fictionlab team, who were previously best known for support sites for shows such as *EastEnders*, *Top of the Pops* and *Ab Fab*, which give fans magazine-style coverage of their favourite shows. With [spooks], though, the idea would be to work closely with Kudos to create an interactive experience that would immerse the audience in the narrative rather than just reporting on it.

As the regular [spooks] characters would generally be locked into their own story arcs on television, the characters that the viewers would interact with had to be able to do so without contradicting what was going on in that week's episode. The story that was developed by the Fictionlab team would focus around Danny's brother Bruno (who featured in an early script but was edited from the transmitted episode). Bruno was a DJ working in a nightclub who had no idea that his brother worked for MI5. When Bruno found himself involved with some 'dodgy characters', he asked Danny for help. In turn, Danny turned to some of his field agents (i.e. the viewers) and asked them to collect information for him. As the mission unravelled, Russian agents, gangsters and ultimately a bomb would be thrown into the mix, with the whole mission timed to conclude on the same night as the final TV episode.

The online drama was first publicised in the classified section of *Private Eye* magazine. The ad read simply: 'Spooks. We're hiring. Have you got what it takes?' along with a telephone number that directed prospective spies to register at www.thameshouse.net. The registration address was also accessible from BBCi's official [spooks] website, www.bbc.co.uk/spooks.

To maintain a level of suspension of disbelief, a number of websites were set up that, although hosted by the BBC, were to all intents and purposes stand-alone sites, from the official Thames House website (which contained over 400 pages of content alone, including detailed information on the cases and characters seen in the TV show as well as additional internet-only cases) and the site for the Skylight nightclub where Bruno worked to the sites for a briefcase manufacturer and a car-hire company. Agents had access to the Thames House intranet (in reality a BBC message board restyled to remove any overt reference to the broadcaster), and, if they searched common search engines such as Google for material or trawled the newsgroups, they could find important clues on mailing lists that had been placed months earlier, way before the show began. Agents would also be guided by regular e-mails from Danny (some preprogrammed, some sent manually by the production team), or by hints fed to the message boards to direct agents to the next link in the chain. Clues were also taken from the ongoing TV episodes, such as the number for Sunnycabs (seen in episode 102) and used to progress the plot further. Such phone numbers led to a prerecorded message from Danny (supplied by David Oyewolo himself).

The response was phenomenal, with over 10,000 registered players following the unfolding mission. The final instalment of the episode required agents to find a code that could stop a biological device going off in central London. Though the first solution was mailed in by a player just 30 minutes after the challenge went live, there were still plenty of participants trying to mail in the following day when the whole project was closed down (as it required such heavy-duty staff maintenance, the plan had always been to only run the 'episode' for the duration of the series).

An ambitious project from the outset, for series two it was decided not to just repeat the experience of the first series. Instead, viewers would be invited to join the 'Spy Academy' and take part in a brand new mission... ■

Series Two (2003) Ten episodes

[Regular Cast]

Matthew Macfadyen (Tom Quinn)
Keeley Hawes (Zoe Reynolds)
David Oyelowo (Danny Hunter)
Peter Firth (Harry Pearce)
Shauna Macdonald (Sam Buxton)
Nicola Walker (Ruth Evershed)
Hugh Simon (Malcolm Wynn-Jones)
Megan Dodds (Christine Dale)
Natasha Little (Dr Vicky Westbrook)
Rory Macgregor (Colin Wells)
Jenny Agutter (Tessa Phillips)
Enzo Cilenti (Carlo Franceschini)

Episode 201

First Broadcast (BBC1): June 2 2003

Written by **David Wolstencroft**
Directed by **Bharat Nalluri**

[C a s t]

Karel Roden (Gradic), **Dragan Micanovic** (Rado), **Esther Hall** (Ellie Simm), **Heather Cave** (Maisie Simm), **Lorcan Cranitch** (Patrick McCann), **Rebecca Johnson** (Trendy Civil Servant*), **Teresa Churcher** (Sarah), **Benedict Cumberpatch** (Jim North), **Ben Fox** (MI5 Officer 1), **Emma Barton** (MI5 Officer 2), **Graham Christopher** (George, Thames House Security), **William Buckhurst** (Bomb Disposal Guy), **Alastair Parker** (1st Policeman), **Martin Cole** (SAS Officer), **Rad Lazar** (Gradic Henchman 1), **Natasha Milkovic** (Rado's Colleague), **Nikolai Claus** (Mugger Kid).
* scenes excised

[W h o ' s   W h o]

Dragan Micanovic (Rado) appeared in the BBC's 2002 revival of *Auf Wiedersehen, Pet*; the same year he played Jorgi in *Cutting It*. He can also be seen in the feature film *Bad Company* (dir. Joel Schumacher, 2001). Teresa Churcher (Sarah) had a small role in *Gosford Park* (dir. Robert Altman, 2001). You might recognise William Buckhurst (Bomb Disposal Guy) from the Nescafé sponsorship adverts used to precede episodes of *Friends* on Channel 4, although his CV also includes roles in *Man and Boy*, *My Hero* and *As If*.

[Case Report]

Tom Quinn could do nothing but watch Ellie and Maisie through the windows of his south London flat as the timer on the bomb counted down. Listening in to Tom Quinn's phone, Danny Hunter and Zoe Reynolds awaited the inevitable explosion from the C4 they'd learned had been planted in McCann's laptop. Then the call came through to Section B that a bomb had gone off – but in north London. As Danny tried to make sense of events, a coded warning came through and Thames House was evacuated. Danny realised what was happening – there were in fact two bombs! At the same time as the one at Tom's house had failed to detonate, another had exploded at the Wandsworth home of Michael Purefoy, Secretary of State for Northern Ireland, killing Purefoy and his two daughters instantly and leaving his wife in a critical condition. Within minutes, Patrick McCann's group – now calling themselves 'The War for Irish Unity' – claimed responsibility.

The bomb in Tom's laptop had clearly been a diversion all along. Presuming Tom would have brought the laptop back to the office, the Irishmen had banked on it setting off Thames House's security alarms as soon as he brought it through the door – in fact, they had even sent in a coded warning to that effect. And while all eyes were on MI5, the other bomb would have detonated.

Tom elected to stay with his family as they went for a medical check-up, but on the way he received a call from Patrick McCann claiming that he wanted to defect as he was scared by the direction his group had decided to take. Realising his branch chief was now aware of his involvement with MI5, McCann was offering a trade of information in return for his own safety. Reluctantly, Tom agreed to his request. However, when two officers went to collect him, they found McCann shot dead with a tag on his toe that read: 'Property of MI5.'

Just as the team were coming to terms with the day's events, a report came in of another explosion, this time at Longcross military base, which had apparently suffered a mortar attack resulting in multiple casualties. When official denials came in from all Irish Republican splinter groups – including McCann's – it became clear that this was the work of another group. Harry Pearce immediately suspected a leak in the MOD and summoned Tom Quinn back to work. As a concession, Tom was allowed to bring his family with him to Thames House and Zoe arranged for a room to be set up for them in the medical centre. But when she learned of the death of Purefoy and his children, Ellie decided to flee Thames House for the safety of her mother's home.

After the dust had settled in Longcross, it was discovered that there was a massive shortfall in munitions supplies, including light arms, mortars, explosives and automatic weapons. All available intelligence placed responsibility for the attack with Miroslav Gradic, a former commander in the Serbian army and now a self-declared freedom fighter (see Security File). When a military vehicle transporting bazookas was hijacked and looted, it became clear that Gradic was beginning to assemble an armoury of very specialised weapons.

Information received from Six indicated that Gradic had managed to evade capture and enter the UK thanks to someone helping him along. Prime suspect was a man known as 'Rado' who had recently started work at the Serbian Embassy. Having identified Rado as a film buff, Zoe arranged for a new video rentals store to open near to where he was living. The store was fitted with surveillance equipment and filled with art-house films that would hopefully catch Rado's interest. Zoe posed as 'Kate', a member of staff (ably assisted by new recruit Sam Buxton, who was eager for her first mission since completing training) with the brief to become Rado's 'new best friend'.

The plan worked and soon Rado was so taken with 'Kate' that he was offering her advice on her career. 'Kate' confessed to him that she didn't have an up-to-date curriculum vitae, and Rado volunteered to help her compile a new one. In return, 'Kate' gave him a present – a pair of cufflinks. This was all an elaborate ruse to plant the bugged cufflinks on Rado (see Gadgets), which enabled Colin of the technical support team to decipher whatever Rado typed at his keyboard at work. This was how the team discovered that Rado was communicating with Gradic via coded messages placed in the classified section of an evening newspaper.

Harry received word that the Prime Minister had decided to convene COBRA away from Whitehall, in the light of the attacks on top secret military installations and the death of Michael Purefoy. Meanwhile, having followed up Harry's suspicion about a leak in the Ministry of Defence, Danny found an irregularity in the private accounts of one Jim North, a civil servant based in defence logistics. Although he was on the same pay scale as Zoe, his accounts showed large sums of money being deposited at regular intervals. When North was brought in for questioning, he revealed that he'd been approached by a Serbian friend – confirmed as Radovan – to help him obtain government documents for a book he claimed to be writing on 'Secret Britain'. He also confirmed that they had communicated via the classified section of the *Evening Standard* in adverts that contained hidden grid references for a dead-letter drop. North would then leave any documents he'd obtained at the drop and the next day he'd collect his payment.

Every person on the Grid was given copies of recent editions of the *Evening Standard* to examine. It was Malcolm who realised that in addition to the adverts placed by North's friend were a second series of adverts conforming to the same code, only these weren't grid references for dead-letter drops, they were for targets such as Longcross and the munitions transporter. A new one had recently been placed identifying the location of the COBRA meeting. Gradic had gambled that in the event of the attacks COBRA would have to convene, and that the meeting would be attended by the Prime Minister, the chief of defence staff, heads of the armed forces, secretaries of state, and the heads of Five and Six – effectively a War Cabinet. A message was sent to Harry, who had already left for the COBRA meeting, and the meeting was reconvened at an alternative location. Gradic's men arrived at the location originally intended for the meeting to find Tom waiting for them. When Gradic ordered his men to shoot Tom, they in turn were shot by SAS officers and Gradic was arrested. With Harry's permission, however, Tom did not send Gradic to The Hague, as expected. Rather, he had him rerouted to Egypt, having called ahead and told them Gradic was a paedophile on a British passport.

Rado was also arrested and detained for questioning. Despite fears that Zoe's life might have been at risk after the discovery that Rado was in fact a trained killer, it would appear he had genuinely liked 'Kate' and was disappointed that she had disappeared so suddenly...

[Previous Missions]

Harry alludes to his well-founded suspicion of McCann (see episode 106) and to Tessa's theft of funds. When Tom tells Danny that Tessa is someone they no longer talk about, it's clear that there's not been time for Danny to be updated about what has happened to her. We also see the dead-letter drop technique (shown in episode 105).

[Miroslav Gradic]

Miroslav Gradic was a Serb commander who holds the UK personally responsible for massacres in Bosnia. He still maintains he has only ever targeted legitimate military targets despite evidence to suggest such targets have in the past included women and children. He sees himself as a political freedom-fighter in the grand struggle for Greater Serbia, a claim given some weight after his two sons were killed in NATO bombing raids on Belgrade: they were porters in a hospital that took a direct hit from British bombs. Gradic's preferred weapon is the mortar; he's used them on mosques, schools, and homes. He also has connections to the Serbian Mafia and has had three narrow escapes with KFOR (the Kosovo Force) troops thanks to tip-offs from Serbian sympathisers in the ground authorities. He is also known to write poems – mainly sonnets.

Gradic entered the UK under a forged passport. On The Hague's most-wanted list, he was previously believed to be hiding in a bunker in Bosnia. He's been on the run for six years, having managed to avoid an MI5-Serbian joint operation to capture him just a couple of months ago, and has also escaped from NATO, KFOR, Interpol, Europol and the Serbian Militias.

[Radovan 'Rado' Gradic]

Though Miroslav Gradic's sons are dead, his brother has two children: one, a daughter, is severely disabled, but the other, from his first wife, is Radovan, who was hired for a clerical post at the Serbian Embassy three months prior to the attack on Longcross, having changed his surname to avoid any obvious connections to his uncle. Known socially as Rado, he is a former foot-soldier in the Serbian army who worked in Belgrade for the then-Yugoslavian government in signals intelligence – mainly cipher work – and was identified as a sympathiser of his uncle's cause.

Intelligence reveals that Rado has a weakness for art-house movies; he has been seen getting off the bus home four stops early to make regular visits to a video rental store.

[Notes]

This episode follows on immediately from the end of 106.

Zoe mentions cipher work, which is the practice of typing coded messages back and forth to agents in the field and then decoding their replies.

The mobile phone number that 'Kate' gives to Rado was 07700 900002. As is standard practice, this number has now been deallocated.

Zoe tells Danny she earns £32,000 a year, though we can assume a proportion of that will be 'London weighting', additional money civil servants receive for working in the capital.

Danny tells Tom 'the sky is falling', an oblique reference to the children's story Chicken Licken. Rado gives 'Kate' a rather dismissive appraisal of The Russia House (dir. Fred Schepisi, 1990), the film adaptation of a John Le Carré novel. Zoe's friend Sarah asks Sam for a copy of Pretty Woman (dir. Garry Marshall, 1990), the film that saved Richard Gere's career and really kick-started Julia Roberts'. Rado introduces 'Kate' to the joys of sljivovica, a traditional brandy in the former Yugoslavia, made by fermenting and distilling plums. Maisie is seen clutching an old, saggy cloth cat. He's baggy, and a bit loose at the seams, but Maisie loves him (i.e. it's a replica of the beloved children's character Bagpuss).

As both he and Tom are too personally involved with Patrick McCann's former group, Harry refers the case files on the 'War for Irish Unity' to Section C (this is the first time this section is mentioned in the series).

Patrick McCann (to Tom): 'Terror game's changed, Davy. I'm telling you, it's scary – particularly right now, I must admit. At this present moment my sphincter is tightening at an alarming rate...'

Zoe: 'Look at Tom and Ellie. They were perfect for each other and the job's made mincemeat out of them. If they can't make it, what chance have the rest of us got? What chance have I got?'

Tom: 'One minute they're innocent, they're just innocent, safe. Then you open your mouth, a few words come out: "I'm a spy." And suddenly they're a target, they're a liability for life, and it's all your fault. They've been branded. It's like a hex...'

Dr Vicky Westbrook (to Danny): 'What d'you do, just walk around in a big T-shirt that says "Please mug me"?'

[D i s i n f o r m a t i o n]

Longcross is a classified military base that doesn't appear on any maps. Though even local residents had always believed it to be an army transport facility, it is in fact a Special Forces weapons-testing centre.

Zoe and Sam set up 'Filmz', a video store that's not that well stocked with Hollywood romances but has a marvellous selection of art-house films that might appeal to your average Serbian terrorist.

[I d e n t i t y C h e c k]

McCann still addresses Tom as 'Davy Crockett'. Tom calls himself 'Matthew' when speaking to Ellie's mum – who wastes no time in revealing she's already been briefed of his real name. While at the hospital after the mugging, Danny uses the name 'Palmer'.

We see some of the difficulties MI5 officers have to face in juggling multiple identities, which is an issue that we'll return to later in the series. Even when not working under an assumed identity, Zoe has to adopt a 'safe' cover story when she bumps into an old school friend and immediately tells her she's a civil servant 'pushing paper clips'. Later on, after meeting Carlo the corporate banker (whose surname is not revealed until episode 204), she becomes a legal secretary with a boyfriend called Jamie (or Danny, as we know him), a trader in the city who she's been seeing for six months (and as we'll learn in later episodes, she's adopted another false name here too). Finally, to entrap Rado (who claims to be a journalist), she becomes 'Kate Mills' (born 23/02/71), a bored video rentals clerk with a colourful CV and an unnamed sister. When her old school friend Sarah visits the video shop unexpectedly, Zoe is forced to construct another back-history that involves her friend being romantically linked to 'Kate's' ex.

[Personnel Records Update]

New recruit Sam seems instantly taken with Danny, though she's also showing good 'befriending training' by trying to get the home phone and passport number of the security guard in Thames House reception. Malcolm would appear to be fire warden for the floor, going on his handling of the evacuation procedure.

Zoe reveals an aptitude for Serbian, and we learn that she went to school with a woman called Sarah (now employed by law firm Challon and Partners). Zoe lost touch with her – perhaps intentionally – after she went to university (Oxford), but bumped into her again on a bus on the evening after the Longcross attack. Sarah is still with 'Paul', who presumably Zoe also knew at school. Still, Malcolm seems to like Zoe just the way she is, though Colin, the technician, seems a little irritable about Malcolm's obvious interest in her during the creation of the bugged cufflinks.

After Danny is mugged for his mobile phone by a gang of youths, Tom accompanies him to the hospital and completely fails to notice that the doctor looking after Danny, Vicky Westbrook, is flirting with him outrageously. Despite severe bruising to his ribs, Danny declines time off to recuperate.

Harry learns that during the operation to capture Gradic, Tom lost control momentarily and tried to strangle Gradic. In a private debriefing with Tom he raises the question of whether or not Tom can still do his job.

Though Ellie and Maisie survive the bomb threat, when Ellie hears of the effects of the other bomb on Michael Purefoy and his family she leaves Tom and goes to stay with her mother, Jane Simm. Although Tom tries to reassure Ellie that she and Maisie are his main priority, when he's unavoidably detained from meeting her, Ellie tells him their relationship is over. A tearful Tom leaves the Simm family to rebuild their lives without him and returns home to pack away all of the items he associates with Ellie and Maisie, just as he would do once a legend has ceased to be useful.

[Gadgets]

Colin prepares a set of cufflinks for Zoe to give to Rado. The cufflinks have audio receivers secreted inside them that can then transmit the keystrokes from Rado's computer keyboard back to Thames House. The CV that 'Kate' gives Rado has been specially designed to contain all the letters of the alphabet – including symbols – so that once Rado has typed up the entire CV, the keystroke for each letter can be isolated, recognised and converted into text, courtesy of a handy program on Colin's computer.

Tom's car is fitted with a GPS (Global Positioning System) that allows Danny to track him. Gradic's soldiers are equipped with night-vision goggles, almost certainly acquired during the raid on either Longcross or the transporter.

[Missing in Action]

A scene was shot where a 'trendy civil servant' gave Harry a hard time, effectively laying the blame for the bombing of Michael Purefoy on MI5's shoulders. Later, Sam gives Zoe some fashion advice, suggesting she should wear more green as it suits her. Suddenly realising how that sounds, she tells her she's 'not a raving lesbo or anything' before hastily adding, 'Not that there's anything wrong with lesbians.' A slight dig at Keeley Hawes' stint as a lesbian in *Tipping the Velvet*, perhaps?

A nice exchange between Sam and Malcolm was also lost, where Malcolm shows Sam that he can complete a German crossword in record speed, something he believes is good practice, though for what he doesn't say.

An exchange between Gradic and one of his men regarding where to shoot into a heart would have served to illustrate that the Serbian general has a good understanding of human anatomy. The connection between Rado and Jim North of the MOD was originally a little more convoluted. To confirm their suspicions, Tom calls the *Evening Standard* and phones in a correction to the advert. Then, when Jim North calls the newspaper office from his desk at work to check that the ad was correct, his call is traced and he's brought in for questioning as per the transmitted episode.

[Expert Witnesses]

Producer Simon Crawford Collins: 'This series builds on that sense of topicality, as threats to national security have never been greater and our team of spies have to match the growing sophistication of an often unseen enemy.'

David Oyelowo: 'These guys rely on such trust and friendship because effectively day-to-day their lives are in each other's hands. This is where life imitates art for us because Matthew, Keeley and I all get on very well too. But we are terrible gigglers, which can get in the way sometimes when you're supposed to be all serious and saving the world! Matthew is the worst and sometimes you can't look him in the eye!'

Rory Macgregor (Colin): 'I know the first series was massively popular, and I think it surprised everybody how successful it was. I wasn't really involved that much in the first series, but it just blew me away – I think it blew everyone away… And everyone still keeps asking me what happens in the first episode, and how the storyline's going to turn out!'

Natasha Little (Dr Vicky Westbrook): 'I've been very lucky in that I've never had to spend very much time in hospital, so it was hard playing a doctor. Fortunately there was someone on hand to advise me how to check someone's ribs. I prodded David a lot when we were filming the scene when he and Tom come into my emergency ward, and it seems I have very cold hands which I think is a very doctorish thing!'

Awaiting Series 2

By the end of June 2002, Stephen Garrett's initial thoughts about finding 'a new precinct' to play in had paid off in force.

The series had already been graced with a front cover on the *Radio Times*, and reviews were enthusiastically positive: *The Times*' Joe Joseph compared it to its American rival *24* – to which [spooks] admittedly had coincidentally superficial similarities, such as the split-screen technique – but was pleased to declare that '[spooks] had established a voice of its own'; Gerard O'Donovan of *The Telegraph* reserved praise for David Wolstencroft's 'wry and knowing script'; and Alison Graham of the *Radio Times* felt compelled to ponder, 'It's presumably not meant to be taken too seriously, because surely life in MI5 can't be this exciting?'

In *The Guardian*, Jonathan Wright was in a jingoistic mood when he wrote: 'If you want proof that British TV drama can be as glossy, smartly scripted and as seat-of-pants exciting as *24* or *CSI*, then here it is.' And *Heat* magazine's reviewer Chris Longridge declared it to be 'the finest British thriller series in years'.

The series was a ratings winner too; it was cited by many as a major factor in the BBC grabbing a greater share of the ratings than ITV for the first time in decades. The first episode of [spooks] captured the attention of 9.2 million viewers and a 41% audience share between 9pm and 10pm, compared to the ITV Amanda Burton vehicle *Helen West,* which had just 4.8 million viewers and a 22% share of the overall audience. It was a share that **[spooks]** maintained throughout its six-week run.

The series won its share of awards and nominations too: winner of Best Drama Series at the Broadcast Awards; nominated for a Royal Television Society Award; winner of the much-coveted BAFTA for Best Drama Series; and short-listed for Best Continuing Series at the Banff Awards, the sole British contender alongside such US TV heavyweights as *Six Feet Under, The Sopranos, The West Wing* and *Oz*.

But all this paled into insignificance when the second series of **[spooks]** was finally announced as imminent. As the massive billboards went up at the end of May 2003, and as the show's stars once again graced the front cover of the *Radio Times*, the only thing every loyal viewer wanted to know was 'WHAT ABOUT THE BOMB?!'

When the official BBC message board reopened the week before the second series began, that was the question visitors were invited to discuss. Everyone had his or her own pet theories. Some fell completely for the fact that the first season's concluding episode had ended with a flash of white light, suggesting that the bomb had indeed detonated – presumably these viewers had forgotten that every episode had ended in pretty much exactly the same way, which was exactly as it had been intended. Another common theory was that there wasn't actually a bomb ('Not enough space in the laptop for all that explosive' was one fan's comment – sorry to break this to you, but there was), while visitor Clare Hogan postulated that the SAS might break through the wall of Tom's neighbour's house and get Ellie and Maisie free

that way ('It's just like the BBC to keep us on the edge of our seats,' she noted cheerily). Many picked up with some relief on the fact that Matthew Macfadyen featured heavily in the TV trails and billboard posters for the second series, which – though reassuring them that Tom at least must survive – led to them growing increasingly concerned for his family instead. And a few managed to get quite near the mark when they guessed that McCann himself had been misled by his bosses and the bomb-laden laptop was not what it seemed. As one poster to the message boards phrased it: 'There are endless possibilities, aren't there?'

Having already been responsible for one of the great 'watercooler' moments in British TV with the chip-fat-related demise of Helen, the **[spooks]** team had, it seemed, also managed to pull off another TV coup in the creation of the biggest and most anxiety-ridden 'What next?' cliffhanger since the shooting of J.R. in Dallas… ∎

Episode 202

First Broadcast (BBC3): June 2 2003
First Terrestrial Broadcast (BBC1): June 9 2003

Written by **Howard Brenton**
Directed by **Bharat Nalluri**

[Cast]

Quarie Marshall (Mohammed Rachid), **Alexander Siddig** (Muhammad Ibhn Khaldun), **San Shella** (Javaid/Johnny Patel), **Roshan Seth** (Fazul Azzam), **Taahir Husain** (Abu Hassan), **Praveen Sond** (Aminah), **Sam Bond** (Vinny, PC outside Scotland Yard), **Lucy O'Connell** (Doctor), **Simon Snashall** (CID Officer), **Kammy Darweish** (Mr Hussain), **Rez Kempton** (1st Man – Aaqil), **Gary Bakewell** (Uniformed PC).

[Who's Who]

Alexander Siddig (Muhammad Ibhn Khaldun) was born in the Sudan but was raised in England. At the start of his career he used his real name – Siddig El Fadil – but changed it after discovering too many people had trouble with its pronunciation. He is best known for playing Dr Julian Bashir in the *Star Trek* TV spin-off *Star Trek: Deep Space Nine*. His film roles include *Vertical Limit* (dir. Martin Campbell, 2000) and *Reign of Fire* (dir. Rob Bowman, 2000).

Roshan Seth (Fazul Azzam) played Pandit Nehru opposite Ben Kingsley in Richard Attenborough's *Gandhi* (1982). He can also be seen in *Indiana Jones and the Temple of Doom* (dir. Steven Spielberg, 1984), *A Passage to India* (dir. David Lean, 1984), Hanif Kureishi's *My Beautiful Laundrette* (dir. Stephen Frears, 1985), and *Monsoon Wedding* (dir. Mira Nair, 2001).

Gary Bakewell (seen here as the PC who is singularly unimpressed with Tom's 'spook' status) starred as Paul McCartney in the film *Backbeat* (dir. Iain Softley, 1993), the story of the birth of the Beatles. He reprised the role in 2000 for *The Linda McCartney Story* for CBS Television. He first found fame in the Scottish soap opera *Take the High Road*, playing Mark Torrance, and his other TV work includes the Lenny Henry series *Chef!*, mystical fantasy *Neverwhere*, and the BBC adaptation of *Man and Boy*.

[Case Report]

Tom, Zoe and Danny were on an operation outside Parkmount Community Centre and Mosque, Birmingham (see Security File below). Inside was Tom's agent, Javaid Patel (known as Johnny) who had been recruited to infiltrate the mosque, which intelligence suggested had been taken over by an extremist, Mullah Mohammed Rachid. When Johnny's wire had been down for 50 minutes, Tom decided to break cover and enter the mosque to rescue the boy, but before he could do anything, Johnny was thrown from the top of the mosque directly onto the roof of the surveillance van.

Johnny was immediately sent to MI5's clinic in Truro. Before the drop, he'd been subjected to 'fallaq', a particularly nasty torture technique that involves breaking every bone in his feet, the intention being to cause blood clots that can, in time, severely damage the victim or even lead to death. When Tom went to interview Johnny, the visibly distressed youth spoke of suicide bombers being trained from the mosque, which he referred to as a 'nest of angels'. The agitation of recalling what he had endured caused Johnny to suffer a fit. The cause was later identified as a haemorrhage which, sadly, left him permanently brain-damaged.

Harry called a meeting in order to brief Ruth Evershed, the new intelligence analyst recently seconded from GCHQ. With Tom's agent blown, there was now a serious need for a replacement so that the level of threat to national security posed by the mosque could be properly assessed. The situation was so desperate that Harry gave Tom permission to speak to Tessa Phillips, who, since leaving the service had set up her own security firm, but her bitterness and resentment of Harry made the visit unfruitful. However, just as things were looking bleak, Ruth made a breakthrough.

The previous day, Ibhn Khaldun, a former agent of the Algerian Secret Service (see Security File), finally made it into Britain illegally after months of living undercover. He'd presented himself to Scotland Yard and asked to speak to someone in Special Branch but was assumed to be simply a vagrant. Tom gave orders for the man to be released from jail and then arranged to meet with him in Kensington Gardens, on the edge of Hyde Park. There, Ibhn told Tom that the GAJ – the Group for Algerian Jihad – were funding extremist groups in the UK and confirmed that this included Mohammed Rachid. Harry, who had been waiting nearby, swapped places with Tom and promised Ibhn a British passport in return for him becoming an MI5 agent.

Although at every stage Khaldun appeared to be genuine – even allowing himself willingly to be submitted to debriefing – there was still a serious concern that he might be a highly dangerous double agent. However, this didn't stop Christine Dale of the CIA from requesting a meeting with Tom in the hope that she might gain access to Ibhn Khaldun. Tom denied all knowledge of the man, despite the fact that it was CIA intelligence that had led MI5 to Rachid in the first place.

Zoe arranged for Khaldun to be hired as a refuse collector at the University of West Midlands in order for him to make contact with known followers of Rachid. Having won his fellow workers' trust, he was invited to the Parkmount Community Centre and Mosque and eventually he was invited to meet with Fazul Azzam. Though Azzam suspected him of being an extremist and dismissed him, by then Khaldun had already realised that the key to gaining access to Rachid was Azzam's daughter, Aminah. As he left Fazul Azzam's house, Khaldun managed to give a message to Aminah for Rachid. Soon after, he received word that Rachid wished to speak to him.

Tom's team debriefed Khaldun and supplied him with a transmitter, camera and small internet browser so that he could collate information on Rachid and get it back to them straight away. He was also given a substantial amount of money with which to buy his way into Rachid's cell. It later transpired that he disposed of the equipment almost straight away, and had handed the money over to Rachid claiming it to be from mutual Algerian contacts.

Tom began to grow concerned after Khaldun missed three meetings, but decided to give him 24 hours to show himself. Fortunately, that night Khaldun made contact. He said that he'd been under constant watch ever since he'd met with

Rachid. He was pleased to say he had managed to infiltrate the martyrs group and had learned that they were preparing a new martyr, a 16-year-old boy named Abu Hassan, who would detonate a bomb on his person somewhere in the centre of Birmingham very soon. Unfortunately, the exact time and location would not be revealed until the last moment. Tom felt that the situation had grown too dangerous and told Khaldun that he was going to withdraw him from the operation. Khaldun begged for more time to rescue the boy and when Tom refused, Khaldun punched him and escaped.

With no other options open to him, Tom mounted a raid on the mosque. Unfortunately, by the time the team got there Abu had already been taken. Tom then went to Fazul Azzam, who suddenly realised his daughter's involvement in Rachid's cause. He forced her to tell him where the martyr was being kept. As Rachid's men prepared their martyr, Abu, Khaldun took his chance and fought with the men to free the boy. Startled and confused, Abu ran away. Ibhn

pursued him towards a school playground with Tom's team arriving seconds later. Ignoring Tom's instructions to back away, Khaldun tried to talk Abu down, but when Abu realised that he could claim Ibhn as his 'unbeliever', he detonated the device, killing them both instantly.

[Disinformation]

Tom's team gain access to the mosque claiming that Rachid has been keeping false records, according to the 1967 Charity Commission Act. It's enough for Rachid's followers to throw him out.

[Parkmount Community Centre and Mosque, Birmingham]

The Parkmount Community Centre and Mosque was founded by Fazul Azzam in the early 1960s, but in recent years the mosque has been influenced by Mullah Mohammed Rachid. Originally from Afghanistan, Rachid came to Britain in 1995 on an extended visa granted by the British government at a time when Afghanistan was still seen as a victim of Soviet oppression; as there was a shortage of leaders in the British Islamic community, the government were keen to help. After seven years' residence in the UK, Rachid is entitled to full citizenship, unless an impediment to his application can be found.

Despite Rachid's reputation as a thug, Fazul Azzam has so far stopped any complaint being made. The mosque is bitterly divided between support for its founder and for the interloper. The CIA believes Rachid to be an Afghani intelligence officer with links to Al Qaeda. There is strong evidence to suggest he is training teenage boys as suicide bombers. Attempts have been made to bug the mosque but Rachid's supporters perform regular sweeps and a lack of agents with the right ethnic profile has further hindered infiltration of the mosque. Additionally, the Home Office has advised sensitive policing of communities that might erupt and lead to race riots.

Tom Quinn's agent Ibhn Khaldun was able to confirm that Rachid had connections to an extreme terrorist organisation known as the GAJ (the Group for Algerian Jihad).

[Muhammad Ibhn Khaldun]

CLOSED

Muhammad Ibhn Khaldun, former university lecturer. Arrested by the Algerian Secret Service and threatened with death if he did not help them penetrate the GAJ. He succeeded in doing this, but when his cover was blown a car bomb meant for him instead killed his wife and daughters. Using his life savings, he bribed his way onto a boat and left Algeria. He went to France and sent back fake reports that he was infiltrating a GAJ cell in Paris. His last report was that his cover had been blown; as far as his former Algerian masters were concerned, he was dead. Khaldun disappeared and escaped via a Channel Tunnel freight train to the UK where he was eventually recruited as an MI5 agent.

FILE UPDATE

Khaldun managed to infiltrate a British mosque and brought an end to the 'nest of angels'. Sadly, while trying to talk a teenage suicide bomber into surrendering his explosives, the boy instead detonated the bomb, killing himself and Khaldun in the blast.

FILE CLOSED BY TOM QUINN, SECTION B

Tom: 'We don't get medals for what we do. All we get is respect. And respect you have, Johnny. Big time.'

Rachid: 'MI5: what a sad apology for an intelligence service. Secret policemen in other countries can arrest, beat, electric-shock, even kill. But what can you do? A smear in the press, a meaningless threat? The world I come from must seem utterly uncontrollable to you. And dangerous.'

Zoe (to refuse contractor): 'We have an employee we wish you to hire... It doesn't quite matter who we are. I have your VAT returns in front of me and there is a problem...'

Khaldun: 'The only paradise we will see will be one we make on earth...'

[Identity Check]

Tom poses as Mr Anderson from the Home Office Immigration Service (for his meetings with Rachid). When he first meets Ibhn, Tom is Mr John Steadman, again from the Home Office. At the university he becomes John Culper, a Cambridge graduate from Derbyshire with first-class honours in history who's doing a PhD on Gladstone in Ireland.

[Personnel Report Updates]

Ruth speaks perfect French. After Harry learned of Tessa Phillips' 'phantom agents' deception (and stealing over £150,000 of fictitious expenses), Tessa was dismissed from the Service. She now runs Phillips Security, a private security consultancy. In talking with her, Tom realises that she has always resented not

Ibhn first meets Tom in Kensington Gardens, near the famous statue of Peter Pan. Sculpted by George Frampton, the statue was donated to the park by Peter's creator, author James M. Barrie. The statue was put in place in secret on the night of April 30 1912, so that the next morning it would seem to visitors to have arrived by magic.

When discussing the 'nest of angels' with Harry, Tom makes mention of Hamas, an Islamic movement in the Palestinian territories. Formed in late 1987, the organisation demands a complete Israeli withdrawal from the Palestinian territories and has in the past used both political and terrorist means to achieve its long-term aim of an Islamic Palestinian state in place of Israel.

This episode was premiered on BBC3 on June 2 2003, half an hour after the first episode had been shown on BBC1.

getting Harry's job, something Harry is all too aware of.

Happy that her vetting has come back clean, Tom begins a relationship with Dr Vicky Westbrook. During her meeting with Tom, Christine Dale also suggests that she's interested in going for a coffee with him out of hours. Though this might just be a clumsy attempt to sweeten him up so he'll help her get access to his new agent, the kiss she gives him (to show her relief that he didn't get himself killed by the suicide bomber) suggests otherwise.

Zoe loiters in the pub where she met Carlo (see episode 201) and has a drink with him.

[Gadgets]

Malcolm builds a small, single-purpose net browser housed in a double-tray box of chocolates. Khaldun is given a match-box camera compatible with the chocolate browser, as well as a pen containing a hidden transmitter.

[Missing in Action]

Before the meeting where Ruth is introduced, Sam and Zoe speculate on who the new officer is going to be and decide it'll be 'a rival alpha male and he'll be gorgeous'.

Also lost was one short scene of Zoe waiting in the pub for Carlo in vain before she actually finds him again. Tom calls Vicky to tell her he's going away for a few days – buying time for her vetting to come through. A short exchange between Harry and Ruth was dropped where Harry accused Ruth of being at GCHQ too long: 'This job isn't all about sneaking on people with microphones and CCTV cameras and then sending others in to do the dirty work!' Sensing Ruth's embarrassment, Harry quickly says 'apology' and Ruth says equally quickly 'accepted', suggesting both of them are keen to forget the conversation ever happened.

One edit from the final confrontation with Abu has Khaldun educate him on the Taliban's regime: 'The Taliban in Afghanistan banned football. They used the stadium in Kabul for executions. They cut off people's heads in the centre circle. What do you think of that? Mind you, if they were Man United supporters…'

[Expert Witnesses]

Executive producer (BBC) Gareth Neame: 'We did extensive research on the programme and there were Muslim advisors involved in the development of the script... There was also a Muslim advisor present during filming... This is a drama series and it's fictional and its main orbit is about the world of terrorism and counter-terrorism. The notion of suicide bombing is absolutely within the remit of [spooks], to look at the growing international concern there is about suicide bombing and the quite well-documented debate about what on earth would happen if such a terrible act were ever committed within the UK.'

Series producer Jane Featherstone: 'The second episode is a very sensitive subject that's been handled brilliantly by Howard Brenton. All throughout we were very careful about how we did portray people, and indeed the BBC has a responsibility to portray things with as much balance as possible. I think if you inflame both sides of the argument then you're doing the right job.'

Writer Howard Brenton: 'I didn't worry about causing offence. What I wanted to do was create an Islamic hero at the centre of the story. His name is Khaldun, and I took that because one of the greatest pieces of medieval Islamic literature was written by a man with that name.'

Nicola Walker (Ruth): 'When I came in for my first episode, I was probably the most nervous I have ever been on a job without a doubt. The first day was in the meeting room and I was looking round at the main group feeling completely out of my depth. The fact that Ruth arrives very overexcited and keen was very lucky for me, because that was exactly how I felt.'

Islamaphobia

'Viewers complain over TV "Muslim plot": More than 150 viewers complained after BBC1 screened a controversial episode of *Spooks* on Monday, taking the total number of objections to the episode towards 1,000.'

That was how BBC online news reported the reaction to this episode the morning after its BBC1 broadcast. For a show that deals with the kind of sensitive issues as

[s p o o k s] does, complaints might possibly be seen as an occupational hazard, but after the time and care the team had taken with the episode (as suggested by the quote from Gareth Neame), it must have been more than a little surprising that the reaction was so strong. What was even more unexpected was that the vast majority of the complaints had been received before the BBC1 transmission itself – and some of them (almost 200 in fact) had been logged by the BBC based purely on a reaction to the trailer.

In among the many complaints came accusations that the episode was unrepresentative of Islamic life, that it was just another example of the 'racist' BBC refusing to show Muslims in anything other than a negative light and that it could cause (and indeed was later accused of causing) racial incitement against Muslim communities. What might have come as some surprise to the non-Muslim viewers was not that Muslims complained but that they did so in such numbers. Though areas such as Bradford and Birmingham are known to have a high Asian population, for example, and in the last census the amount of people registering as Muslim was just over 3% of the population, many white, Anglo-Saxon Christians might well be surprised by how many 3% actually is – some two million people at the last count.

In 1959, the American current affairs programme *The Mike Wallace Show* broadcast an edition called 'The Hate That Hate Produced' that focused on the Nation of Islam, a growing organisation of African-Americans that had until then managed to avoid the scrutiny of the almost exclusively-white ruling press of America. The American press's reaction was one of panic. In his autobiography, former minister for the Nation of Islam Malcolm X described the effect that the show had:

'Every phrase was edited to increase the shock mood. As the producers intended, I think people sat just about limp when the program went off.'

The press wasted no time in condemning the Nation of Islam as 'hate-teachers'... 'black fascists'... 'anti-Christian'... 'possibly Communist-inspired...' as if such phrases might help suppress a movement that had been slowly growing in numbers since the 1930s to the point where their members counted in the hundreds of thousands countrywide.

The point of mentioning this is that although the white majority of the population is aware of other religions that make up the diverse ethnic mix of Britain , the likelihood is that when the word 'Muslim' is heard in media reports, it is invariably in association with the words 'extremist', 'fundamentalist' or, alarmingly, 'suicide bomber'.

There have been more than 70 Palestinian bomb attacks aimed at Israelis since 2000; in 2002 alone, 185 people died and many hundreds more were injured by bombers, almost 20 of whom were killed – seemingly willingly – by their own bombs. Many of these attacks have been attributed to militant Muslim groups such as the Islamic Jihad or to Hamas. Such tragic events are, of course, worrying to Muslims themselves, who have been quick to condemn the groups behind the attacks on the World Trade Center and Bali, and distance themselves from extremists such as the radical Muslim cleric Sheikh Abu Hamza, who in April 2003 was stripped of his UK citizenship. Hamza had been a regular preacher at the Finsbury Park Mosque in north London until his suspension by the Charity Commission in April 2002, and has angered many with praise post 9-11 for Osama Bin Laden and condemnation of Britain, the US and Israel. As usual, though the events depicted in the series are fictional, they can't help but be shaped by the world outside of the

[**spooks**] world. Though the show's critics might cry 'Islamophobia', it has to be noted that the Western world at least still considers Palestinian and Al Qaeda terrorists to pose the number one threat to international security. Had [**spooks**] not acknowledged these fears at any point, it would have been open to accusations of being afraid to discuss the major issues that our real-life Security Service faces more and more. In the end, it's a fictional drama; as such, it can only really be true to itself. ■

Episode 203

First Broadcast (BBC3): June 9 2003
First Terrestrial Broadcast (BBC1): June 16 2003

Written by **Matthew Graham**
Directed by **Rob Bailey**

[Cast]

Robert Bowman (I.T. Project Manager), **Chris Fairbank** (Gordon Blaney),
Augustus Prew ('Peter Ellis' / Noah Gleeson), **John Hopkins** (Anton), **Rory
Feeney** (MI5 Officer), **John Salthouse** (James Crowe), **Laurence Mitchell**
(Johnny D), **Cate Fowler** (Schoolteacher), **Carlie Falco** (Cloe), **Jack Doolan** (Jason
Sweeney), **Marsha Crosby** (Daniella), **Leigh Funnelle** ('Bryony Ellis'), **William
Gaminara** (Victor Gleeson).

[Who's Who]

Though you might well know Christopher Fairbank (Gordon Blaney) from playing
the Scouser, Moxey, in the long-running *Auf Wiedersehen, Pet*, it's a testament to
his versatility that he's also appeared in other productions where you might not have
spotted him. He played the Gotham-accented thief who gets on the wrong side of
Batman in the first of Tim Burton's reimaginings of the popular comic-book
character (1989), the Player Queen opposite Mel Gibson in Franco Zeffirelli's
Hamlet (1990) and one of the many victims of the xenomorph creature in *Alien 3*
(dir. David Fincher, 1992). He has also appeared in both *Spender* and *Crocodile
Shoes* alongside *Auf Wiedersehen* co-star Jimmy Nail and was a Chief Inspector in

Prime Suspect 3 – with a different accent almost every time.

John Salthouse (James Crowe) was originally a footballer, having played for Crystal Palace FC, but after a knee injury effectively ended his career he turned to acting. He starred alongside Alison Steadman as the repugnant Tony in the TV adaptation of Mike Leigh's *Abigail's Party* (1977), though he's remembered more as DI Galloway, original (and best) head of CID for the first few years of *The Bill*. He returned to his roots with Sky One's football 'soap', *Dream Team*, on which he also worked as series producer, and has since moved on to produce holiday-rep romp *Is Harry on the Boat?*, again for Sky One.

Actor and writer William Gaminara (Victor Gleeson) has played a fair few doctors in his time: he was Dr Andrew Bower, a series regular in *Casualty* between 1989 and 1992 (and Duffy's husband in the series) and played Dr Richard Locke in the long-running BBC radio series *The Archers*. Other TV work includes the dotcom drama *Attachments*, *Hope and Glory* and, in 2003, *Silent Witness* alongside Amanda Burton. He's also written episodes of *This Life* and *The Lakes*, and adapted Rachel Morris's novel *Ella and the Mothers* for TV.

Cate Fowler (Schoolteacher) was Princess Anne in the mini-series *Charles and Diana: Unhappily Ever After* (1992) and also had small roles in *Our Mutual Friend* (which also starred [**spooks**] regular Keeley Hawes), *Berkeley Square* and *The Cazalets*.

Augustus Prew (Noah Gleeson) can be seen in the film *About a Boy* (dir. Chris & Paul Weitz, 2002) playing the ranting spoilt brat son of Hugh Grant's girlfriend.

[Case Report]

During an urgent transmission to two MI5 officers in Nok Kundi, Western Pakistan, a computer hacker decided to target the security firewall on Thames House's mainframe. The attack scrambled the line to Pakistan and left the officers isolated in a life-threatening situation. The cause of the breach was traced to the Stoke Newington Community Centre, north London, where an I.T. open day was in full swing. The computer doing the damage was eventually found, but when it was disconnected it released a 'spider' (a program designed to pull information off servers, which in this case was depicted by a literal on-screen graphic of a spider) that triggered a high-frequency pulse that stunned the officers and severed the link to Pakistan.

Further investigation revealed that the hacker had entered the mainframe via the MI5 public website but fortunately had failed to gain access to the 'inner sanctum'. Aware that Ruth had been presented to them from GCHQ – and therefore could still be reporting back to them – Harry cautioned Tom, Danny and Zoe to play down the crisis level in front of her. Meanwhile, Ruth would be kept busy trying to decode an apparent threat that the hacker had sent shortly after the attack, a quote from Homer's *Iliad*:

Zeus spoke and nodded with his darkish brows and immortal locks fell forward from the Lord's deathless head, and he made great Olympus tremble.

With Ruth distracted, Tom's team were able to brief Harry on the Pakistan situation. The officers in Pakistan (known as 'Antony' and 'Cleopatra') had been in the process of infiltrating an arms-trafficking ring at an illegal weapons fair. When the fair's own security went off and the guns began to sound, the officers relocated and awaited instructions to guide them to a safe location – at which point the hacker's damage occurred. The very real threat was that every single agent in the field could potentially end up isolated if the hacker was not traced and closed down. MI5 could be rendered powerless.

Digi-cam footage of the I.T. fair revealed the presence of Gordon Blaney, a schoolteacher at Highdale Secondary School, Stoke Newington, and a former member of the Socialist Freedom Movement (SFM), a known terrorist organisation (see Security File below). Zoe was assigned to take on the role of a recently qualified schoolteacher placed at Blaney's school in the hope that she could gain Blaney's trust. Meanwhile, having posed as a Socialist-inclined journalist for the last seven months, Danny had managed to made good connections with James Crowe, editor of the *Red Cry* newspaper, official voice of SFM. He arranged a meeting with Crowe and told him that he'd heard via his contact at the Home Office about a raid by MI5 trying to seize computers. When James asked him why he didn't just go straight to the broadsheets with this, 'Ray' reminded him of where his loyalties lay.

Despite the best efforts of Colin, the Thames House mainframe was again attacked from outside of the firewall. To limit the attacker's routes of entry, Harry ordered the shut-down of all non-essential systems.

By the time Zoe started her first day at Highdale, most of the rooms in the school had been fitted with bugs and minute cameras, except – annoyingly – the I.T.

room, which was being refurbished, meaning there was a slight risk of the decorators finding the bugs. Though Zoe tried to persuade Blaney to join her for a drink after work, he politely declined, saying he had to work late. Despite round-the-clock surveillance on Blaney, there was still no genuine connection between him and the mainframe attacks. Although phone calls between him and James Crowe of SFM had been intercepted, all they revealed was unwillingness on Blaney's part to discuss matters over the phone.

While Zoe again failed to get Blaney to take her out for a drink, Danny met with James Crowe who revealed that his plan was to persuade those traditional Labour supporters disillusioned with New Labour to join their cause. He also told Danny that he was trying to arrange a meeting between him and Blaney. During a briefing back at the Grid, Tom told Harry that he believed Blaney was priming school computers for another hacking operation. Danny told the team about Crowe's planned meeting

with Blaney and arranged for backup in case things got ugly. Zoe however remained unconvinced of Blaney's guilt; unlike most other terrorists she'd ever met, Blaney still displayed enough compassion and care for his students to convince her he was less involved than everyone seemed to think.

During a class the next afternoon, Zoe saw Blaney heading towards the rear of the school. She followed him and discovered that he'd gone to fetch a fizzy drink for a young student – Peter Ellis – who was being picked on and had decided to hide in a shed on the school grounds until home time. Reassured that Zoe was in no danger, Tom's team withdrew to provide backup for Danny while Zoe volunteered to take the boy home.

Danny went to Crowe's office for the meeting with Blaney, but Crowe's comrade Johnny D seemed uneasy about Danny's presence there. When Johnny noticed the MI5 undercover vehicles outside the office and drew Crowe's attention to the fact they were in triangular formation, Danny had no choice but to call in backup. As MI5 officers swarmed the building, Blaney arrived and was surprised to find 'Jane' blocking his way. As she revealed her holster under her coat, he realised Zoe was not a schoolteacher after all. Under interrogation, Blaney claimed that although Crowe had tried to recruit him from time to time, he'd already told him he wasn't interested. He also claimed he was innocent of trying to hack into MI5. But when Zoe showed him the surveillance photos of him storming police barricades, he reacted in a way she had not been expecting. He began insisting that the pictures were fakes and that whoever had fed her the information was giving her 'crap'.

Another attack on the firewall breached the system and scrambled everyone's screens. Spiders appeared and dragged a message across – '94' – which Ruth quickly deduced was a reference to Plutonium, located at the school. Tom's team led an immediate evacuation of the school and began to investigate. While the rest of the team either withdrew or helped Tom, an unseen assailant sneaked into Malcolm's work-tent and managed to access the mainframe directly from Malcolm's computer. The 'radiation' turned out to be a Geiger scrambler (see Gadgets) hidden in the water-shed where Zoe followed Blaney. Again she confronted him with the evidence, saying he couldn't play dumb this time as she'd caught him in the shed. That was when Blaney realised that he hadn't been alone, and that Peter Ellis must somehow be connected. A review of the footage from the IT open day confirmed that Peter Ellis had been present.

Contact with Cleopatra was re-established after two days of silence. She was tired, dehydrated, suffering a suspected broken wrist and hiding in the north quadrant of Nok Kundi. Just as Danny was about to transmit safe co-ordinates to her, the hacker began work again, sending a message that warned them:

We have access to every part of you. Even the Inner Sanctum. We will now download everything. We will expose every one of your dirty secrets. Your people will be free and Olympus will crumble. Good riddance.

Ruth cracked the message. The coded references to Zeus led her back through Greek mythology to Zeus's father, Kronos, so she realised the reference was to a powerful child. That led her to Noah Gleeson, son of the late Victor Gleeson (see Security File below). Zoe and Tom managed to get to Gleeson's home and close down his computer before he could do any more damage. With the crisis over, Danny was finally able to send co-ordinates for a safe house to Cleopatra.

[Gordon Blaney]

Gordon Blaney, 45. Born in Sunderland, his grandfather marched on the Jarrow Crusade but died due to blood clots two days later. Blaney has been a member of the Socialist Party since 1976. Former member of the Socialist Freedom Movement, an organisation that supports the under-class through sabotage, extortion and, more recently, computer warfare. Membership runs into the hundreds and they are well funded. They detest 'New Labour' which they view as a presidential government that must be dismantled. MI5 infiltrated them during the miners' strike in the mid 1980s. The SMF are still active, believed to be responsible for the hacking of sensitive computer files at the 2002 Labour Party conference.

Blaney was seen at the industrial summit riots in Leeds in 2002. He was not arrested at that time, unlike in 1984 when he used protests in Nottingham against the miners' strike to push civil disobedience into other sectors on behalf of the SFM. He is alleged to have thrown a nail bomb into a police car, and is also one of two men believed to be responsible for an assault on a WPC in Bolton in 1985.

Blaney is currently employed as a history and I.T. teacher at Highdale Secondary School, Stoke Newington, where he has an exemplary record. He helps with the initiative to bring computer technology to the inner cities.

FILE UPDATE
As Blaney was handing out leaflets just yards from where the computer hacking into MI5 was found, he became the prime suspect. Though subsequent investigation revealed that Blaney was still in contact with members of SFM, it became clear that the evidence pointing towards his involvement in the breach of MI5's firewall was completely falsified by Noah Gleeson. Blaney was exonerated and relocated to another school with MI5's apologies.

[Previous Missions]

An old codename, Zeus, referred to Algerian dissidents trying to buy a dirty atomic weapon (a mission Harry recalls as 'giddy days').

[Disinformation]

Danny informs the project manager of the technology fair that the building is contaminated with 'blue asbestos'. An observation hut is installed outside of the school, and one of the officers posing as an engineer there, Anton, has a very dodgy 'Bow Bells' accent that miraculously drops when he enters the hut.

[Identity Check]

The two officers trapped in Pakistan were known as 'Antony' and 'Cleopatra'. Cleopatra's real name is Rebecca Hughes, and on her return to the UK she is due to be married.

Zoe becomes 'Jane Graham', 25, born in Slough, graduated six months and currently working as an English supply teacher. She had a canoeing accident in France a year ago and has just come out of a relationship. 'Jane' tells Peter/Noah that she once plucked chickens for a living. Simultaneously she is maintaining the name of Emma (the legal secretary) for her meetings with Carlo and shares an anecdote with him about something she did at work – a job she doesn't actually have – involving hiding the floppy disks of a colleague – who doesn't exist – in the plant pots around the building – which she doesn't work in. It's no wonder Zoe is growing anxious about the number of personalities she's running. Zoe phones in to the Grid calling whoever answers 'Auntie Doris'.

Danny goes under the name of Ray, a journalist with Socialist allegiances, to infiltrate *Red Cry*. An officer trailing Blaney is given the codename 'Apple'. Bryony Ellis, Peter's mum, is revealed to be an actress trying to earn money to fund her drugs habit.

[Security File]

[Noah Gleeson]

Noah Gleeson is the son of Victor Gleeson, a former MI5 officer who died 18 months ago while on an overseas assignment. A child with an intelligence way beyond his years, Noah had accompanied his father to Greece, where Gleeson Senior had accepted a job at an embassy. However, the embassy post was really a cover to enable Gleeson to infiltrate a cell of Albanian terrorists. When his cover was exposed, both he and his son were kidnapped and taken to a remote farmhouse in a mountain range known as Titan's Reach. Though Gleeson's fellow officers had been able to establish an audio link to the farmhouse and were outside listening to the events within, they were wary of making any attempt to storm the house for fear of what might happen to the boy. With young Noah locked in a cupboard, the terrorists tortured Victor in an attempt to make him talk. When they realised Victor would never talk, they decided to torture Noah instead. Hearing the boy's cries, the MI5 officers had no choice but to move in. Noah was rescued but Victor was shot in the crossfire.

Severely traumatised, the child genius became psychotic, imagining his father was still alive and helping him plot revenge on MI5. He created a plan that he believed would stop other agents being betrayed by their country. He escaped from Social Services and created a new life for himself as Peter Ellis, using cyber-cafes to steal money, renting a house via the internet and even 'buying' himself a mother to avoid any awkward questions. Having found Blaney on an old police list, he realised the teacher would be the perfect patsy, so he doctored photos to incriminate the teacher and cheated himself a place in Highdale School, confident that MI5 would install an officer sooner or later. Noah believed that by infiltrating MI5 he could bring the system crashing down so that all the agents abroad could be brought home.

Once Noah had been found, Harry Pearce personally arranged some very specialised care for him at a private psychiatric hospital. Though the signs were that Noah still believed that his father was alive, it was hoped that in time he could be cured to see the truth.

[Notes]

Classical references abound in this episode. The field agents, Antony and Cleopatra are named after Marc Antony, Roman lover of Cleopatra, the tragic young queen of Egypt. The threat issued after the first attack comes from a translation of Homer's Iliad, a 24-volume history of Ancient Greece that begins with the battles over Helen of Troy and ends with the death and burial of war hero Hector. That the epic poem also examines the relationship between the gods and mortals — questioning whether everything is preordained or whether mankind can make decisions away from the gods' influence — is of course relevant.

During initial surveillance on Blaney, he is heard listening to Alchemy, Dire Straits' live album recorded at the Hammersmith Odeon, London, in July 1983 and released the following year. In her class, Zoe gets her students to discuss Dido's 'Don't Think Of Me' from the No Angel CD, having abandoned any attempt to excite them with Charles Dickens' Great Expectations.

James Crowe makes reference to the discontent in Britain lasting longer than 'one winter', a reference to the 'winter of discontent' of 1978/9 that brought down the Labour government (which in turn was a reference to the speech that opens Shakespeare's Richard III).

This episode was premiered on BBC3 on June 9 2003, half an hour after the end of the first transmission on BBC1 of the previous episode.

[Quote/Unquote]

In a rather dodgy protracted metaphor, the team reacts to the hacker's work. Harry: 'Someone thrust their hand up our skirt.' Ruth describes it as 'rape', but Tom qualifies this as merely 'groped', explaining 'we weren't penetrated'.

Tom (explaining the level of threat to Ruth): 'It's like demonstrators breaking into Parliament and letting off fireworks. Alarming but hardly a threat to the constitution.'

Zoe: 'Know what scares me? That one day I'll get a bump on the head and all these people I have to be are all going to get fused in my psyche. I'll be one helluva schizophrenic.'

Gordon Blaney: 'That's teachers for you – left-wing for life, fascist in the staff room.'

Tom (to Zoe): 'Wear a tight sweater tomorrow...'
Zoe (arch): 'Any particular sweater in mind?'
Tom and Danny (as one): 'The blue one.'

Harry: 'You see, you always knew where you were with a public school traitor. Just look for the pipe-smoking 16-year-old sodomite with a copy of E.M. Forster under his arm...'

[Personnel Report Updates]

Sam is allowed to go on her first raid with Danny. Ruth reveals a working knowledge of classical Greek literature. Tom tells Vicky that he's an officer for Her Majesty's Secret Service, though she doesn't seem that impressed.

Zoe continues to see Carlo without declaring the affair to her superiors. Zoe's favourite teacher at school was a Miss Forbes. Both Danny and Tom agree that Zoe's blue top is the most flattering. Malcolm lets slip to Tom that he thinks Zoe is 'splendid'.

[Gadgets]

Aside from the array of laptops and other computers on show here, we see Danny and Malcolm (with another officer) install cameras and bugging devices into the security detectors at the school. Peter/Noah uses a Geiger scrambler, a device for confusing scintillation counters to make them read as if they're in the middle of a meltdown.

[Missing in Action]

In the script, it's made clear that Danny's undercover work infiltrating *Red Cry* has been conducted without Zoe's knowledge. She's surprised and impressed that he'd found the time to maintain an additional legend, though when he reveals that a school reunion he went to recently was for his cover identity rather than himself Zoe remembers that he returned home from that event rather drunk, which is worrying.

A small scene was scripted where Colin installed all the modems in Harry's section with a new state-of-the-art firewall. Another, during the shutdown of non-essential systems, showed Harry announcing that the crisis would also affect the 'motion-sensitive' urinals in the gents' toilets. Using MI5 jargon, Cleopatra tapped Morse code into her cellphone to inform the team that Antony was dead and that she was moving eastwards towards the nearest town.

[Expert Witnesses]

Keeley Hawes: 'I certainly have a new-found respect for teachers. You have no idea what it's like and I wasn't really teaching them. I think it must be an incredible thing to be able to do.'

David Oyelowo: '[Danny]'s meant to be the gadget/computer expert, and I'm so not. I only got a computer about a year or so ago… Friends of mine dismay at the fact that I'm so bad.'

Peter Firth: 'The dialogue in **[spooks]** is very difficult to learn because invariably you're speaking about things that you've never spoken about before in your life. You've got no frames of reference. I find that enormously difficult as there's some real tongue twisters in there, but it keeps you sharp and it's good to be challenged.'

Matthew Macfadyen: 'We use the word "debriefed" a lot, and "penetrated", and that sort of leads to giggles sometimes. Y'know, you "debrief" a terrorist suspect… or sometimes you get blown. You "blow your cover"…'

Promoting [spooks]

It's a fact of modern drama production that it's not enough to make the best programme around – you have to be able to sell it to an audience who are already faced with hundreds of other possible viewing choices. The promotions have to be strong enough to make the viewer want to choose to watch one terrestrial channel at a specific timeslot rather than any of the others, or any cable/satellite channels, or even a DVD or (heaven forbid) a VHS tape of another show entirely. Part of this work is done behind the scenes to seduce the press. CD-ROMs are created exclusively for journalists that contain a selection of images and quotes from the cast as well as background material on the show itself. The reason for this is that – as they themselves would probably admit – journalists are much more likely to be positive about a series if the production team make things easy for them. Handing them recyclable material that they can use for their articles saves them a lot of time, and of course if you get the press on your side then part of the battle's already won because hopefully they'll then be the ones bigging up the show in advance in their weekly columns and TV roundup features. But winning over the press is only part of the challenge. The press might love you, but you still need to make sure the audience is there on the first night.

With billboards and print advertising, you have just one image, a single frame, to hopefully capture the imagination. So far, both series have benefited from extensive billboard advertising – huge oversized photos of the cast placed in prominent positions (such as roads that get gridlocked regularly) so that the bold image of three attractive-but-stern people staring down on the driver or passengers like the Gods of Olympus can make a lasting impression. Of course, it can also be a little startling for the people in the photo. David Oyelowo recalls driving through London and seeing himself, Keeley and Matthew on a billboard by a roundabout near Old Street: 'It's bad enough negotiating a roundabout at the best of times but when you're going "Oh my God, that's me up there!" it's even harder. I think I went round a few times so that I could take it in!'

For David's co-star, Matthew Macfadyen, the coverage was even harder to escape: 'There was one billboard right outside my flat! I would walk out of my front door and think to myself, Oh, there I am! which was the weirdest thing. But then, after a while, it became strangely normal to see my face staring back at me every day!'

The next stage in the promotion trail is the sacred art of the TV trailer, which has the difficult task of trying to capture the mood, the tone and the basic subject matter of a 60-minute episode in just under a minute. For series one, these trails took the form of mini-adventures outside of the context of the episodes. For example, we see Danny Hunter park his very flash car outside a school playground. A cheery 11-year-old boy collects his backpack and lunchbox and steps out of the car to wave Danny off. This is Danny's little brother (who, like the rest of Danny's scripted family, is never seen in the transmitted episodes), who is met at the gate by a schoolfriend.

'Nice motor,' says the friend. 'Your brother Danny got a new job then?'

'Yeah,' Danny's brother sighs unenthusiastically.

'Whassee do?'

'Computers or something.' We then see Danny in action, working with 'computers' as 'DJ Spookman' from episode 101 and leading the assault on Johnny Marx's team at the bank in episode 103. We cut back to the playground.

'Booooring!' says the friend.

'Yeah,' little Hunter agrees. 'What does your brother do?'

'Lorry driver!' the friend replies proudly, a disclosure that Hunter Jnr is much more impressed by. 'Wi-cked!' The trailer is rounded off with that iconic clip of the three leads walking away from Christine Dale's car at the end of the first episode as actor Jack Davenport (one of British TV's most popular voice artists as well as the star of shows such as *This Life*, *Ultraviolet* and *Coupling*) delivers the series' tagline: 'MI5, not 9 to 5.' So through this campaign, we learn that these are characters who lead lives that even their families are not a part of, we see that they have jobs that frequently put them in danger, and we also get a hint that there's a bit of a glamorous side to their lives too.

In comparison, the trailer for series two was a little less tongue in cheek and a little more portentous as we hear specially recorded voice-overs from the cast intercut with footage from the new series:

Tom: 'I live in a parallel world to you... I'm beside you, behind you, next to you.'

Zoe: 'I'm several people, all at once.'

Here we see a clip from episode 203 where Zoe explains the different personalities she's playing.

Danny: 'Your safety and your future are in my hands... I can go places you can't.'

We hear Malcolm's line from episode 204: 'No-one sees us, we go through walls.'

Zoe: 'I deceive my enemies and sometimes my friends.'

Tom: 'It's a life of danger, but a risk I'm willing to take.' Again, this trailer ends with Jack Davenport and the all-important tagline.

It was a clever campaign, not least because, unlike the trailer for every Hollywood blockbuster, it didn't actually give much away about the new series, aside from possibly revealing that Tom survived the blast that had kept a nation on tenterhooks for the last year. To understand the context of each brief clip, the audience would have to see the finished episode. The result was conclusive – excluding soap operas, [**spooks**] became the top-rated programme on British TV. ∎

Episode 204

First Broadcast (BBC3): June 16 2003
First Terrestrial Broadcast (BBC1): June 23 2003

Written by **Howard Brenton**
Directed by **Rob Bailey**

[C a s t]

Rade Serbedzija (Victor Shvitkoy), **Oliver Ford Davies** (Sir Richard 'Dicky' Bowman), **Sophie Okonedo** (Amanda Roke), **Robert Hardy** (Sir John Barry), **Peter McDonald** (Tim Prachett), **Julie Cox** ('Maxi Baxter'), **Daniel Kruyer** (Jack Brampton), **Robert Sebastian** (Hotel Manager), **Tom Nolan** (Young Russian Man).

[W h o ' s   W h o]

Rade Serbedzija (Victor Shvitkoy) is one of Croatia's most highly respected stage and screen actors. He had well over 40 feature films under his belt before his performance in the Academy Award-nominated *Before the Rain* (dir. Milcho Manchevski, 1994) brought him to the attention of Western audiences. Since then, he's played a succession of sinister or mysterious characters in films such as *The Saint* (dir. Philip Noyce, 1997), *Eyes Wide Shut* (dir. Stanley Kubrick, 1999), *Stigmata* (dir. Rupert Wainwright, 1999), *Mission: Impossible II* (dir. John Woo, 2000) and – as Boris 'The Blade' – *Snatch* (dir. Guy Ritchie, 2000).

Though Oliver Ford Davies (Sir 'Dicky' Bowman) has appeared in TV productions such as *Tenko*, *Kavanagh QC* and *David Copperfield* and the films *Mrs Brown* (dir. John Madden, 1997), *An Ideal Husband* (dir. Oliver Parker, 1999) and

Johnny English (dir. Peter Howitt, 2003), it's highly likely that he's more famous (among nine-year-olds and the young at heart, at least) as the Governor of Naboo, Sio Bibble in the Star Wars films *The Phantom Menace* (dir. George Lucas, 1999) and *Attack of the Clones* (2002). Sophie Okonedo (Amanda Roke) appears in the films *Ace Ventura: When Nature Calls* (dir. Steve Oedekerk, 1995) – as the Wachati Princess – and *This Year's Love* (dir. David Kane, 1999). On television she appeared in TV series *Staying Alive* and *Clocking Off*, and co-starred with Paul McGann in the two-part romantic thriller *Sweet Revenge*.

Robert Hardy (Sir John Barry) will forever be associated with the role of genial vet Siegfried Farnon in *All Creatures Great and Small*, which ran on British TV screens from 1978 until 1990. He played Britain's best-loved Prime Minister in *Winston Churchill: The Wilderness Years* (1981), a part he recreated in *The Woman He Loved* (1988) and *War and Remembrance* (1988). He's possibly about to be rediscovered by a whole new generation thanks to taking on the role of Cornelius Fudge in the Harry Potter movies.

Dublin-born Peter McDonald (Tim Prachett) starred in the films *I Went Down* (dir. Paddy Breathnach, 1997), the Roddy Doyle-scripted *When Brendan Met Trudy* (dir. Kieron J. Walsh, 2000) and *Blow Dry* (dir. Paddy Breathnach, 2001). He also appeared in *Felicia's Journey* (dir. Atom Egoyan, 1999) with Bob Hoskins, as did Julie Cox ('Maxi Baxter'), whose CV also includes a turn as Diana, Princess of Wales in the TV movie *Princess in Love* (dir. David Greene, 1996) and as Princess Irulan in the Sci-Fi Channel's adaptations of Frank Herbert's *Dune* books.

[C a s e   R e p o r t]

As part of the first economic summit between President Bush of the USA and President Putin of Russia, America granted the Russian Federation $20 billion in aid from the International Monetary Fund. Then, somehow, the money went missing. A day later, Tom and Harry were asked to attend a meeting with Sir Richard Bowman, Chairman of Bowman & Co Bank, Sir John Barry, the Governor of the Bank of England, and Amanda Roke, the political counsel for the Chancellor of the Exchequer. It seemed that John Lightwood, one of Bowmans' employees, had stolen $1 billion from one of the accounts they handle. MI5 was approached as all concerned wanted to avoid alerting the Fraud Squad, as that would necessitate a court case; as one of Britain's oldest 'family' banks, such a scandal could have conceivably sent Bowmans to the wall, causing a shock across the City that could result in a major economic depression. There was also the matter that Bowmans also handled certain government accounts used, for example, for 'strategic aid'; effectively, Bowmans acted as the British government's 'dirty bank', something they were also keen to hush up.

Morale among the Section B team was understandably very low; everyone felt this particular assignment was beneath them and resented being treated like footsoldiers for the Bank of England. It was to everyone's great relief then that Harry decided to sanction some 'good old-fashioned spying'. Danny was installed as a trader at Bowmans as John Lightwood's replacement, while Zoe was placed as a cleaner to give her access to office refuse that might contain vital information. Danny wasted no time in getting to know Lightwood's former colleagues – indeed, he was placed at a desk in between Lightwood's best friend at the firm, Tim Prachett, and Maxime Baxter, who Danny learned had grown very close to Lightwood before his disappearance. During a heavy night of drinking, Tim revealed to Danny that Lightwood had been helping to launder money through the bank via the Banco Co-operativo in Lugarno, Switzerland. Money had come through Bowmans as part of a chain of money laundering – moving the sums so fast their origins can't be traced – and Lightwood had decided to skim a little off the top for himself (in this case, though, 'a little' meant $1 billion).

With help from Special Branch, Ruth was able to ascertain that Lightwood had gone to ground; his mobile phone had not been used in days and his apartment was abandoned. But it was with some surprise that the team learned that Lightwood had been murdered – his body was found on Hampstead Heath nailed to a tree. Ruth found an example of Russian art that matched the form of crucifixion used on Lightwood, which would indicate that he had been

[Victor Shvitkoy]

Victor Shvitkoy is an ex-KGB General, art collector and criminal – one of most powerful psychopaths in the Russian mafia, now believed to be living in hiding somewhere in the UK...

[Maxime Baxter]

Maxime Anne Baxter, born December 31 1978, in Victoria Gardens, Farnham, Surrey, daughter of John and Sandra Baxter. She attended Salehill Boarding from the age of 13, and prior to that she was a pupil at Farnham Park. She is asthmatic, which makes her career choice – the stressful world of share trading – all the more puzzling. She is currently one of the most successful traders at Bowmans Bank.

FILE UPDATE
The real Maxime Baxter died March 31 1979, aged three months. Her birth certificate was used to obtain a minor's British passport in 1990. Farnham Park School have no record of her and her entire career history appears to be a legend created to hide her real identity – the daughter of Victor Shvitkoy.

UPDATED BY D. HUNTER, SECTION B

[Carlo Franceschini]

Carlo Franceschini was born in Milan. His father is Italian-born Alberto Franceschini, his mother, Magherita (née Pollini) is Italian-Swiss, which is how Carlo has both Italian and Swiss passports. Currently employed by the Banco Co-operativo, he is married to Maria, daughter of Antonia Gustino, Italian Minister of Finance.

deliberately left there as a warning to someone.

The Banco Co-operativo had a suite of rooms permanently booked at a hotel in Mayfair for the purpose of providing 'hospitality' for their clients. While Tom and Malcolm arranged to have the Mayfair suite bugged, Ruth began collating information on Maxi Baxter at Danny's request. Meanwhile, Malcolm had managed to reassemble a shredded document from Bowmans that revealed that Richard Bowman had personally opened an account for John Lightwood containing $500,000 on the day the billion went missing. As bonuses were only paid to employees at the end of the year, it looked as if Lightwood had been paid to steal the money.

Suddenly, there seemed to be a little too much interest in Section B activities from outside. First, CIA liaison Christine Dale asked Tom outright if the British government had decided to steal the American money intended for Russia. Then Amanda Roke came to Thames House to order Harry to remove his mole from Bowmans. Ms Roke's actions unintentionally alerted Harry that he in turn had a mole in his department. Thanks to the endeavours of a reluctant Colin, communications of the bank operation were traced to Ruth's terminal. Tom met with Ruth offsite to discuss her future. Though she claimed that passing information from one government department to another couldn't be classed as treason, she knew she was being a little naïve. She confessed that she'd so desperately wanted to work for MI5 that GCHQ had granted her a transfer on the condition that she occasionally reported back to Downing Street on certain operations. This was only the first time she'd done so. To Ruth's great relief, Tom agreed to let her carry on at MI5 on probation.

For some time now, Zoe had been conducting an affair with a man called Carlo. However, scared of having her relationship broken apart by her job as she'd witnessed happen to Tom, she did not declare the relationship to Harry, nor did she request Carlo be put through vetting. So it was with great embarrassment that, after joining him for a lunchtime of passion at a Mayfair hotel, she later learned the entire thing had been conducted in the very room that had been bugged to keep an eye on the affairs of Banco Co-operativo. Realising she would be asked to use her relationship to spy on her boyfriend, Zoe instead ended the relationship, leaving Tom to recruit him. Persuaded by photos of his affair with Zoe and threats that they might be shown to his wife, Carlo was asked to trace the account that the money had been transferred to. He revealed that the account was held in the name of Victor Shvitkoy, a known leader in the Russian criminal underworld.

In a meeting with Harry and Tom, Sir Richard Bowman finally revealed that he and Amanda Roke had been withholding vital information. It transpired that Shvitkoy had approached Sir Richard and asked him if he'd be interested in handling a large sum of money very quickly. Sir Richard had informed MI6 straight away and was advised to go along with whatever Shvitkoy asked of him with a view to stealing the money back for the Americans. Sir Richard subsequently arranged for Lightwood to handle the transactions, but when he decided to steal the money instead, Shvitkoy had him executed. Convinced that Sir Richard was now in his control, Shvitkoy ordered that he proceed to launder the remaining $19 billion. With all the cards now on the table, Sir Richard was informed of a small matter that had recently been uncovered by Ruth: Shvitkoy had an insider at Bowmans – his daughter, Maxime Baxter.

Shaken by this revelation, Sir Richard stepped outside to take a call, but a few minutes later he collapsed, having suffered a stroke. Struggling to speak, Sir Richard told Harry that Shvitkoy had phoned to inform him he had transferred the rest of the Moscow money to Bowmans and was expecting it to be on its way to Lugarno within minutes. Danny had just five minutes to access the accounts and divert the funds.

Having successfully stolen $19 billion, Danny was in the mood for a celebration and invited Maxi to join him for a drink (although he had already been briefed regarding her lineage) and then invited her back to his flat (Harry had refused to fund the kind of penthouse apartment suitable for a banker's lifestyle, but had sanctioned a few 'installations' at Danny's own flat, including a fridgeful of Moet). There, he confided in Maxi that he'd stolen the money to return it to its rightful owner, and asked her if she knew who that might be. As Danny opened some champagne, however, Maxi found a gym card under Danny's bed that bore his face and real name – the 'cleaners' had somehow missed it. Using the excuse that she'd left her inhaler at home, Maxi lured him to a flat where Shvitkoy's thugs overpowered him and handcuffed him to a chair. As one of the thugs was instructed by Shvitkoy to pierce Danny's eye with a knitting needle, Maxi discovered a tracking device hidden inside a toothpick in Danny's jacket. At that moment, a team of Special Branch officers released a stun grenade into the room and seized Shvitkoy and his men.

Christine Dale let Tom know that she'd heard a new rumour that the British government had recently acquired some £13 billion to regenerate the NHS, which she correctly calculated would equal $20 billion. Tom naturally claimed all ignorance of the matter. Meanwhile, her own government were forced to give the Russians another $20 billion, as much to prove that they could afford it as anything else.

[P r e v i o u s   M i s s i o n s]

Harry chooses Danny to go undercover as a trader as he has a history of swindling credit cards, making him perfect for the task (see episodes 102-104). The fact that Ruth seems aware of Danny's past indiscretions would suggest that either his credit card deceptions are now common knowledge within Section B or Ruth has done her homework. The respective roles Danny and Zoe are given for the Bowmans operation are strangely similar to the ones they claimed to have for the benefit of Danny's girlfriend in episode 105.

[Q u o t e / U n q u o t e]

Sir Richard: 'Nature intended me to sit behind a desk balancing books, not go double-crossing Russian gangsters.'

Tom: 'Are we ready with the flat?'
Colin: 'All concurrent surveillance systems are operational.'
Tom: 'Colin, when the word "Yes" will do, use it.'

Malcolm (to the hotel manager): 'No-one sees us – we go through walls…'

Shvitkoy (to Sir Dicky): 'It was a warning to you, you genitally-shrivelled English pant-pisser… That is so much better in Russian. If only you spoke my language.'

[N o t e s]

Note the location of where Tom and Ruth have their off-site meeting. We will see this again in episode 210.

Victor Shvitkoy quotes from Fyodor Dostoevsky's The Idiot. Sir Richard is seen to own an icon by the Blessed Dionysius the Carthusian (Denys van Leeuwen, 1402-1471). At the strip club, we hear 'Just A Little Bit More' by Popstars runners-up Liberty X.

This episode was premiered on BBC3 half an hour after the transmission of the previous episode's first screening on BBC1.

[Identity Check]

Danny poses as Joshua Ikoli, fast-tracking trader at Bowmans. Ikoli's dad is Nigerian, though he himself was born in Peckham.

[Personnel Report Updates]

Sir Richard Bowman is an old schoolfriend of Harry Pearce. Ruth was once in love with a 'big swinging dick' (slang for a trader) and so has a healthy knowledge of trader-speak. She also reveals she has a passion for art. Christine Dale seems determined to treat her off-site meetings with Tom as if they were conducting a clandestine love affair. Malcolm approaches the reassembly of shredded documents like the most exciting jigsaw puzzle in the universe.

In possibly the single most embarrassing way, Zoe's affair with Carlo is now out in the open. Good to his word, Tom personally ensures that any evidence of the liaison is destroyed, but whether the emotional damage to Zoe can be erased that quickly remains to be seen.

[Missing in Action]

A nice little exchange between Danny and Sam was scripted where Sam observes that she's being used as a 'custard cream' lady. Danny notes that 'the tea tray can be an office weapon', which Sam takes to mean that she could poison her way to the top. All said in jest… probably.

A few scenes involving Tom's girlfriend Vicky were also lost. The scenes would have shown how Vicky is beginning to become a bit of a liability, arriving at Thames House uninvited and calling him 'Spook-man' loudly in public.

[Expert Witness]

Keeley Hawes: 'I think [Zoe] is a bit wary of romance. I think it's hard enough for anyone who's single to meet someone but when you do what Tom and Zoe do for a living then it's especially difficult – you can be called out anywhere at any time. They don't have much of a social life really apart from with each other. The easiest way sometimes is if they date each other which Zoe says to Danny when he fancies Sam.'

Nicola Walker: 'Ruth absolutely adores Tom. She thinks he's brilliant at his job and would just love to be like him. I think her main ambition would be to be allowed to go out and be involved in an undercover operation just like him. And I think she would be thrilled to get involved with the gadgets too. That would be her dream as that's real spying for her, but sadly her life is pretty much rooted in the Grid.'

GCHQ

Often forgotten in favour of the more 'glamorous' MIs 5 and 6, GCHQ – or the Government Communication Headquarters – is the civil service department responsible for providing various governmental departments with what's known as 'signal intelligence' or 'Sigint', which it does by intercepting and extracting information from communications such as radar transmissions and telephone calls and then sharing that intelligence with other security and defence agencies in the UK. Like MI5 and MI6, GCHQ also works in liaison with intelligence and security services abroad.

The department was established in 1946 from the ashes of the Government Code and Cipher School (GC&CS), which had been set up in 1919 with just 25 cryptologists and 30 support staff based in Bletchley Park, Buckinghamshire. In the late 1930s, the GC&CS began recruiting mathematicians, linguists, chess masters and academics of all disciplines to work towards gaining an advantage against Nazi German intelligence. Though the GC&CS made an enormous contribution to fight against Germany in World War II – most notably in the deciphering of the German ENIGMA machine – their efforts were kept secret for decades (indeed for many years, the ENIGMA machine was believed to be the work of a team of Americans). During the war, over 10,000 people worked in the department. Though this number was reduced to about 6,000 people when the team moved to London as part of the newly formed GCHQ, they still continued their codebreaking duties even after the war, eventually transferring their attentions to the perceived threat from Soviet groups. In the early 1950s, GCHQ moved to two sites on the outskirts of Cheltenham, where they remain as the central hub of intelligence gathering.

As with MI5 and MI6, the work of GCHQ remained shrouded in mystery until the 1980s, when its existence was finally acknowledged by parliament. Throughout that decade, the statutory grounding for the department was developed, leading to its legislation as part of the 1994 Intelligence Service Act. As the Cold War thawed, new threats were identified to national security and the economic stability of the country. In line with MI5, GCHQ assumed its share of responsibility for collating Sigint for the prevention and detection of serious crime

With the rapid growth in the variety of

communication systems, GCHQ has been forced to evolve swiftly to ensure it can handle any type of intelligence available. The remit of GCHQ has therefore been extended to additionally include providing advice to other government departments and the armed forces on their own communications and security of their communications and I.T. systems. The section that handles such advisory matters, the Communications Electronics Security Group, doesn't actually manufacture security equipment, but it does work alongside industry in the development of products and systems for the greater good of security in the UK. As a consequence, GCHQ has emerged as the world's leading signals intelligence and communications security experts.

Though its technology resources might allow the department to spy on any telephone or internet-based communication, the reality is they are bound by the European Convention on Human Rights and the provisions outlined by the Intelligence Services Act 1994 and the Regulation of Investigatory Powers Act 2000. These acts stress that they are only permitted to intercept communications in the interests of national security, safeguarding economic well-being and the prevention and detection of serious crime. ■

Episode 205

First Broadcast (BBC3): June 23 2003
First Terrestrial Broadcast (BBC1): July 7 2003

Written by **Howard Brenton**
Directed by **Justin Chadwick**

[Cast]

Robert Willox (Interrogator), **James Holmes** (Christopher John Jennings),
Annabelle Apsion (Bridget Macey), **Marty Cruikshank** (Dot), **Mark Lewis Jones**
(Mark Woolley), **Jo Joyner** (Stephanie Mills), **Dale Rapley** (Paul Dunbarton),
Alastair Galbraith (John Macleish), **Richard Braine** (Phil), **Robyn Kerr** (Mary).

[Who's Who]

Director Justin Chadwick's CV includes work on *The Vice* (1999), *Helen West*
(2002) and *Red Cap* (2003). Robert Willox (the interrogator in the opening
montage) played DC Ted Donachie in *Thief Takers* (1996), Bill Ferguson in *Two
Thousand Acres of Sky* (2001) and, in 2003, played Constable Dunning in the
feature film *The League of Extraordinary Gentlemen* (dir. Stephen Norrington).
James Holmes (Christopher Jennings, the interrogator's subject) is more used to
comedy than torture (though some might argue they amount to the same thing) as
a cast member on shows such as *The Office*, *Rhona*, *My Hero* and E4's *TV Go
Home*.

Annabelle Apsion (Bridget Macey) played Joy Wilton in four series of *Soldier,
Soldier*. In 1996 she starred opposite Christoper Eccleston in Jimmy McGovern's

harrowing drama-documentary *Hillsborough* and with Eccleston again in 2003 for Russell T. Davies's *The Second Coming*. Her other TV work includes *The Lakes*, *Goodnight Mister Tom* and *Micawber*.

Mark Lewis Jones (Mark Woolley)'s CV includes lead roles in *The Knock* (1994) and *Lenny Blue* (2002), while Alastair Galbraith (John Macleish) previously worked with Kudos on *Psychos*.

[Case Report]

Harry had arranged an early meeting with Mark Woolley and Bridget Macey from St Albans for a debriefing on the interrogation of a suspect connected with the abortive attack on Sefton B (see Previous Missions below). Meanwhile, Ruth was in work early to prepare the weekly threat assessment for Downing Street. As the rest of the team gradually settled down to their morning duties they were distracted by an alarm, which Harry identified as the major incident alert and declared Tom as Em-Ex (Emergency Executive) officer for what was clearly a drill. Danny arrived customarily late for work to find himself locked out of the pods. Despite the rule that no-one enters or leaves the Grid during a lockdown, Tom helped him through the pods to join the team. Though Harry deferred to Tom over Danny, he insisted that the rules were upheld regarding Bridget and Mark – from that point, no-one was to leave the Grid until the emergency was over.

In the event of a drill being called, the standard procedure is to put all other work aside until the end of the exercise. With that in mind, Tom warned everyone that an EERIE group (see Notes below) would be in the building measuring the team's group and individual responses to the emergency. It was therefore vital that everyone treated the exercise as if there had genuinely been a major incident.

Tom's team convened around a monitor on Danny's desk that had been linked via CCTV to 'Dot', the officer in charge in the Thames House duty room. She informed them that a bomb had gone off in Parliament Square and that, according to procedure, she had already sealed off every floor in the building in case the device had contained nuclear waste (Ruth noted that the latest intelligence had indicated that at least ten such 'dirty bombs' might be under construction in London alone). Dot then revealed that she'd been unable to lock down the other departments aside from the control room and Section B – the Grid was effectively cut off from the rest

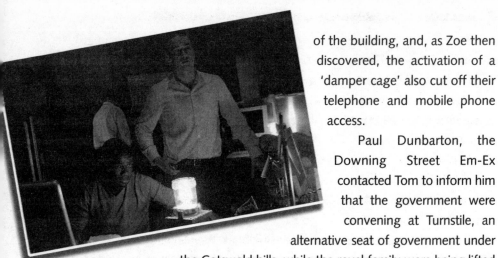

of the building, and, as Zoe then discovered, the activation of a 'damper cage' also cut off their telephone and mobile phone access.

Paul Dunbarton, the Downing Street Em-Ex contacted Tom to inform him that the government were convening at Turnstile, an alternative seat of government under the Cotswold hills, while the royal family were being lifted by helicopter to Windsor Castle. The link to Dunbarton was left open while Tom focused his attentions on the Grid staff. Everyone was issued with the procedural manual for use in an emergency, and protective suits were also issued, though after Malcolm drew everyone's attention to their complete inadequacy, the suits were abandoned. Despite the alarm, everyone remained in high spirits, but when a panicking Dot in the control room severed their link to her and then both Radio 4 and the main television channels stopped broadcasting, the team began to suspect that they were not experiencing a drill after all.

Danny managed to hook up one of the monitors to a computer link in a mobile incident van. Though the link was only up for a short time, the officer on site was able to write a brief but chilling message to them on a notepad: 'VX.' Even the mention of this was enough to frighten Ruth – a lethal gas that could kill everyone within its radius within two hours (see Security File below). The air conditioning had already been switched off during the first minutes of the lockdown, but the water supply on the roof – which they had to assume to be already contaminated – would still be servicing the toilets. Tom ordered Colin to close the bathrooms and set up temporary toilets in the stationery room.

Colin managed to re-establish a connection to the mobile incident van complete with audio link-up. The officer identified herself as Stephanie Mills, a firefighter trained in handling major incidents whose air supply was already exhausted. Tom asked her to inspect the area for them, knowing full well he could be sending the woman to her death. She left the van and returned minutes later to reveal that the source of the bomb appeared to be a white van marked with a sign that read 'Pluto's

[V X   G a s]

A stronger member of the same family as Sarin (which caused devastation to Tokyo's subway), the formula for VX Gas is given as CH3CH2O-P(O)(CH3)-SCH2CH2N(C3H7)2. First developed and tested by British scientists at Porton Down, Wiltshire, in 1952, it was found to be a Grade AA-effective weapon with devastating potential. Britain traded VX technology with the USA in return for information on their H-bomb.

It is an odourless gas, and in its liquid form it is found as a green, viscous slime. It is almost indestructible and as its molecules are also adhesive, it is virtually impossible to remove it from any surfaces the molecules stick to. The effect on humans is it stops nerve ends communicating with each other. VX can be absorbed through the skin or eyes. It acts almost immediately and can take from an hour to two hours to result in death. The lethal dose for humans can be as little as ten milligrams. The antidote, Atropine, is itself highly toxic. For it to be effective it has to be injected directly into the heart.

A VX canister of ten kilograms – in a liquid state and under pressure so as to convert it to a gas state – could conceivably be as effective a weapon of destruction as the atom bomb on Hiroshima. If such a device were to be detonated in central London, it is estimated that a million people would be infected within the first hour. Within 24 hours the gas cloud could cover three-quarters of the south-east of England.

The only countries known to still have stocks of the gas are the United States, France and Russia. Britain abandoned stocks in favour of thermonuclear weapons. However, stocks of the gas from Soviet sources have been found in many locations.

[Patmos]

Patmos comprises a group whose primary ideology is survivalist. They have been under surveillance by Special Branch after a van registered to one of their members had been left unattended in an East End car park for 48 hours. The group named themselves after the Greek Island where St John wrote Revelation – the book of the New Testament that describes the end of the world. They have issued a threat to bomb ten cities across Britain: London; Edinburgh; Cardiff; Leeds; Nottingham; Birmingham; Bath; Coventry; Newcastle; Portsmouth. The threat has been assessed as the typical fantasy of survivalists who believe that if they can destroy the cities, the pure of heart can live in peace in the hills. The final line of the threat warns of 'The British Whore's Last Breath'. Level of threat: Blue, A/B.

FILE UPDATE
Note to the EERIE team – thanks for the worst day of my life, you bunch of utter swines! :)
RUTH EVERSHED, SECTION B

Removals'. Realising the danger she'd been placed in, and resigned to her fate, Steph left the van, despite the pleas of Tom for her to protect herself. Steph's report alerted Ruth to something she'd read in the weekly threat reports – a group calling themselves 'Patmos' threatening to bomb ten cities across the country (see Security File below). Now the entire team were beginning to take things seriously, and their suspicions were confirmed when Colin managed to access the London traffic congestion cameras to reveal a city of still cars and empty of any signs of life. Bridget began to panic, telling everyone that her daughter was in Guy's Hospital and all thoughts turned to the loved ones outside.

Tom called everyone together to pool their comments. They now knew the threat to the country and who was responsible for the incident but were unable to do anything about it for the moment, and thanks to Dot's moment of insanity they'd lost all internal and external telephone connections as well as the satellite link, though their cable link was still working, temperamentally. Though Bridget campaigned for them to leave Thames House and try to set up an ops room elsewhere, everyone else agreed that they were safer staying put.

Tom contacted Dunbarton at Downing Street again to brief him on everything they'd learned. Dunbarton revealed that the Prime Minister and his party were believed to have died in a helicopter crash – as had the royal family. In a chilling echo of Steph's departure, Dunbarton realised he was isolated and most probably already infected by the gas, and so told Tom he was stepping outside…

The government had apparently died without declaring a state of emergency. Trying desperately to maintain control of the situation, Tom asked Mark and Bridget to collect all items of food and ration it out for everyone. In the meantime Malcolm was given the task of trying to establish a link to all the other major cities at risk. The only location Malcolm was able to raise a response from was the Edinburgh section where John Macleish was acting as Em-Ex officer. In the absence of an alternative seat of government, Tom declared the Grid as the control centre for the British Isles. Though Macleish initially resisted Tom's authority, he was eventually persuaded to declare a state of emergency in Edinburgh and begin evacuation procedures.

Throughout the morning, many members of the team had commented on Harry's behaviour. But when Harry revealed to him that he had been infected by the gas after using the toilets before they were sealed off, Tom had no choice but to quarantine him. As if matters couldn't have got worse, Macleish informed the team that a bomb had been detonated in the Morningside area of Edinburgh –

coincidentally where Sam's family were from. He was able to inform them that the emergency bunker in Edinburgh had not been completed, and then the link to his terminal was severed...

After a further eight hours of trying in vain to contact the outside world, tempers were running high. After Colin suggested that Danny's tardiness could have led to the infection, the two nearly came to blows. Food and water rations were almost completely spent, the floor had been ripped apart in search of communication cables and Bridget and Mark were continuing to undermine Tom's authority by demanding to be released from the Grid. Realising that the situation might call upon him to make impossible decisions, Tom authorised Zoe to issue him a firearm. When Mark and Bridget decided to force the pods and make their escape, threatening the lives of everyone on the Grid, Tom had no choice but to hold them at gunpoint – at which point all the lights came up, and connections to everyone's computers were restored... and a perfectly healthy Harry stepped through the pod doors (having spent the night at home in bed) to reveal that the entire distressing affair had indeed been a training exercise, monitored by Mark and Bridget. The team passed the test with flying colours, with special praise reserved for Tom's strong leadership. Proud of his understandably emotional team's responses under pressure, Harry invited them all for a drink off-site.

[Previous Missions]

The source of the information fed to Asabiyah (see episode 106) is identified as Christopher John Jennings, a maintenance engineer at Sefton B nuclear power station. Jennings accepted £100,000 in return for information on the power station's weak points. The last time Section B underwent an EERIE, Tom was stationed in Ireland but Malcolm remembers that it was an 'absolute farce' that revealed all the national emergency systems to be ill equipped for an attack.

[Disinformation]

Although the events of this episode are clearly an exercise in disinformation, the examiners do seem remarkably well informed about the Section B staff, knowing

[Notes]

Tom acts as Em-Ex officer — Emergency Executive officer — meaning he has overall responsibility for co-ordinating the team's efforts and has the final say in any decisions. The crisis is revealed to be an 'EERIE', or 'Extreme Emergency Response Initiative Exercise', just as Tom had suspected at the beginning. We also hear of a document called the London Emergency Services Liaison Major Incident Procedure Manual and EPCUs — Emergency Protective Clothing Units.

Zoe notes that Radio 4 going off air is a signal to Britain's nuclear submarines.

This episode takes place between 8.30 on a Friday morning through to Saturday lunchtime.

Under the 2001 Anti-Terrorism and Crime Act, Tom suspends article five of the European Convention on Human Rights to empower the Edinburgh police to arrest anyone they suspect of terrorist involvement.

Mark alludes to Emperor Nero, who was reputed to have played his fiddle while watching Rome burn. Harry quotes from St Paul's Letter to the Philippians, Chapter 4, Verse 8: Whatsoever things are true, whatsoever things are honest...'

Danny tries to use Morse code to contact other floors within the building. Morse code is generally accepted to have been invented by Samuel Finley Breese Morse (1791-1872), though as with any major invention, many others have laid claim to its creation. Having served the world for nearly 160 years, the system was abandoned in 1998 after the development of satellite-monitored safety systems.

Two new Section B team members — Phil and Mary — are seen here for the first time. Tom instructs them to keep a check on the drinking-water supplies.

This episode was premiered on BBC3 half an hour after the transmission of the previous episode's first screening on BBC1.

Thanks to coverage of Wimbledon overrunning (for the match where Tim Henman qualified for the quarter-finals), the BBC1 transmission of this episode was postponed for a week.

Danny: 'Running a country without people sounds like a politician's dream.'

Ruth (to Tom): 'You don't suddenly go all moody and sensitive. That's for us, we're the troops, you're the leader, and leaders don't have feelings, as you well know, Mr Tom Quinn!'

Mark: 'What are you going to do, Tom? Shoot a fellow officer? In Thames House?'

that both Sam and Danny have enough of an emotional attachment to family members currently in Edinburgh to make it the perfect location for the second biological weapon. Ruth has received intelligence on the very group believed to be behind the attacks and it becomes difficult to distinguish how much of that information was genuinely placed by the examiners for Ruth's test and how much they relied on existing information to add to the mix.

[Identity Check]

It's not clear how many of the participants in the exercise worked under their own names, but it's a fair assumption that they were all in character.

[Personnel Report Updates]

Colin regularly arranges barge trips for the staff, and though Sam is initially unwilling to risk joining him for this year's excursion in case she catches 'that rat's disease', she soon changes her mind when she learns Danny has agreed to go. She later tells him why she decided to go and finally their mutual attraction is out in the open. Whether or not they'd have been so honest without the intervention of the EERIE is uncertain. Zoe is still very emotional over the end of her relationship with Carlo, and confides in Sam that she's scared the whole team have had a laugh at her expense. Sam reassures her that Tom made Colin 'lose' that section of the surveillance tape and that no-one is laughing at her.

Ruth reveals that she has a cat. Danny mentions to Sam that his mother is a singer in a gospel choir touring Scotland, while Sam tells him that her family are from Morningside, Edinburgh. Zoe's father lives in Battersea and she has an Aunt Sylvie who lives in Bristol. Sam was not taught Morse code in training, but Ruth and Danny are conversant in it. Zoe has had advanced weapons training – it would appear she's the only one to have been trained to that level in the Grid.

Vicky books two tickets to Egypt without speaking to Tom first. When Tom points out that he wouldn't be able to get clearance to travel to Egypt, Vicky grows irritable and begins to speak loudly about his 'spooky' bosses. Though Tom reassures her that he's not going to end their relationship, when he calls her after the exercise to receive a mouthful of self-obsessed abuse, Tom dumps her.

[Missing in Action]

Included in the script was the revelation that Harry's office has a hitherto undiscovered secret exit – an exit he had used once he had been quarantined to spend the rest of the night safely in bed in his own home.

[Expert Witnesses]

Matthew Macfadyen: 'It was very exciting to film that episode, which was brilliantly written by Howard Brenton. The team are doing everything by the book, but as the episode unfolds the team become unsure whether it is an exercise or not. The whole episode was shot entirely on the Grid. No-one can leave and no-one can enter. It was also shot in sequence, which was fantastic – you almost never get to do that in television. For me, I finally get to use a gun in that episode so I was thrilled! I love all the physical stuff where you get to charge around!'

Hugh Simon: 'The nice thing about episode five was that we'd have to shoot it in sequence – in fact there was no other way of doing it, which is fairly unusual. Doing an episode of anything it's all out of sequence and all over the place so you have to remember where you are in each scene. But the only way to do episode five was to go from A to B to Z. Great fun for us because it was more like being in a play in the theatre, all working together with this great "company spirit".'

Nicola Walker: 'We were all on the Grid together, day in, day out, filming in sequence, ripping the Grid apart, and getting increasingly cabin-fevered... and in my case, typing! The thing is, my typing skills are very poor and Ruth's are meant to be brilliant, so I had to ask our second assistant director, Sasha [Mann], to be Ruth's speedy typing hands in the opening scenes...'

Peter Firth: 'I like Harry's turn of phrase. It comes out of him being well read rather than educated. He's trying to improve himself so he reads quite a lot and likes to pepper his dialogue with the odd quotations and bits of moral or religious philosophy which are pertinent to the situation.'

The Grid

Although the Grid has been at the heart of every episode since the series began, it hasn't really been a story's focal point – until now. With its modern chrome-and-wood furniture and its low-level lighting, it's the designer office that's part 'fantasy work environment' and part 'last place you'd want to be in an emergency'… especially if the emergency looks like it's wiping out millions of lives across the country.

Of course, [**spooks**] is not filmed inside the real Thames House (indeed, the 'real' Thames House is never seen in the series), but at Pinewood Studios, not far from the legendary James Bond sound stage. As we step onto the set, the first thing to catch the eye is the glass-tubed entrance to the area. With its three revolving sections, it's not surprising that these are known to one and all as 'the pods'. Though they look far too futuristic to be based in reality, as set designer Stevie Herbert explains, they're very much modelled on the real thing: 'The pods really exist! They can be seen from Lambeth Bridge in the real MI5 building. I don't think that ours are as flashy as theirs – ours are mechanical and theirs will be all electronic, but yes, we did use that as a model for the Grid.' Similar pods can also be seen by visitors to the BBC Television Centre main reception in White City, west London, which boasts pods of its own.

As we walk across the Grid, we might notice that everyone here has definitely chosen a side in the great Mac v IBM PCs debate; cool white monitors on hemispheres reveal the familiar Apple branding. Just as we'd expect, considering the widespread belief that 'Good Guys use Mac, Bad Guys use PC' that seems to run through many fictional worlds, from *The West Wing* and *24* to *Buffy the Vampire Slayer* and *EastEnders*.

To the right of the pods, there's a small side-room that is usually home to Malcolm and Colin. The walls are a very dull green and the low lighting matches every IT department I've ever been in. It's here that shredded paper jigsaws and utterly impractical robot communications devices are assembled, where snooping on the rest of the team is an occupational hazard and where the geek shall inherit the earth.

Back in the main room, we can see the desks of the regulars. Ruth's area is instantly recognisable with her many reference books piled high and a rather depressed angle-poised lamp slung to the corner of the room.

Next to her, Sam, and in the centre of the floor the double desks where Danny and Zoe sit opposite each other and try to score points off each other. At the far end is Tom, who has the vantage point of a clear view of the entire floor. Harry of course has his own office, which has a window that looks past Tom onto the main Grid, though sometimes the partitions are closed to hide what Harry gets up to (such as treating himself to a glass of brandy while the rest of the team are on rationed water and fearing for their lives, for example). Harry's décor needs little analysis – the red back wall and the arc of chairs facing his desk assert his authority on anyone who dares enter his domain. Stevie admits she was very much aware of the character of Harry and his own perceptions of his authority when designing the set. 'It's Harry's empire and we wanted him to be able to see anything at any given time. He can see out, but it's not quite reciprocal – no-one can quite see in – lending to the very definite feeling of power he has.'

Finally, we come to the boardroom. It maintains that connection between the traditional and the modern, with wooden panels, black leather seats and the sleek chrome TV monitor. But we are very much aware that this is the room outsiders will be brought to, and as such it's dominated by a floor-to-ceiling crest bearing the portcullis and the motto of the Security Service,

'Regnum Defende'.

Having been responsible for the creation of the set, it must have been quite depressing to have to then undo all that work and tear it down purely for the purposes of this episode. Stevie is fairly amused by it all: 'When I designed the Grid, it wasn't planned with this in mind!' Stevie had to not only redesign the set, but to do it in such a way that it could be reassembled neatly in time for the next episode. 'I had to make the Grid look like it had gone into self-destruct mode, take it apart for episode five and put it back in one piece 24 hours later... I am lucky to have a very professional team! I had to plan it with precision as we only had something like an inch leeway to loosen floors, lay cables down, put metal frames in, and dress the set with heaps of cable drooping onto the set like spaghetti. In short, looking for a visual effect that works – destroying a set without really destroying it. A tall order!'

It's the attention to detail that makes the Grid such a successful design. For example, the coffee machine is handily situated near the printer, providing the perfect excuse for officers to stop to make a cuppa while printing out huge documents. However, that doesn't mean that it's the perfect working environment; in the next episode we see how newcomer Sam has already recognised a number of design and layout flaws and created a list of improvements... ■

Episode 206

First Broadcast (BBC3): July 7 2003
First Terrestrial Broadcast (BBC1): July 14 2003

Written by **David Wolstencroft**
Directed by **Justin Chadwick**

[Cast]

Philippe Smolikowski (Francois, the French Delegate), **Ruth Gemmell** (Miranda),
Todd Boyce (Troy), **Steven Kirby** (Trevor), **Fred Ridgeway** (Jarvis, the Seedy
Man), **Aaron Swartz** (Trent), **Robert Harrison** (MI5 Operator).

[Who's Who]

The credits of Ruth Gemmell (Miranda) include the TV series *Band of Gold* and
Silent Witness and the film *Fever Pitch* (dir. David Evans, 1997).

Fans of *Coronation Street* might remember Todd Boyce (Troy) as Audrey's long-
lost son Stephen (the one who characters go to Canada to visit every time they want
to recast one of them). He also appeared in three series of *Fields of Fire* and the
films *Spy Game* (dir. Tony Scott, 2001) and *Behind Enemy Lines* (dir. John Moore,
2001).

Despite numerous appearances in *The Bill* and other London-based dramas,
Fred Ridgeway's most famous role would be that of Father Ken Dillon, one of a
gaggle of priests in the superb Channel 4 sitcom *Father Ted*. Aaron Swartz (Trent)
had a small role in *The 51st State* (dir. Ronny Yu, 2001).

[Case Report]

When President Bush announced a whistle-stop visit to the UK, Section B was instructed to assist the CIA liaison Christine Dale in the security preparations for his time in the country. Harry received a tip-off that the visit was in fact a feint to enable Bush to meet with representatives of Libya. Harry asked Ruth to intercept some of the presidential crates to see if there was any evidence of the Libyan meeting, but unfortunately a loose mug of tea happened to find its way into a crate, staining a significant number of presidential documents. Sam quickly took control of the situation and recruited Malcolm in helping her duplicate, replace or otherwise bleach the contents of the crate.

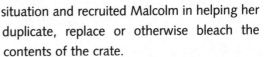

Christine Dale organised an initial briefing for the visit, and it was clear from the word go that she intended to take advantage of the precedent set by Prague for the CIA to maintain absolute control of every second of the visit, regardless of existing diplomatic protocols. In addition, she wanted her team to be granted access to the Registry. Harry granted permission for this – after all, sensitive documents had been removed.

After a radio ham getting lucky with a random search, news of the President's visit was soon widespread across the internet. As a consequence, MI5 received two threats to central London's water supply and one to the reservoir that supplies Chequers, five warnings of civil disobedience along the motorcade routes; unofficial calls to protest from two Palestinian groups, three anti-death penalty campaigners and four anti-globalisation bodies. To appease the Americans, raids were arranged on ten potential threats to provide the impression that MI5 were taking the situations seriously.

Discussions between Tom and Christine became heated when she requested additional vetting and a stringent background check into one of the policemen assigned to guard the motorcade for the President's visit on the grounds that he was

[The Presidential Visit]

PHASE I: PREP

PHASE II: EMBASSY

PHASE III: HORSEGUARDS

PHASE IV: BUCKINGHAM PALACE

PHASE V: CHEQUERS

PHASE VI: WHEELS UP

TOTAL ELAPSED TIME: 15 HOURS

The advance teams land two-and-a-half hours ahead of Air Force One, consisting of two C-5 Galaxy cargo planes into Brize Norton. Inventory includes: bullet-proof limousine plus stand-by limos and decoy limos; private ambulance; sundry Secret Service vehicles; Marine One plus one other helicopter; the presidential podium.

a Muslim. Sadly, the Home Office overruled Tom and DC Khan was removed from that particular duty.

The presidential visit was timed to the second, so when the President suddenly went off schedule, the personnel of Thames House were alarmed. Although this was later explained away by Christine as just a deviation to allow the President to visit Harrods, intelligence received by Ruth and documents unearthed by Malcolm during his clean-up operation revealed the likelihood of a secret meeting between the President and certain representatives of Libya to discuss a proposed deal between the two countries. In return for accepting responsibility for the Lockerbie plane bombing and handing over $7 billion in reparations, the US offered to end unilateral sanctions and help remove Libya from the 'Axis of Evil'.

Every presidential visit since the assassination of Kennedy has involved the assembly of a 'trip file', a document listing every contact, every threat, in effect anything and anyone that poses a problem for the President's visit in every geographical area he'd be expected to pass through. But one name came forth that had been missing from the trip file for this visit but was on MI5's files as a potential suspect – Dmitri Bubka. Late of the Moscow Mafia but now based in Britain, the latest intelligence suggested he was believed to be cannibalising radiotherapy machines for their Cobalt 60 to create a dirty bomb. So when a microlite aircraft was detected on a direct course for Buckingham Palace, the possibility that he might be a suicide bomber could not be dismissed. Christine authorised for the pilot to be shot down by nearby Tornado jets, a decision which could have been potentially disastrous had Tom not countermanded the order. When the aircraft eventually corrected its course without intervention from the armed forces the news was received to the great relief of everyone concerned. It was later discovered that the pilot had indeed wandered off course by accident, due to a faulty radio.

The diplomatic crates were returned to the American Embassy. Meanwhile, thanks to the tip-off from Thames House being passed to the relevant people, Libya was persuaded to include Britain in their deal with the United States – much to the surprise of the Americans brokering the deal.

[Previous Missions]

An officer by the name of Barry Mitchell once approached the staff psychologist to say he couldn't cope with the stress of the job. Few people remember him.

[Disinformation]

Airforce One is, as the movie of the same name revealed, the presidential aircraft, transport and a mobile office in one. Christine and her CIA chums have a nice line in acronyms and codewords: 'POTUS' stands for 'President of the United States', while there are also acronyms for the Vice-President (V-POTUS) and the First Lady ('FLOTUS'), though neither of them join POTUS on this visit. The presidential podium is also known as 'Blue Goose', 'Cowpuncher' is Air Force One, 'LZ' is the abbreviation for Landing Zone (i.e. the helipad at the American Embassy) and 'Kittyhawk' is code for HM Queen Elizabeth II.

[I d e n t i t y   C h e c k]

Harry, Tom, Zoe and Danny pose as delegates at a trade reception at the Italian Embassy. Tom (posing as 'Steve') takes Christine Dale (or 'Diane') as his guest. As a French delegate seems aware of Harry's true role there, it can be surmised that many, if not all, of the guests are attending under false names and positions. Christine later calls Tom 'Bob', her husband of six years, in an attempt to diffuse a tricky situation with Vicky.

[P e r s o n n e l   R e p o r t   U p d a t e s]

Much of this episode is taken up with the various responses to the deeply tactless and fear-inducing Miranda, the staff psychologist at Thames House. Although we never get to find out what it is that Zoe believes Danny has said about her, we do get an insight into the wonderfully practical Sam, whose complaints and suggestions for improvements come too thick and fast for Miranda to cope with. Thankfully, although she leaves a trail of paranoia wherever she goes, she is forced – with what appears to be disappointment – to inform Tom that his team has passed her tests. Tom, however, cannot be so reassuring about his own appraisal of her working methods.

Although Tom has made it quite clear to Vicky that he doesn't want to see her again, she persists in calling him up to 50 times a day. Eventually she resorts to placing adverts for 'Tom Quinn of Her Majesty's Sexy Service' in the phone boxes, lavatories and windows of gay establishments in Soho. The advert carries Tom's home and mobile phone numbers and his home address, which leads to him receiving a visit from a rather seedy gentleman hoping he's still 'working'. Tom immediately calls Sam, who manages to remove and destroy most of Vicky's cards during a late-night dash around Soho. Vicky is not that easily quelled, however. After following Tom during his walkthrough of the presidential route with Christine, Vicky decides to confront him personally and accuses him of two-timing her. As the angry doctor becomes more and more uncontrollable, Christine is forced to use some of her staff to remove her from the scene. Later on, Christine visits Vicky along with a couple of very intimidating CIA officers who manage to frighten the young doctor off for good. Which conveniently leaves Tom unattached enough to accept Christine's later invitation to meet her friend 'Jim Beam' at her apartment…

[Notes]

Vicky would appear to own a copy of the best-selling book Why Do People Hate America by Ziauddin Sardar and Merryl Wyn Davies. Christine references Fyodor Dostoevsky's The Idiot (see Notes, episode 204). Vicky's ad for Tom's 'Sexy Service' places Tom in the generic poster pose of almost every James Bond, while the caption specifically targets On Her Majesty's Secret Service (dir. Peter Hunt, 1969).

Miranda, the MI5 staff psychologist, is based on the fifth floor of Thames House.

According to Tom, The CIA World Factbook contains an entry on Britain, written by Christine Dale, that describes it as being 'slightly smaller than Oregon'.

The real CIA World Factbook (available online via the CIA website — see the Internet References section at the end of this book) does indeed contain a section on 'Area Comparison' where it does indeed state that the UK is 'slightly smaller than Oregon'.

Danny tells Miranda that the freephone number for the public to call in with tip-offs on terrorist threats is known within Section B as the 'Weirdo Line'. Incidentally, in real life, that number is 0800 789321.

As with the rest of the season, this episode was premiered on BBC3 the same evening as the first screening on BBC1 of the previous episode.

[Expert Witnesses]

Writer David Wolstencroft: 'I wanted to lift the lid on what it must be like behind the scenes of a presidential visit – the Security Service getting involved, the CIA, the way that plays out in terms of personal relationships as well. In the espionage community, there's friendship, but there can't be trust. It was the most fun I've ever had writing a script.'

Hugh Simon: 'What the characters do, inevitably because it's drama, is probably more interesting than what the people in MI5 do. Most of them probably do sit in front of computers trawling through the most boring acres of information and collect and collate. It's probably long periods of boredom punctuated by brief moments of high drama. For us it's high drama all the way though punctuated with bits of humour and irony.'

Natasha Little: 'Vicky's a great character. She's a very good doctor but she doesn't take life too seriously. She has a mischievous sense of humour and is quite cheeky with Tom. What sets her apart from the agents is that although their work is terribly important and serious, she realises that she has her own life. And I don't think she takes their work quite as seriously as they would like her to.'

The CIA

Though President Franklin D. Roosevelt had already commissioned an examination of American Intelligence deficiencies before Pearl Harbor, the Japanese assault on a fairly obscure part of America played a major part in the creation of what became the CIA. The first step was the creation in 1942 of the Office of Strategic Services, which would collect and analyse strategic information required by the Joint Chiefs of Staff and conduct special operations not assigned to other agencies. However, after the war, President Truman was under pressure to dismantle the agencies set up during wartime (no-one wanted a reminder of what they'd just endured). The OSS was closed down in October 1945, its counter-intelligence work handed over to the State and War Departments.

But even Truman saw the worth in having a central intelligence organisation. Just three months after the OSS closed, he set up the Central Intelligence Group with the help of the FBI and the military. The CIG would report to the National Intelligence Authority and would have access to intelligence from all sources. Within two years, the CIG and NIA were superseded by provisions made by the National Security Act which led to the creation of the National Security Council and the Central Intelligence Agency. The National Security Act empowered the CIA to take on all of the tasks of the CIG and more. It did, however, prohibit the CIA from engaging in law enforcement activity and restricted its internal security functions, effectively establishing the parameters of the law enforcement agencies and the FBI.

The CIA's remit remains to this day to co-ordinate, evaluate and disseminate intelligence according to how it affects national security. Its mission is to support the President, the National Security Council, and other officials involved in the nation's security by providing 'accurate, comprehensive, and timely foreign intelligence on national security topics'. They also handle counter-intelligence activities and any other functions related to foreign intelligence and national security as directed by the President. You might notice in all this how it's the President who has made the decisions all along. One major reason for this is that, thanks to the way American elections are run, there is every chance that a President from one party can find himself with both houses of government governed by his opposition. This makes it harder and harder for a President to get laws passed across the States – in effect it means that the President is often impotent in his own country. The only area where he has any real power at all is in foreign policy. That, naturally, puts the President in a position where foreign groups might target him for attack, which in turn necessitates someone back home to watch his back for him.

Is it any wonder then that Christine Dale is so uptight? ■

Episode 207

First Broadcast (BBC3): July 14 2003
First Terrestrial Broadcast (BBC1): July 21 2003

Written by **Simon Mirren**
Directed by **Ciaran Donnelly**

[Cast]

Philippe Caroit (Jean Luc Goyon), **Geoff Cotton** (Henri Durand),
Heshima Thompson (JJ Franks), **Aaron Martins** (Denton Franks), **Tyrone Lewis**
(Kyle), **Adam Deacon** (Billy), **Philippe De Grossouvre** (Richard Bertrand).

[Who's Who]

Director Ciaran Donnelly previously worked on ITV1's romantic comedy-drama
Cold Feet. Star of TV and film in his native France, Philippe Caroit (Jean Luc) might
possibly be more familiar to British and American viewers from his guest appearance
in the TV show *Highlander: The Raven*. Geoff Cotton (Durand) played Johnny
Ritzenella in the Sky One series *Dream Team* (and no, he's not French). Heshima
Thompson played Eric in the first two series of *Babyfather*.

Philippe De Grossouvre (Bertrand) had a small role in *The House of Mirth* (dir.
Terence Davies, 1999) and plays a young Gaul in the forthcoming *Smack the Pony*
feature film *Gladiatress* (dir. Brian Grant, 2003). Viewers with good memories might
also recognise him from *Coronation Street* where he played the artist who painted
a not-very-flattering portrait of Maxine Peacock while she was on holiday in Paris
with Ashley.

[Case Report]

Officers from MI6 arranged a meeting with Harry in the early hours of the morning to pass on information regarding Henri Durand, a French scientist responsible for the development of the technology-killing missile 'Firestorm' (see Security File). Aware that if sold to the wrong side it could be used to cripple the defence systems of any opposition, MI6 briefed Harry to 'acquire' the technology at any costs. Unfortunately, the information on 'Firestorm' existed solely on Durand's laptop, and as Durand has always maintained the utmost security by keeping it inside his briefcase or in a safe, the opportunity to snatch it had, up to that point, not presented itself. MI6 had traced Durand entering the UK from Paris and had followed him to the offices of Frank Hastings, CEO of Hastings Defence Solutions. Firestorm itself existed only as a 'jigsaw', encrypted on numerous sites on the web so that the only way to complete the jigsaw was with a series of nine 12-digit codes. MI6 had managed to discover the codes and gave them to Harry, who put them in his own briefcase and then headed home, as his house was nearer to the meeting place than Thames House. Though Harry knew that taking the codes home was against the rules (to the point that it could potentially be career-threatening), he gambled that he would be able to put the case in his safe at home, catch up on a few hours' sleep and then get the codes to Thames House first thing before anyone was any the wiser.

A few hours later, Harry was on his way to work when he realised he'd forgotten the all-important case. Turning back, he reached his house to see a large transit van speeding out of his driveway. Somehow, burglars had managed to bypass his state-of-the-art security system and had stolen a few electrical goods before they'd been disturbed by his return. That in itself was worrying, but then Harry found that the thieves had also managed to trip the lock on his safe and steal the briefcase.

Back at Thames House, the Section B team were already working on the Firestorm case. Intel indicated that the likelihood was Durand and Hastings would sell 'Firestorm' within 48 hours. With the diplomatic situation so precarious over this, the problem facing Section B was that they needed an agent who would not lead anyone to MI5 if caught trying to steal Durand's access codes – in effect, they needed a 'clean skin'. Unfortunately, all this had to be done with the French watching; one of their operatives from the DGSE, Jean Luc Goyon (an expert in surveillance techniques) was expected at Thames House any minute. Danny was entrusted with the responsibility of keeping Jean Luc out of the way on a surveillance operation at Hastings' offices.

As Harry tried to work out his next course of action, he found a small dribble of blood on his desk. Reasoning that it must have belonged to one of the burglars, he arranged for a sample to be sent for analysis. With the hope that the blood might lead him to whoever took the case, Harry made his way to Thames House to inform his team of everything that had happened.

Although everyone understood the severity of the situation (and indeed both Ruth and Zoe voiced their concerns), Tom decided to grant Harry some time to recover the briefcase, reasoning that without it, all of their careers would be at risk.

Harry felt compelled to inform Tom that, as if the situation wasn't bad enough, the briefcase had also contained a prototype for a weapon being developed by Hastings – a gun, disguised as a mobile phone.

The blood sampled matched the record of a 14-year-old black youth called JJ Franks (see Security File). Tom followed a lead to JJ's brother's flat to find a frightened JJ, another youth called Kyle who had been accidentally shot by the phone gun... and two other youths, Billy, and JJ's brother Denton, both pointing guns in Tom's direction. Though Harry was able to talk the boys into dropping their weapons, it was too late to recover the contents of the briefcase; the boys had burned all of the files in a panic.

Ever the pragmatist, Harry had read the file on JJ and discovered that among his list of petty crimes was a mention that he possessed an astounding photographic memory. With a little training, Harry believed JJ could well become the clean skin they were looking for. Zoe was outraged that Harry could suggest manipulating the boy in such a dangerous way, but even she could see that they had no other choice. Tom offered JJ a deal – help them in acquiring Firestorm and they'd not only waive the charges against him for breaking into Harry's house, they'd also ensure JJ's

[Henri Durand]

Durand is known for two things – his brilliance and his inflated ego. In the 1980s he worked in missile development, though he is thought to have sold certain secrets to Argentina – an act that caused MI6 to monitor his activities for the best part of two decades. More recently, he was the brains behind the development of 'Firestorm', an air burst missile that when detonated emits an electromagnetic pulse over half a square mile that kills technology instead of people (just a few such missiles could bring London to a standstill). In 2002 he resigned from his post in the French military, taking his technology with him. He's received financial backing to develop the EMP from Frank Hastings, a middle-weight arms dealer.

[Jason James Franks]

14 years old, known as JJ. Older brother Denton. Their mother handed them both over to care when JJ was just four. He was fostered for a short time, but when Social Services learned that his foster father had been abusing him, they removed JJ. He spent some time in Feltham Young Offenders' Institution, but recently broke the rules of his probation and a warrant was issued for his arrest.

wounded friend received the best treatment available. Though he was resistant at first, JJ was eventually persuaded by his own brother to comply with Tom's request.

Tom, Zoe and Colin began training JJ. Using a simulation of Hastings' offices, they showed JJ the route he would have to take to find Durand's briefcase. Although Colin would be able to control the security cameras inside the real Hastings building to stop them picking up JJ, it would only be for a short time before Colin's hacking would trip the alarms, which meant that JJ had just a few minutes to find his way in, access Durand's laptop and mail the codes to Section B. JJ realised that this left him no time to escape, and that he had been selected for the mission so that MI5 could claim no knowledge of his existence. But he also knew that if he succeeded he wouldn't have a criminal charge hanging over him and a death sentence over his friend.

Thanks to a tip-off from Christine Dale, Tom had learned that Zheng Jing Hui, a military scientist and missile expert from China, had recently entered the country. Taps on Jing Hui's telephone calls connected him to Hastings Defence Solutions. Meanwhile, during surveillance with Jean Luc, Danny realised that the Frenchman was not being entirely honest with him. Looking back through airport surveillance footage, he recognised a man who had entered the country with Jean Luc who Danny had also seen during the surveillance on Hastings. The man was soon identified as Richard Bertrand, a former soldier in the French Foreign Legion who had served with Jean Luc and was currently listed as being on attachment to the French Secret Service.

JJ's break-in operation began well, but almost as soon as he was inside the building, Zoe and Colin detected interference from an unidentified source – someone else was trying to hack into the system, and it soon became obvious who was responsible when the security cameras picked up a shot of Bertrand, clearly set on exactly the same target as JJ. JJ made it to Durand's office, empty except for the laptop. But then Durand himself returned unexpectedly. JJ snatched the laptop and hid just as Bertrand also reached the office. Bertrand shot Durand dead but was surprised when he could not find the laptop. As the security system crashed, the alarm sounded throughout the Hastings building and Bertrand had no other choice but to make his escape. With Hastings unable to supply the Firestorm program, Zheng Jing Hui cancelled his offer and returned to China empty-handed.

Naturally, Jean Luc denied all knowledge of Bertrand's mission, claiming that although he knew him, the last he had heard the man had been working as a gun for hire. Jean Luc was not, however, too concerned; although he had not managed to acquire Firestorm, neither had the British or the Chinese. As Jean Luc left Thames House, Tom spied a smug JJ across the road. The boy handed over the laptop in return for £1500 and a bowl of fruit for his friend. To JJ's incredulity, Tom asked him to consider working for MI5 and left him with his home phone number.

[Disinformation]

Durand's murder is reported as a burglary gone wrong.

[Personnel Report Updates]

Danny can speak fluent French; Sam cannot, though she can cope with a few phrases.

[Gadgets]

In addition to JJ's personal codebreaker, Colin indulges in a little James Bondery by giving JJ a false fingerprint to access the security doors (the fingerprint was acquired after much rummaging through the refuse of Hastings Defence Systems).

[Expert Witnesses]

Keeley Hawes: 'I think the audience often aren't given enough credit. A lot of the jargon I don't understand, so nobody else could be expected to understand that. But if you get the drift you are quite capable of understanding the stories even though they can be very complex. I think it gives the audiences some credit.'

David Oyelowo: 'I would be a terrible spy. Lying is an occupational hazard. In terms of relationships you can't go home and tell your wife or your friends and family what you've done that day. And my vanity as well – if I had saved the world that day, I would want people to know. It's as simple as that.'

[Quote/Unquote]

Ruth (on hearing Tom's plan to steal Firestorm from the French): 'If that isn't illegal it's… very, very naughty.'

Sam (en-route to collecting Jean Luc from reception): 'I saw him first!'

Zoe: 'I outrank you.'

Sam: (Mouths the word 'Bitch')

Denton: 'They say mobiles are bad for you. No shit. One call from dis does the job.'

Tom (to JJ): 'We could frame the Pope – so what chance have you got?'

[Notes]

The access code to Harry's house was 9832 (though it's almost certain he changed it after the events of this episode). His car registration number remains KY03 RUH.

Harry listens to silver-tongued broadcaster Terry Wogan on Radio 2. Kyle calls JJ "Moby Dickhead", an interesting variation on the title of the classic whale-chase novel by Herman Melville that JJ is reading. Tom narrowly avoids having to endure a performance of Tosca, Puccini's controversial opera first performed in 1900 at Teatro Costanzi in Rome. The idea of transferable fingerprints comes from the James Bond film Diamonds are Forever (dir. Guy Hamilton, 1971).

Tom gives JJ a watch that he says came from 'an old girlfriend' (presumably Ellie).

As with the rest of the season, this episode was premiered on BBC3 the same evening as the first screening on BBC1 of the previous episode.

Episode 208

First Broadcast (BBC3): July 21 2003
First Terrestrial Broadcast (BBC1): July 28 2003

Written by **Steve Bailie**
Directed by **Ciaran Donnelly**

[Cast]

Leo Bill (Corporal Eric Woods), **Reece Dinsdale** (Major Sam Curtis), **Alex Palmer** (Sergeant Major Baker), **Kieran Bew** (Bryant), **Conor Ryan** (Wallace), **Michael Hodgson** (Derek Hanson), **Roger Brierley** ('Mr Getty').

[Who's Who]

A familiar face to British TV viewers, Reece Dinsdale (Curtis) really came into the public eye when he played John Thaw's cheeky son in the sitcom *Home to Roost*. After that, he led an ensemble cast in the drama series *Thief Takers*. He starred in the film *ID* (dir. Philip Davis, 1995) and played Guildenstern in Kenneth Branagh's adaptation of *Hamlet* (1996).

Leo Bill (Woods)'s television credits include *Crime & Punishment*, the second series of *Attachments*, *Midsomer Murders*, *The Canterbury Tales* and *Beethoven's Eroica*. He's also appeared in the films *Gosford Park* (dir. Robert Altman, 2001), *All or Nothing* (dir. Mike Leigh, 2001) and *28 Days Later* (dir. Danny Boyle, 2001). Michael Hodgson (Hanson) played Robbie in the third series of *Two Thousand Acres of Sky*.

Another of those character actors who manage to appear in lots of things and always avoid being typecast, the CV of Roger Brierley ('Mr Getty') includes the sci-fi

series *Doctor Who* (twice, playing two different roles, 21 years apart), *Jeeves and Wooster* (as regular guest Sir Roderick Glossop), *Young Sherlock Holmes* (dir. Barry Levinson, 1985), *A Fish Called Wanda* (dir. Charles Crichton, 1988), *Ali G Indahouse* (dir. Mark Mylod, 2002) and *About a Boy* (dirs. Chris & Paul Weitz, 2002).

[C a s e   R e p o r t]

A series of strikes had plunged the country into the worst period of industrial action since the late 1970s with many sources citing the government's focusing on overseas matters as the cause. While various unions went on strike, the government depended more and more on the resources of the armed forces, who were often called upon to step in and maintain essential services. So when a report came through that one major was organising a strike within the army itself it was a serious cause for concern. If the army decided to strike, they would leave the country vulnerable to attack and unable to provide back-up in the event of a terrorist incident.

The information came via Eric Woods, a corporal who had decided to give evidence of the potential mutiny after being arrested and held on a disciplinary charge. Tom was placed undercover in the same company as Woods, reporting to the man believed to be behind the mutiny, Major Samuel Curtis. Once in place, Tom wasted no time in being vocally critical of the standard of equipment and weapons he was forced to use, all the time acting like an ideal potential recruit for any future industrial action.

Meanwhile, Ruth learned of a sudden strike brewing among the rail unions. As a consignment of spent nuclear fuel was on its way to Dover by rail, the consignment was at risk of being left in the middle of the countryside for any terrorist to take a pot-shot at. The Nuclear Authority arranged to provide an alternative means of transport, a low-loader that could make the journey overnight to Dover. With Tom away, Harry made Zoe acting section head; as such, she was entrusted with the responsibility of ensuring the low-loader convoy made it to its destination safely. Zoe then faced an additional complication when she learned that Dover dockers were also planning to strike, meaning it was even more important that the convoy reached Dover on time.

Danny made contact with one of Curtis's former colleagues, Derek Hanson.

Hanson refused to talk with him initially, but with a little encouragement, Hanson told Danny that he'd been approached by Curtis with a driving job. Hanson had turned the offer down, too proud to become a 'chauffeur' and still too full of resentment over the way his career had been ruined by Curtis's ego.

After two weeks at the barracks, Tom was finally invited for a chat with Curtis, who revealed he'd done some background checks on him. The conversation remained relaxed however. After

everything he had heard about the man, Tom was relieved when Curtis asked him to help him with a protest he was planning – and handed him a petition. Tom signed it willingly. Returning to his room, he sent a message to the Grid with his mobile phone informing his colleagues that Curtis was not to be considered a threat to national security. He had managed to get hold of Curtis's private mobile phone number and urged his team to confirm Curtis's innocence by accessing the phone's logs with his service provider.

In the early hours of that morning, the door to Tom's quarters was kicked in and three masked men dragged him out of bed, down a corridor where the whole platoon were standing (having apparently been given a similarly rude awakening) and into an interrogation room. Tom maintained his identity throughout the interrogation and was dutifully informed that the incident had been a training exercise. He returned to bed just as Corporal Woods was brought in for his interrogation…

The next morning, Tom woke up to find his mobile phone had been shattered when he'd been dragged from his bed. Having failed to receive Tom's morning check-in message on time, Danny went to see him and confirmed that he was about to hand over papers that would free Tom from the operation and allow him to leave the barracks with his cover intact. Tom left Danny and returned to the platoon to find Curtis and his old colleagues waiting for him. It appeared that Woods had decided to inform Curtis about his arrangement with MI5. Curtis bundled Tom into

[Samuel Curtis]

In 1991, during 'Desert Storm', Major Samuel Curtis led a team of men across Iraq to safety. He subsequently released a book – under the pseudonym 'Soldier C' – in which he recounted the operation in detail. The survivors of Curtis' team include Sergeant-Major Baker, Sergeant Philip Wallace and Corporal Harry Parks, all of whom still serve in Curtis's platoon. Two other survivors, however, have now left the army; William Scoby was last seen in a hostel 18 months ago and Derek Hanson has been claiming benefits ever since. Though he applied for the SAS and indeed passed all exams, the high profile Hanson received after the release of Curtis's book made him an unattractive prospect for undercover work.

Curtis has written 86 letters to the Chief of Defence over a period of five years, including suggestions and complaints on topics such as the personal army kit to pension rights that have largely been ignored.

the back of a truck and the platoon prepared to leave.

At Thames House, Malcolm managed to trace a call from the convoy to Curtis's mobile phone. Ruth checked the Nuclear Authority personnel records and found a match – the driver of the convoy was William Scobey, one of Curtis's old friends. He'd clearly been placed there by Curtis for some purpose and it wasn't long before Curtis himself provided the answer.

Curtis's men had captured the nuclear convoy and taken it to an oil storage depot on the bank of the Thames, just a few miles east of the City of London. There, he held both Tom and Danny as hostage while he made his demands via a webcam on a laptop. He had already faxed a list of demands to the Chief of Defence Staff which included compensation, treatment and acknowledge of the existence of Gulf War Syndrome and post-traumatic stress disorder and a 50% pay increase across the board. Having exhausted every legitimate method of campaigning for change, Curtis had decided to hold the country to ransom. He gave the authorities just 30 minutes to agree to his terms, after which time he would transmit images of the stolen nuclear tanker to every major broadcaster in the West, confident that the news would spread quickly. If his terms remained ignored within an additional hour, he would blow up the oil storage tankers. The resulting explosion would heat the nuclear load to such an extent that the resulting explosion would irradiate most of the south-east of England.

A 20-mile cordon was quickly established around the depot and civilians were evacuated from the area while a counter-terrorist team got into position. Harry spoke to Curtis by remote and claimed that they had been aware of his activities for a while – including his use of Scobey as the driver of the convoy. Curtis thought this was a bluff until Harry told him that the nuclear tanker was in fact empty – a decoy to draw him out, which would mean all he would be doing by detonating the oil supplies in the depot would be killing his own men. Tom realised what was happening and tried to talk Curtis down, telling him that he was being manipulated into self-destruction so that his superiors could silence him and undermine all of his campaigning. Curtis refused to listen and threatened to shoot one of his hostages instead. Despite Tom's pleas, Harry gave the order and a sniper took Curtis out.

Tom returned to the Grid during the birthday party for Harry. Christine Dale had dropped by and on seeing her very friendly reaction to Tom's return, Harry requested a quick chat with his section leader. Behind the closed door of his office, Harry ordered Tom to end his relationship with Christine. Tom was already furious

Danny (referring to a government minister): 'Isn't he the man who had the fling with the guy –'

Zoe: 'Who knew the girl who sold the thing? Yep.'

Army barracks leaflet: 'Fancy spending nine months away from home on crap pay, provide strike cover for firemen earning twice as much money for six months' work and face the possibility of being killed for a country full of greedy, pathetic and selfish individuals? Sign below. Army – Be Depressed.' (Someone later scrawls underneath it, 'We are!')

Harry (on the subject of asking the army to investigate Curtis): 'It'd be like asking the Vatican to prove Mary wasn't a virgin.'

Zoe: 'If we went on strike, who'd notice?'

Curtis: 'War is shit. Anyone who tells you otherwise has never been in one. Train hard, fight easy. Train easy, fight hard, and die.'

Ruth (to Zoe): 'I don't want to go back to GCHQ. Too many bloody mathematicians for one thing...'

[N o t e s]

The dissenting leaflet that Tom finds on the army barracks notice board is a parody of an army recruitment campaign that urged recruits to 'be the best' rather than 'be depressed'.

Curtis owns a painting of George Bingham, 3rd Earl of Lucan, who led almost 500 men into the Valley of Death during the Charge of the Light Brigade.

The final scenes of this episode occur on Harry's birthday.

As with the rest of the season, this episode was premiered on BBC3 the same evening as the first screening on BBC1 of the previous episode.

with Harry for allowing himself (and Tom) to be manipulated into removing the problem of Curtis, and he was certainly not going to let Harry dictate to him who he could and could not see in his private life. But Harry was resolute – the affair with Christine Dale was to end.

[Disinformation]

Tom uses a code in all his messages for times of the day. Whatever time he gives is six hours ahead of the real time. Hence '1100 hours' means 5.00am. Sam employs a little deception by hiding a bottle of 25-year-old malt for Harry's birthday inside a file labelled 'UK EYES ALPHA: TOP SECRET'. Only in MI5 would the words 'Top Secret' ever stop someone prying where they shouldn't.

[Identity Check]

Danny poses as 'Rob Simkins', staff writer for *Today's Soldier* magazine. Tom becomes Lieutenant David Getty, number 541232. His record includes operational tours in Bosnia, Sierra Leone and, most recently, six months in Belfast under Tim Derbyshire. While in Belfast, Tom faced a minor disciplinary charge after it was discovered that he had 'liberated' a supply of whisky from an IRA arms dump in Armagh and handed it over to the Junior Ranks mess. 'Getty' had been due three weeks' leave but that was cancelled after he was placed on fire-fighting duty during the most recent strikes. He had still not made up the leave by the time he was sent to Curtis's barracks.

Corporal Woods is given the codename 'Nightingale', Curtis 'Eagle One', the nuclear convoy 'the Stick' and the Nuclear Authority Central Control is called 'Polestar'.

[Personnel Report Updates]

Ruth receives a memo from GCHQ informing her that her secondment to MI5 is about to come to an end. Thanks to a recommendation from Harry, however (which in turn is thanks to some very generous work on Zoe's part), Ruth's services are retained.

We learn here that as Section Leader, Tom has to attend a fortnight's training with the SAS on an annual basis, training that makes him the natural choice to go undercover with Curtis's company.

After a little encouragement from Zoe, Danny finally asks Sam out for a date, while Tom's relationship with Christine comes to the attention of Harry.

[Gadgets]

Harry tries to persuade Danny and Zoe to use some specially designed, standard-issue waterproofing equipment – an umbrella. Slightly more sophisticated is Tom's mobile phone, which contains sweeping technology to enable him to check for bugs. It also allows him to prerecord a message that can be digitally compressed and encrypted before being transmitted in a 0.1-second burst, rendering it impossible to intercept. He uses a tack-mounted camera and places it on the pin-board of the army barracks to enable Section B.

[Expert Witnesses]

Matthew Macfadyen: 'Part of the fun of being an actor is to explore those parts in you that you wouldn't normally be able to do. I think I've influenced Tom and he has also influenced me. Tom's quite a serious character and concentrates on his job, sometimes to the expense of other areas of his life. He has difficulty when his work spills into his personal life, and he finds it hard to keep things secret.'

Peter Firth: 'I think for anyone working for a Security Service then there has to be a degree of trust between the team. You don't do that job for the money, you do it for your country and as such there has to be a camaraderie which is rare between work colleagues.'

Jennie Muskett – Spooks' composer

'… It starts from the moment he says, "Move it."

That's the point at which Tom is in danger, that's when he's got a real problem and it stops when that tension's resolved, or in this case increased.'

It's the middle of May and I'm sitting in the studio of [**spooks**] composer Jennie Muskett while she puts the finishing touches to the score for episode eight of the second series. We're watching the scene where Major Curtis has just revealed that Tom's cover has been blown. The MI5 officer is bundled into the back of a truck and taken to the oil storage depot where Curtis intends to broadcast his demands. As the scene plays out on Jennie's screen, we follow the action as the truck storms along the motorway right into the oil storage (where I notice the music getting a little more electronic, almost *Bladerunner*-like),

and then some interesting textures develop, which Jennie explains are to draw the viewers towards that laptop: 'It's all designed to make them feel very uncomfortable without them really thinking about it too much. Often, people call it "background" music but it's much more than that. It can have such a profound effect on you.'

Jennie sits surrounded by an array of keyboards, monitors and buttons, the likes of which have probably never been seen outside of an episode of *Star Trek*. Apparently it's a combination of a G4 Mac dual processor, three emulators and a program called Logic and another called Pro Tools… and a few other toys. Although it sounds orchestral, almost all of the music for the series comes from the kit in front of me. I begin by asking whether the decision to use synthesised music was a budgetary decision or a stylistic one. 'Oh it's a very conscious choice. [**spooks**] is such a fast-paced, modern show. We knew from the start that it had to be that kind of sound.'

Jennie confesses that, having trained as a classical cellist, she fell into composing rather by accident after she began combining her interest in music with an enthusiasm for natural history. 'I felt that a good way to be involved with ecology and conservation might be to do the music for some documentaries, so I started out scoring films for IMAX, and TV shows for National Geographic, the BBC and others, such as *Great White Shark* and *People of the Rain Forest*. That was going really well, and then I found myself wanting to have a go at a movie. I was really lucky because I got to do a couple of movies for Miramax, including a film called *B. Monkey* [Michael Radford, 1998]. I was brought in by [producer] Harvey Weinstein. I was a bit worried because up until then I'd only done orchestral things and all of a sudden he was asking for this very edgy sound. I confessed to him that I wasn't sure I knew how to do what he wanted and he just said, matter-of-factly, "You gotta learn." It was a vertical learning curve, but it was great because it was how I got involved in doing all this programming and using computers. I'd never dream of going back to writing all this with paper and pencil now.'

In 2001, Jennie was invited to work on a three-part thriller series called *Shockers* on an episode called 'Cyclops', which was directed by Bharat Nalluri. 'That was a really brave, dark show and Bharat was great because he pushed me in new directions. I had an image of my music as beautiful and great and then Bharat comes along and says "I want this to be really uncomfortable", really pushing it as far as it could go, to the point of being almost ugly. When I went in to meet the dubbing engineer for the first time, he'd already heard my music for it and when he heard I was at the door he lunged for a crucifix and started calling me "The Scary Woman".'

When it came to [**s p o o k s**], although Jennie was Bharat's first choice, she still had to provide audition tapes for the producers, who were looking at other people at the time. 'I played the producers a few of my pieces, and they really responded well to the pace of the music. I just listened to what they and Bharat wanted and how fast-paced they wanted it, and it just felt right to do that here. If you had an orchestra on something like [**s p o o k s**], you'd still have to have that mix of sounds in there just to get that contemporary feel.' How did it feel working to impress the three producers like that? 'The producers are all collectively passionate about the series, and although they all have their own ideas, they're all generally working together and in the same direction. There isn't an apathetic moment in sight and they all want it to be right as much as each other. So when they decided to go with what I could offer it was great as I knew I had their complete support.'

After being commissioned, Jennie sat down to work with Bharat Nalluri on a few ideas – which she tells me wasn't as straightforward as that might sound. 'When we started work on the first episode, Bharat came round to the studio at about half past nine in the morning and at about 9.45 in the evening he finally said "I think we're ready to start now" because we'd spent the entire day just discussing the concepts.' So presumably you were encouraged to go into great detail about the themes and motivations in the story? 'Absolutely. Bharat's great like that. He wants to discuss every single detail and he really understands what the music's all for and what he wants from it. Like the rest of the team, he's really passionate about it all. Those early discussions set the tone for the whole series.'

I ask Jennie about the timescale she works to. How long before the series airs does she begin composing the score? 'On the first series, I started work about four weeks before the first episode aired. When I was nominated for a BAFTA, I told myself it was for "Fastest Work in the West" [laughs]. I've got a lot more time this year, almost twice as long, but then I've got twice as much music to produce too.'

So, how did you both come to decide on that distinctive sound of the series? 'We started off by discussing what kind of music we liked. Bharat likes artists such as Fatboy Slim and so do I, so initially I came up with a lot of similar sounds to that, which Jane (Featherstone, series producer) thought a bit too "garage", too "techno". So at Jane's suggestion I started putting the strings in and making it more weighty. The main thing they all wanted was something really contemporary and cool, so the music had to always be really tight on the images, like Bharat would ask for a subtle "swush" on the movement of a Venetian blind to draw the audience's eyes to it without the sound being distracting. If there's a little hint in the music, they'll be less likely to miss something important.'

Although each episode boasts a completely original soundtrack, there are a few elements that Jennie was keen to maintain for continuity and thematic reasons. 'One of the first "themes" I worked on was the relationship between Ellie and Tom… or Matthew… or whoever he was then [laughs]. It was a question of finding the right pitch; were they really in love or was it something else? Their love is always weird, she doesn't know who he is, and most of the time neither does he. Another theme I looked at was what I call the "betrayal" theme, because the women in the show all got betrayed by their men – like in the Turkish episode where Tessa says to

Johnny Marks "that's twice you broke my heart", which is really sad. Ellie gets betrayed in a way because Tom's never there for her. Whenever they look for this ideal love it melts away.'

Much of the music is atmospheric rather than necessarily melodic, but what dictates the kind of sounds you select for each episode? 'I usually look at it in terms of either what the story is or where the characters are going. In episode seven, JJ has his own theme because it's very much about his character's journey within himself.' She points to the monitor, where the image is paused on Tom's face as he tries to talk Curtis out of self-destruction. 'With this episode, when there are trucks and helicopters, this is "the [**s p o o k s**] thing". I have a cue called "Boyz n Toyz" on the soundtrack album, which I use for when one of the guys is up to his neck in gadgets and loving it. Then there are times when the three of the leads walk towards the camera in a certain way that's very cool, so if it's one of those moments when they're at the peak of their game and they know what they're doing, then that's when I use the cue that Bharat named "Spies on Top".

It's not all synthesisers though. A couple of episodes have soundtracks with recognisably human elements in them. 'For episode two of the second series I brought in a fantastic singer called Paul Gladstone-

Reid. I've worked with him a hell of a lot on loads of projects. We even did a song together, a "James Bond-style" [**s p o o k s**] song just for the fun of it. For that episode, I wrote the music and then told Paul the kind of emotions I wanted to represent, what the characters are feeling and hopefully what the viewers will feel, and he becomes a sort of conduit. He sings and the feeling on-screen just comes out. He's got an amazing range, from deep and bassy to sweet. So I wanted him to represent the inner thoughts of the boy [Abu] and his innocence. It was one of the most thematically interesting episodes. When Rachid holds up that jacket as if it's the most beautiful garment on earth that could grace anybody's shoulders. For me it felt like a horrible abuse, but in his mind, we can imagine, it came from the best of intentions, from maybe a good place. Really curious, like a creepy seduction.'

There were also some vocals in series one. 'I really liked that one, the lament for the second episode – the one with the chip-pan.' Jennie suddenly erupts with laughter. 'It's supposed to be really beautiful, but it's "The one with the chip-pan," isn't it! We had a soprano called Catherine Bott who came in for that, and she gave us the vocals for a beautiful lament over Helen's funeral scenes.'

Episode five of Series Two was another

challenging one, especially as it's largely set in the same location for the entirety of the story. '[Director] Justin Chadwick, who directed that one, was after something quite different from the music for the other episodes in that it's very sound-designy to enhance the feeling of being trapped. And at the end, when they realise they're all safe, you'd usually feel drawn to celebrate it, but this stays with the sadness. Despite being "saved", the overall feeling in that room at the end is "What are our lives about? What are we doing here?" And it's a feeling that stays with the characters from this point to the end of the series. It's a fantastic piece of writing. I really love that episode. But then, they're all good, in their own ways.' ■

Episode 209

First Broadcast (BBC3): July 28 2003
First Terrestrial Broadcast (BBC1): August 4 2003

Written by **Ben Richards**
Directed by **Sam Miller**

[Cast]

Sophie Lombard (Mariela Hernandez), **Daniel Cerqueira** (Rafael Morrientes), **Michael Cochrane** (Ross Vaughan), **Santiago Cabrera** (Camilo Henriquez), **Abigail Hercules** (Jenny Thomas), **Gary Sefton** (MI5 Operative).

[Who's Who]

Director Sam Miller was the man responsible for, amongst other things, the innovative documentary-style direction for legal drama *This Life*. Daniel Cerqueira (Rafa) played a soldier in the harrowing WWII epic *Saving Private Ryan* (dir. Steven Spielberg, 1998), as did Gary Sefton (MI5 Operative). Michael Cochrane (Ross Vaughan) is the voice of Oliver Sterling in *The Archers* on BBC Radio 4. He's also made appearances in numerous TV shows including *Doctor Who* (twice), *A Touch of Frost*, *Sharp* and *Longitude*.

[C a s e   R e p o r t]

Tom was placed undercover on a major Customs & Excise operation to halt the trafficking of drugs via Dover by the Chala Cartel, a Colombian group in a league of their own. Tom's aim was to collect a Chala Cartel soldier and escort him to a safe house in Dover. But as Tom slipped out of the surveillance van for his hourly status report, masked Cartel soldiers slaughtered the customs officers in the van. Other operations were hit in the same way, with a total death toll of eight. Tom was convinced that no-one could have arranged an ambush on such a scale without insider help.

All this appeared to be the work of one man, Rafael Morrientes – AKA Rafa – who (conveniently for his alibi) was in his hotel room while his soldiers did his dirty work for him. Surveillance placed on his hotel for the last week revealed the existence of a girlfriend, Mariela Hernandez, also from Colombia. She was later seen getting into the limousine of Ross Vaughan, finance director of PETCAL, one of Britain's leading oil companies. There, she would exchange briefcases with Vaughan and that way act as a go-between for the two men.

Having applied a little pressure on one of Rafa's workers, Danny secured himself a job as a cleaner at PETCAL, a position that enabled him to place a bug inside one of the Cartel's meeting rooms. Meanwhile, Tom and Zoe began their own mission – to befriend Mariela. Zoe made first contact at Mariela's gym.

Thanks to Danny's bug, Ruth discovered that the Cartel were planning to trade drugs for surface-to-air missiles (SAMs), presumably to repeat the kind of retaliation they took in the 1990s when the Colombian government tried to crack down on the Cartel's activities and suffered civilian air crashes as a consequence. Tom advised Harry to allow the weapons to enter the country in order to give them the chance to place a tracker on them with a view to finding the Cartel's armoury. Harry initially refused to sanction such a dangerous operation, but when Tom challenged him to offer an alternative he reluctantly conceded.

A second meeting between Zoe and Mariela was staged during which Mariela's briefcase was swapped for an identical one. The contents were copied and the briefcase returned under the pretext of the other briefcase's owner picking up the wrong one. This enabled the Section B team to learn that Vaughan's briefcase contained details on drug shipments as well as bearer bonds – dummy shares in anonymous companies that could be exchanged as easily as cash. This suggested

[Rafa and the Chala Cartel]

Chala is the provincial capital of a lawless region of Colombia ruled by left-wing guerrillas, right-wing paramilitaries, drug lords and American Special Forces. Anyone wanting to build a pipeline from the Colombian oilfields to a sea port has to go through Chala, which means one of the many groups will offer 'protection'. One of the leading figures in the Chala Cartel is Rafael Morrientes, also known as 'Rafa'. In the 1980s, a group of Spanish special operatives were in Colombia directing a guerrilla training mission around Chala. Rafa took exception to their presence and the mission ended unpleasantly. Ever since, the Spanish have been trying to ally themselves with organisations that could help them gain retribution against Rafa.

Since the late 1980s, it's been alleged that a representative of a British company, PETCAL, cut a deal with the Chala Cartel. That representative is believed to be Ross Vaughan; he would certainly have met Rafa during this time. Since Rafa's move to the UK, however, he and Vaughan have never met in person – they use Rafa's lover Mariela as a go-between. Rafa's foot-soldiers work as cleaners at PETCAL, using the basement of the building for meetings and arranging drug drops and the odd massacre.

Tom (to Zoe): 'We're family. We'll always look after each other.'

Tessa: 'Ah Zoe, you're so like me in some ways. Always wanting the last word…'

that Vaughan was in fact using PETCAL to launder Chala Cartel funds. Despite all this information, and the clear evidence of a mole, Ruth had been unable to find a link to the Customs & Excise.

'Katy' and 'Jack' invited Mariela for dinner, during which she confided in them that her parents, brother and sister were murdered back in Colombia when she was just 15. Her mother had given her a lapis lazuli ring, identical to her father's bar the inscription 'A mi querida hija. 4-5-91' (to my darling daughter). Her father had been the mayor of Chala and when he and his wife were murdered, the killers stole their jewellery.

Seemingly out of the blue, Tessa contacted Zoe and promised her information on the Chala Cartel. Representing her own Spanish clients' interests, she offered Zoe information that could help her turn Mariela into an agent for MI5 in return for MI5 allowing the Spanish the chance to dispose of Rafa themselves.

Tessa made good on her side of the bargain; her information revealed that Rafa and his men, disguised as guerrillas, had been responsible for the slaughter of Mariela's family, after which Rafa had taken her as a souvenir. Taking the chance that Mariela could be convinced of the truth about her lover, Tom decided to risk telling her everything. To help their case, however, a copy of her ring was commissioned (complete with the inscription 'A mi querido marido' to match the one on Mariela's late father's ring) and placed within a box of other 'treasures' that Tom and Zoe would claim came from Rafa's hotel room. Tom and Zoe met with

Mariela and told her that they had targeted her as she was their best chance of stopping Rafa from ever harming anyone else ever again by getting information from Vaughan. Once they showed her the ring, an emotional Mariela agreed to help them discover the level of Vaughan's corruption.

Having discovered that some classified information had already escaped from their contacts in Spain, Ruth followed the trail of information until it led her to a shocking discovery – the leak was coming direct from inside Thames House, from Sam. Sam had been seen by Zoe with an expensive palmtop device, which she had claimed had been a birthday present. In reality, she was downloading files and passing them straight onto Tessa.

Sam was hauled in and interrogated by Harry. Though she held up well under questioning, it was clear that Sam was lying. But then a message came through on Harry's fax: 'Tell Sam that the bar is now open.' Harry returned to the interrogation room and passed on the cryptic message only for Sam to visibly relax, kiss Harry and request a cup of tea. Only then did she reveal what she had been led to believe had been going on all along. While still in training, she had been approached by a woman calling herself Jane, who asked her to take part in an exercise at some point in the future. As she had claimed to be Harry's boss, Sam had naturally trusted her, and from the moment she saw an advert in a shop window containing the key words she'd been given, she'd realised that the training exercise was now live. She'd also assumed that the reason no-one else had ever mentioned the exercise was all part of the test. Of course 'Jane' was Tessa all along, which was how she had been able to obtain the information about Section B's activities.

Danny's operation with the tracking device was a success. Confident that the device could bring the operation to a close, Tom was prepared to keep the deal with Tessa on behalf of the Spanish. Harry, however, vetoed the agreement, despite warnings from Tom of what might happen if Tessa was crossed.

Mariela seduced Vaughan as agreed and was able to get him to unconsciously confess that he had been able to achieve much thanks to the protection he received from a senior figure in the government. Before Vaughan could go too far, Zoe called Mariela and gave her an excuse to leave.

Aware that Harry had doubled-crossed her, Tessa decided to tip Vaughan off about Mariela's involvement with MI5. She then sent Harry a VCD proudly warning him of her actions. Aware that Tessa's spite had placed Mariela in great danger, Tom raced to the young woman's apartment to find her lying in a pool of blood. It seemed that she had confronted Rafa about the death of her family and then told him of her betrayal. Rafa had responded by cutting the tendons in her arms and legs so she could not move. After an agonising amount of suffering, she died in Tom's arms.

It was later learned that Rafa also killed Vaughan before he himself was killed, garrotted by Spanish assassins.

Although it was clear that Vaughan had been assisted by someone high up in the government, Harry refused to bring charges against the main suspect as that could cause a scandal for the government, and also because he might prove a useful pawn in the future. Tom was furious and not for the first time recently did he and Harry have a blazing row. Angered both by Sam's naivety and Tom's increasing insubordination, Harry warned his staff that the very next person to disobey his orders would be out.

That night, Tom made a decision to continue his relationship with Christine, regardless, or maybe even in spite of, Harry's instructions.

[Disinformation]

The operation with Customs is codenamed 'Braveheart'. The Chala Cartel bombing of a nightclub in Madrid that killed 30 teenagers is reported as the work of ETA. In reality it was a Cartel revenge attack after two leading Chala members were arrested and deported from Spain.

[Identity Check]

This episode it's Tom's turn to juggle multiple identities again. During the Customs & Excise operation, Tom is 'Peter', married with two children, 'Danny' ('at that difficult age, always getting into trouble') and 'Zoe' ('too clever for her own good'). Later, he and Zoe become 'Jack' and 'Katy'. 'Jack' is a risk analyst, withdrawn, slightly aloof. His younger sister 'Katy' works in publishing, is impulsive, generous-spirited, and a little over-the-top at times. Their mother was a lecturer, their father a top civil servant and keen ornithologist with a longing to visit Latin America. Their parents were killed in a car collision with a lorry after a family holiday in Sherringham. Katy was just three

[Notes]

Tessa calls herself 'Durbeyfield', a reference to Thomas Hardy's Tess of the d'Urbervilles (Peter Firth of course appeared in Roman Polanski's film adaptation of the novel in 1979). Christine's comment about Britain being a 'nation of shopkeepers' refers to a famous quote by Napoleon.

The card in the window that Sam sees contains trigger words that she has already been briefed on, namely an advertisement for a laptop that has games called Giraffe and Hardball.

'Katy' claims to be a fan of Colombian recording legend Joe Arroyo (born Alvaro Jose Arroyo Gonzalez). A former member of leading salsa band, Fruko y sus Tesos, Arroyo is famous for fusing the traditional sounds of salsa with more Caribbean sounds. He has played with his band, La Verdad (The Truth), since 1981.

Jenny, the Customs officer, refers to Thierry Henry, the French footballing legend currently playing for Arsenal.

Zoe mentions Julio, her Spanish counterpart in CESID (Centro Superior de Información de la Defensa).

As with the rest of the season, this episode was premiered on BBC3 the same evening as the first screening on BBC1 of the previous episode.

years old at the time and remembers nothing about the accident, but Jack was five and remembers it clearly. They are both learning salsa, though Katy's not doing as well as Jack as her tutor's a PE instructor from Stockport. Jack meanwhile has, according to Katy, just split up with his girlfriend.

Danny is placed undercover as a cleaner at PETCAL. Tessa communicates with Zoe under the guise of 'Durbeyfield' (see Notes) and with Sam as 'Jane', who she cheekily claims is Harry's boss.

[Personnel Report Updates]

Despite plenty of opportunity, Danny has yet to actually take Sam on the date they have been promising each other since episode 205. Tessa boasts of Spanish clients in her 'substantial client portfolio'.

[Gadgets]

Tom would appear to have another mobile phone unit similar to the one he lost in the previous episode.

[Expert Witnesses]

Shauna Macdonald: 'Sam's intelligent, enthusiastic, versatile and very keen to learn but she's also very naive for someone who is supposed to be working in MI5 and she's got a lot to learn. I think she'll make a good spy, but at this stage she sees it all as more of a game whereas the more hardened characters like Tom and Zoe are more aware of the implications of the job.'

Nicola Walker: 'I heard that the costume vans always get the scripts in advance of the actors, so I went in there spy-fashion to get a sneaky-peak at the next episode down the line and when I got to the bit about me going back I just thought, Oh no! It's over! But we've always joked that the only way Ruth could ever really leave now is in a horrific photocopying accident.'

Jenny Agutter: 'Some of the **[s p o o k s]** episodes focus on MI5 in action out in the field – the adrenaline-fuelled moments and the thrill of the chase. But Tessa's story is about the intellectual subtleties, the dangers of corruption from within. When you have so many bright, excitement-driven people in one place, someone's bound to get bored and wander off the beaten track. The inherent Security Service paradox is that if someone wants to bite the hand that feeds it, they are fully trained. Lying and manipulation are part of the job, and you are your own moral guardian, so the lines can get very blurred. Tessa's just dabbling on the side and I expect she doesn't even think she's doing anything wrong.'

Episode 210

First Broadcast (BBC3): August 4 2003
First Terrestrial Broadcast (BBC1): August 11 2003

Written by **Howard Brenton**
Directed by **Sam Miller**

[Cast]

Tomas Arana (Herb Ziegler / Hermann Joyce), **Samantha Coughlan** (Lisa Joyce), **Bruce Payne** (Michael Karharias), **Mac McDonald** ('Hard-Faced Man'), **Elizabeth Chambers** (Woman).

[Who's Who]

Tomas Arana (Joyce) should be used to playing characters who return from the dead, having been cast as Lazarus in Martin Scorsese's challenging *The Last Temptation of Christ*. In a career of more than 40 films to date, his other major film roles include Quintus in *Gladiator* (dir. Ridley Scott, 2000), one of the rogue cops in *L.A. Confidential* (dir. Curtis Hanson, 1997), Whitney Houston's stalker in *The Bodyguard* (dir. Mick Jackson, 1992) and a Russian saboteur in *The Hunt for Red October* (dir. John McTiernan, 1990).

London-born Bruce Payne (Karharias) is invariably cast as a villain in films such as *The Fruit Machine* (dir. Philip Saville, 1988), *Passenger 57* (dir. Kevin Hooks, 1992) and *Dungeons and Dragons* (dir. Courtney Solomon, 2000), though he has occasionally played the hero – he was one of the leads in the Hong Kong ensemble cop series *Yellowthread Street* in 1990. Fans of *Red Dwarf* should recognise Mac

McDonald ('Hard-Faced Man' who sits in on Harry's interrogation of Christine), who has played Captain Frank Hollister in the comedy sci-fi show on and off for 15 years. Elizabeth Chambers (the woman who visits the pensioner whose house Tom enters) is currently in a TV commercial as one of a pair of old ladies 'getting down' to some 'kicking beats' from a new hi-fi system courtesy of their insurance company. However, in the 1980s she was better known as Mrs Dominica Van Meyer, inmate of Japanese WWII women's camp in three series of *Tenko*.

[Case Report]

Although Harry has transferred responsibility for liaising with Christine Dale to Zoe, Tom continued to conduct his affair with the CIA agent in secret. After a stolen afternoon at a hotel in Pimlico, Christine told Tom that she had recently received a telex that was flagged for security clearance way above her level. She handed it to him and begged him not to reveal its contents to Harry as he'd be duty-bound to inform her bosses and passing on such sensitive material would almost certainly be viewed as treachery, putting an end to her career.

The telex revealed the existence of a clandestine CIA operation on British soil to 'desensitise' a known assassin – former New York hitman Mickey Karharias – who had been hired to target a then-unknown British figure. Tom took the decision to investigate the matter further. Having memorised the telex, he burned it to remove any direct connection to Christine. The couple then left the hotel separately.

Returning to the Grid, Tom decided to tell Zoe and Danny of Christine's discovery. Partly an order and partly a favour, Tom asked the pair not to inform Harry Pearce until such time as they had enough evidence to prove Christine's claim without implicating her. Instead, Tom took Danny and Zoe to Heathrow airport to keep an eye on the CIA agents that would undoubtedly be watching the arrivals from the USA. Although Zoe did air her concerns that Tom's judgement might be clouded by Christine, she was ignored. Danny noticed a number of figures at the airport who were clearly identifiable as undercover CIA agents. When Karharias arrived at the airport, Danny went to fetch his car to tail him only to find his tyres had been slashed. As Danny radioed in to Tom, one of the CIA agents in the departure lounge looked up at the security glass and waved directly at Tom. Despite the fact that he could not see through the glass from where he was, he had clearly been aware of Tom's presence at the airport all along.

Zoe was still plagued by her worry that Tom was not thinking clearly. In her update meeting with Christine Dale, Zoe challenged the American woman about her dealings with Tom and the telex, and showed her photos of the waving man from the airport who, Zoe had discovered, did not appear to exist on any of the known CIA agent lists. Christine claimed not to know the man but surmised that he was probably deep undercover in Cland-ops, which would explain why there was no official record of him.

After the meeting, Zoe again tried to convince Danny to inform Harry about Tom's new operation. They were interrupted by Malcolm, who told Danny that a valuable piece of surveillance equipment had gone missing (see Gadgets); the last time he saw it was when he gave a demonstration of it to Tom earlier that day. Tom naturally denied taking it.

By this stage, even Danny found he was suspicious of Tom's motives, so when Tom left Thames House, Danny decided to tail him. Walking east from Millbank, Tom made his way towards Brick Lane where he eventually stepped into a shop, A to Z Leather. Tom left the shop after a few minutes, but Danny loitered until the shopkeeper shut up for the night. Danny then broke into the shop and eventually found a safe in a back room that contained a substantial amount of money and an Irish passport for 'Paul Connors' that bore Tom's photo and an old visa stamp for Slovakia.

After hours, Danny arranged to meet Zoe at the Grid to fill her in on his discovery. But when Harry walked in on their discussion, Danny decided to tell him everything. On learning of the existence of the passport, Harry became alarmed. Suspecting Tom might have prepared a bolt-hole for himself in Slovakia, he realised that he had no other option but to pull Tom back in.

Returning home, Tom was surprised to receive a visit from the silver haired man, who introduced himself as 'Herb Ziegler'. He informed Tom that while the CIA had no problems with his relationship with Dale, he was to drop his interest in Karharias, otherwise Christine would be jailed for leaking top secret information. 'Ziegler' left, unaware that Tom had placed onto his coat the tracking device he had in fact stolen from Malcolm. Using the locator palm device, Tom followed him to Euston station where 'Ziegler' had a dead-letter drop. Tom then called Danny and Zoe, who reluctantly agreed to meet him.

Once at the station, Tom brought them both up to speed. The pair tried to convince him to share his information with Harry, but Tom again stressed his worry that their boss would send in special forces who could compromise their received intelligence and possibly put the life of Karharias' still-unknown target at greater risk. An unidentified person arrived at the dead letter drop and left directions for 'Ziegler' to a safe house, at Salter's farm, Feniston, near Sudbury. Against their better judgement, Zoe and Danny agreed to accompany Tom to the farm.

Once in place outside the farm, the team learned that local interference seemed to be blocking their phones, preventing them from contacting the Grid, and so remained unaware that Harry, increasingly concerned by the situation, had informed Ruth that he intended to issue a warrant for the arrest of Tom Quinn on an anti-terrorist charge as a pretext to get hold of him.

There was no sign of Ziegler or any other CIA personnel at the farm. Just as they began to consider abandoning the operation and returning to base, Tom, Danny and Zoe were taken by surprise by masked men who held them at gunpoint and tied them up in the farm's stables. First, Danny was taken to another room to find 'Ziegler' waiting for him. When Ziegler asked him about Tom's fake passport, Danny denied all knowledge; Ziegler's men beat him savagely, then returned him to the stable and took Zoe away instead. Left alone with Tom, Danny challenged him about the passport, but he claimed to have no knowledge of it. Zoe was returned to the stable unharmed only for her and Danny to be injected with a knock-out drug. When the two regained consciousness the next morning, there was no trace left of Ziegler – or of Tom. Trying his phone, Danny discovered that the interference that had blocked them the previous night had lifted. He immediately called Harry to inform him of developments.

With the help of the CIA, Harry brought Christine Dale in for questioning. He informed her that the CIA registry had no record of any telexes being sent by CIA Cland-ops, nor of satellite-intercepted telephone calls from Saudi Arabia to Wimbledon, as she'd claimed to Tom. They did, however, have a record of her receiving a telex sent from a commercial firm based in Islington, a copy of which Harry presented to her. Christine confirmed that it was the message she showed Tom but asserted that she has done what she felt she had to out of love for Britain, and for Tom Quinn. Harry then showed Christine a photo of the dead body of Mickey Karharias that had been found in a Florida storm drain three days before the man had apparently entered the UK. With that, Harry returned Christine to the CIA for further interrogation and summoned Danny and Zoe into the boardroom.

During the debriefing, Danny confessed that he had begun to suspect Tom of planning the whole affair. Zoe refused to believe the accusations, though she too was clearly beginning to have her doubts.

A few hours later, Zoe received a call from Tom. He told her that he had been kidnapped by 'Ziegler', who he'd since learned was actually a former CIA officer called Hermann Joyce. Some years earlier, Tom had recruited Joyce's daughter Lisa as an agent, but after an operation went wrong, Lisa had been left critically injured. Joyce had apparently told Tom that she was now comatose in a hospital in Maine, USA. Tom realised that Joyce had a vendetta against him and had engineered the situation to ruin his reputation as a loyal MI5 agent. Joyce left Tom unconscious in a ditch but when he came round, Tom had managed to find his way to a nearby cottage to call Zoe on an unscrambled domestic line. Desperately, he told Zoe that he had learned that Joyce was planning to target someone in Ipswich and blame it on him. Unfortunately, Tom's information had come too late as Zoe informed him that earlier that day the Chief of the Defence Staff had been shot; he had died just 20 minutes before Tom had called. Harry had of course been listening in to the entire conversation and chose that moment to ask Tom to come in. Aware of his increasingly dire situation, Tom refused. Instead he gave Harry directions so that he could come and find him. He demanded that Harry should come accompanied by just Danny and Zoe – if he saw any indication that special forces had been summoned, Tom promised he'd disappear.

Harry, Zoe and Danny entered the cottage to find Tom waiting for them. In his hand was a shotgun that he'd found at the cottage. He seemed irritated that they refused to believe his explanation until Zoe blurted out that CIA records show that Hermann Joyce had died five years ago in a car accident. He was buried in Sefton, Maine, and his daughter Lisa Joyce was not in a coma, information corroborated by Joyce's widow. Tom remained convinced that the CIA records had been falsified and that Mrs Joyce was therefore part of a much wider conspiracy. As he tried in vain to convince his colleagues of his innocence, Harry tried to reach a signalling device in his pocket to summon a team of special forces awaiting his command in a helicopter just five minutes from the cottage. Tom realised that Harry was about to betray him and, in a panic, he shot Harry and made his escape.

The gun Tom Quinn had used was eventually found on a beach in Suffolk. Though the scene was searched thoroughly, Quinn's body was not found.

[Michael Karharias]

Michael Karharias – known as 'Mickey' – was an assassin in the New York gangland responsible for the executions of 15 people. Though the FBI got close to prosecuting him on a number of occasions, they never managed to get the evidence to put him away. Instead, they pensioned him off, moving him to a safe house in Miami. There he lived a comparatively normal life (the feeling was it was cheaper for the tax-payer than a prison sentence). Then, two weeks ago, Karharias disappeared, leaving his minder gagged and brain-damaged in the back yard. Karharias was subsequently found dead, murdered in the style of a gangland execution, though CIA involvement cannot be ruled out.

[Hermann Joyce]

Hermann Joyce was a top CIA officer renowned for his deep undercover work – he once managed to remain undercover in the former Soviet Union for four years and escaped undetected. His daughter Lisa was once an MI5 agent run by Tom Quinn until her cover was blown on an operation. Joyce died five years ago in a car accident and was buried in Sefton, Maine. The funeral was attended by his wife and daughter.

[Intercepted Telex]

Received: Sat–Def 10.
Length of transmission – 11 seconds
Two male voices
Language – Arabic

First voice: 'Shark arriving London, Heathrow. What news of money?'
Second Voice: 'The million is in the mountains.'
First voice: 'Please advise us of the movements of the British eminence next 48 hours. Greetings from Algallah.'
Second voice: 'God is great.'
Transmission ends.

Location of first caller: Rihad, Saudi Arabia.
Location of second caller: Wimbledon, London UK.
Extreme weather. Do not advise mice.

Working through the transmission, the shark is Michael Karharias ('Karharias' is Greek for shark). 'Money in the mountains' means they were using a bank in Switzerland to pay Karharias $1 million. The transmission means that someone currently in hiding in Saudi Arabia has hired Karharias to assassinate a British member of parliament. 'Extreme weather' refers to a CIA clandestine operation to desensitise an individual on foreign soil, while 'Mice' refers to MI5.

NOTE: Though records of this transmission do not appear to exist in the CIA registry, the above has been traced to a transmission from an undisclosed private company in Islington to Christine Dale's office in Grosvenor Square, which suggests the above is actually a forgery made to look like a CIA transmission (Sat-Def 10 is a known CIA surveillance satellite that concentrates on phone calls in the Middle East).

[Previous Missions]

When Tom first came to the Service he did an operation in Slovakia on secondment to MI6. He apparently fell in love with the country. It's Harry's suspicion that he might have prepared a bolt-hole for himself over there.

Some years ago, Hermann Joyce came to Tom and asked him for help in rescuing his daughter, Lisa. She had become involved with an anarchist organisation. Joyce had been stationed deep undercover in London and so couldn't intervene himself. Tom showed Lisa evidence of what her anarchist friends were really up to and she left them. Soon after, though, Tom recruited her as an agent. Aged 19, she infiltrated a hard-core anarchist cell. But when her cover was blown, the anarchists tortured her for five days before leaving her for dead.

[Disinformation]

In this episode, it's difficult to sift through the facts to work out what is disinformation to maintain someone's cover and what is the truth. It's clear that the telex received by Christine is not all it seems, but whether that's her masters at the CIA covering their tracks or a red herring designed to lure Tom out into the cold is uncertain. Likewise, it's not immediately clear how much of the evidence of 'Herb Ziegler' is a fabrication and how much is true. Does he reveal the hidden truth about his daughter's disability to shame Tom, or does he simply make it all up? While we must assume that the records of his death are the results of a cover-up, it's not beyond the realms of possibility for them to be true, and for 'Herb Ziegler' to be a double impostor.

[Identity Check]

It appears that Tom has prepared an unapproved identity – Paul Connors, born July 25 1975, Dublin, who has links with Slovakia. In Tom's personnel file, there is a record of him using the legend 'Jack Gateman', a man who is apparently from Worcester.

[Quote/Unquote]

Christine: 'Don't you know I've a brute of a husband whose name is CIA?'
Tom: 'Actually, I'm married too. An older woman called MI5.'
Christine: 'I've spied on the bitch.'

Tom: 'Zoe, sometimes don't you find you want to turn this job inside out? Break all the rules just for the hell of it?'
Zoe: 'No, but sometimes "just for the hell of it" I feel like shaking certain colleagues...'

Herb Ziegler: 'You know, scientists are developing a whole new theory of reality. We live in an illusion. What the world is really like is way beyond what our senses tell us, and very, very frightening.'

Tom: 'What the CIA is doing is espionage as rape. They're trying to destroy my personal life with Christine. Why should I trust them with my country?'

Harry: 'Traitors are often vain people; they want us to think well of them.'

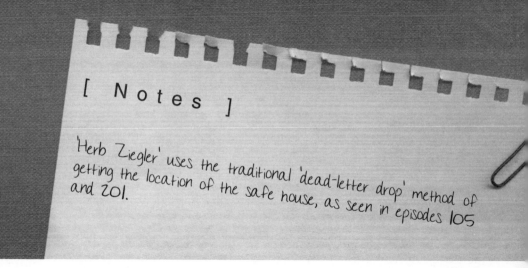

[Notes]

'Herb Ziegler' uses the traditional 'dead-letter drop' method of getting the location of the safe house, as seen in episodes 105 and 201.

[Personnel Report Updates]

Christine Dale's family name was originally Dallich; her grandfather was from Bratislava. Tom has continued his relationship with Christine, despite Harry's direct instruction to end it. Christine finally terminates the affair after growing increasingly worried about the threat of a security breach hanging over her head.

[Gadgets]

The latest in nano-technology, Malcolm's latest toy is a tiny pad, 1cm square. If a person were to touch the pad and then touch anything on a target – clothing, skin, anything – it would place a microscopic transmitter on the target, whose movements could then be tracked via a small palm device. The technology was developed by the CIA, but it somehow fell into Malcolm's lap. His signal to Tom suggests it's something fairly dodgy and questions shouldn't really be asked.

'Herb Ziegler' has a jamming device that can block mobile phones.

[Expert Witnesses]

Nicola Walker: 'My favourite episode is episode ten because Howard [Brenton]'s done such a brilliant old-style spy story. For me, it's that scene where Harry takes

Ruth out of the office and tells her he thinks Tom has turned and says "Are you with me on this?", and poor Ruth has to sit on the same bench overlooking the Thames where Tom had saved her career [in episode 204] and agree to stand by Harry. It's so sad in a way because at that point she finally understands that her loyalty is to the Service rather than individuals within it. She's "proper" MI5 there, part of the machine. I don't know if that's even a good thing yet...'

Peter Firth: 'Harry doesn't enjoy his authority. It's been pushed upon him as a result of his advancing years when I think he would much rather be out in the field like Tom and Danny. But he seems to have become more of an "anchorman", really.'

Matthew Macfadyen: 'I think Tom gets on with everyone in the team, but particularly Zoe and Danny who he really likes and trusts. He's their boss and he does play the boss card when he has to. He also looks out for them in quite a paternal way when he's not that much older than them.'

Producer Simon Crawford Collins: 'There comes a stage where for a show that's the scale of [spooks] you literally can't cope with doing more than a certain amount of episodes and I think ten is probably the maximum that we could achieve, not least for the cast because that's six months of filming.'

'MI5' not 'MI5-not-9-to-5'

As we come to the end of another nail-biting cliffhanger ending for the [**s p o o k s**] team, our cousins across the Atlantic have yet to experience the terrors of boiling chip-fat and exploding briefcases. But it's only a matter of time as [**s p o o k s**] finds itself repackaged for the American market.

Some of the best-regarded TV drama on American screens comes from the UK. It's a boast we Brits have been proud of making ever since we laid claim to the invention of television. Sure, they've got *The Sopranos, Oz, Six Feet Under* and *The West Wing*, but for some crazy reason, the Americans seem to quite like our stuff just as much.

[**s p o o k s**] creator David Wolstencroft has said on occasion that it was the British thriller *Edge of Darkness* as much as the American *Hill Street Blues* that got him wanting to write for television. Shows such as *Brideshead Revisited* and *The Jewel in the Crown* went down enormously well thanks to the fact they perpetuated the image of the British as the snotty 'Empire-builders' that the audiences over there already knew them to be.

Likewise, Joan Hickson's Miss Marple mysteries found themselves a home on BBC America thanks to a rather quaint outlook on death and deception, while *Prime Suspect* and *Cracker* challenged the critics with hard-nosed, often distressing images of life in Britain courtesy of some superbly-honed scripting. Of course, sometimes the way for a British programme to make that vital cross-over is to succumb to 'Americanisation' in the form of reformatted, rewritten remakes: *Till Death Us Do Part* became *All in the Family* with Alf and Else Garnett metamorphosed into Archie and Edith Bunker; *Steptoe and Son* took ten years to be converted into *Sanford and Son*; Russell Davies' Channel 4 drama *Queer as Folk* was picked up by Showtime and somehow turned from ten episodes to three whole seasons' worth of sex, drugs, tears and bitchiness; Steven Moffat's *Coupling*, which some have erroneously described as 'The British *Friends*' is now in the process of relocation, ironically set up as a replacement for the long-running *Friends* huggathon when it finally comes to an overdue end; and *Traffik*, originally a mini-series for Channel 4, became *Traffic*, a feature film directed by Steven Soderbergh, which in turn has become a TV mini-series directed by Stephen Hopkins of *24* fame. Conversely, American shows tend not to make such a successful cross-over (we usually just import it as-is). A rare exception is *The Upper Hand*, a sit-com starring Joe McGann that ran for six years on the strength of scripts recycled from Tony Danza's *Who's the Boss?'*. At the time of writing, [**s p o o k s**] is about to make its debut on American TV, and expectations are running high.

The only real set-back for most British shows is the number of episodes in a series. To be a marketable property, the distributors often have to wait a year or two before there are enough episodes available to form a saleable package. Six episodes might make an attractive mini-series, but that then means the scheduler has got to find an equally strong series to follow it up with, if for no other reason than being able to offer advertisers a strong, consistent run of programming for as long as possible. With the completion of the second series, [**s p o o k s**] is now in the perfect position to be offered to an American network.

While this is not hitting the screens in the shape of a remake (i.e. the show will have the same actors and stories), there are still a number of key differences to the show we know and love. First to go was the title. While the word 'spooks' is widely known in the States, it's perhaps too closely associated with the American CIA and FBI to be of any use to a British spy series (there's also the small matter of the word having certain racist connotations in some areas of America). So [**s p o o k s**] is out and *MI5* is in.

But the biggest change to the show is the duration of each episode. While [**s p o o k s**] is shown on BBC1, a non-commercial channel, it can afford to run for almost a full hour and still fit the available slots in the TV schedule (nowadays, BBC1 tends to only schedule programmes in either 30-minute or hour-long slots). In the USA, however, the schedule has to make room for advertising, usually amounting to around 18 minutes in every hour. Which of course means that each 59-minute episode of [**s p o o k s**] has to cut down to just 42 minutes of *MI5*. For a show that's so tightly packed, with (one would think) not a second of padding, making this happen in a way that doesn't lose any of the story is a daunting challenge for any editor.

The network that was lucky enough to bag such a challenging series was A&E. Nominated for more Emmy Awards in the past two years than any other basic cable network, A&E boasts a strong mix of films especially commissioned for the channel, dramatic series, documentary specials and series such as *Biography*, their award-winning flagship factual series. Available in more than 85 million homes in the United States, it's a major player in the ratings game and a significant coup for [**spooks**] / *MI5*.

The announcement that A&E had acquired the rights to *MI5* was made to the American press in January 2003. Abbe Raven, Executive Vice President/General Manager of the A&E Network was suitably enthusiastic: 'We are very excited to add *MI5* to our primetime summer line-up… This series is drama that's compelling, intelligent, and timely. It speaks to the high stakes in the world around us and it brings our audience high stakes, high quality drama in every episode.' As this book goes to press, the series should have just begun its first run in America. What the American public make of such an uncompromising drama that refuses to pull its punches or throw a veil over criticism of the United States in particular remains to be seen. But guaranteed, they won't have seen anything like it before – and in an era of increasingly formulaic television, that surely will give it a helping hand… ■

[T h e   E n d . . .   f o r   N o w]

Two series, 16 episodes and hopefully more to come. But for the moment, that's it. This book has personally been quite an operation for me. I had to juggle different personalities as my day job, freelance commissions, family and social life all demanded time of me, and I had to make sure that none of the roles interfered with each other or complicated matters more than they had to. I interviewed 'Expert Witnesses' and harangued the staff at Kudos to fuel my addiction with more scripts and viewing tapes each week. I battled an ever-diminishing working schedule as the transmission dates got closer and closer. I faced the trauma of computer infiltration as I acquired a problem with some spyware that had attached itself to my PC and proceeded to assault me with advertising. An attempt to remove this software resulted in a massive system failure that crashed my computer. As a consequence, with just a week to go to my deadline, I had to choose between being able to reboot the machine and continue working (but sacrificing seven years of freelance writing, including the original version of the last quarter of this book!), or losing a week's computer access on the off-chance that all my files could be saved. It was a traumatic decision, but in the end I opted for the short sharp shock solution. I lost everything my PC had once housed and quickly had to reconstruct the last few thousand words of this book again from scratch, all the time trying to put out of my mind the distress at never again seeing the contents of my 'Rainy Day' file where I'd stored magazine feature ideas to pursue another time. I've had to lie, beg, borrow and – well, I won't be so melodramatic to suggest I had to steal...

However, I got to see the second series develop from script to early edit to final transmission and beyond. I was invited to the crew screening of the first episode at an ungodly hour one Sunday morning and got to witness the proud glow the production team gave off knowing they'd each played a part in the creation of something pretty bloody great. I got to play at 'Spooks Master' on the BBCi official site and answer questions from the viewers (although even in the final week, four out of five tended to be 'How can I get a job at MI5?', a question I answered in week two!). And thanks to the BBCi messageboards I also gained an insight into the Muslim community, who despite concerns over their perception of the programme's approach to Islam, on the whole remained articulate and patient with the non-Muslims there as they explained the many differences between the fictional depiction of their lives and the real thing. It's an insight for which I remain truly grateful.

This, then, is my completed report on the mission. My work here is done. Now I think it's time I disappeared for a while. I hear Florida is nice this time of year...

JS,
June 2003
London, UK.

Production Credits

Series Creator	**David Wolstencroft**
Executive Producer for the BBC	**Gareth Neame**
Executive Producer	**Jane Featherstone**
CEO Kudos Productions	**Stephen Garrett**
Producer	**Simon Crawford Collins**

[Series One]

Line Producer	**Leila Kirkpatrick**
Production Co-ordinator	**Annie Gilhooly**
Assistant Production Co-ordinator	**Rachel Peters**
Production Runners	**Emma Brown**
	Wes Gallagher
Director (Eps 1 & 2)	**Bharat Nalluri**
Director (Eps 3 & 4)	**Rob Bailey**
Director (Eps 5 & 6)	**Andy Wilson**
Writer (Eps 1, 2, & 6)	**David Wolstencroft**
Writer (Ep 3)	**Simon Mirren**
Writer (Eps 4, 5, & 6)	**Howard Brenton**
Script Editor	**Karen Wilson**
Script Clearances	**Sarah Hughes**
Production Accountant	**Adrian O'Brien**
Assistant Accountant	**Kerry Bates**
Casting Director	**Gail Stevens**
Casting Associate	**Maureen Duff**
Casting Assistants	**Robin Hudson**
	Claire Saunders
1st Assistant Director (Eps 1, 2, 5, 6)	**Mark Goddard**
1st Assistant Director (Eps 3, 4)	**Francesco Reidy**
2nd Assistant Director	**Paul Morris**
3rd Assistant Director	**Ian Easton**
Floor Runner	**Frazer Fennell-Ball**

Script Supervisors	**Cathy Doubleday**
	Caroline Thomas
Location Manager (Eps 1, 2, 3, 4)	**Ralph Cameron**
Location Manager (Eps 5, 6)	**Malcolm Treen**
Assistant Location Manager	**Jo Manderson**
2nd Assistant Location Manager /	
Unit Manager	**Stephen Chinrey**
Director of Photography (Eps 1, 2, 5, 6)	**Sue Gibson**
Director of Photography (Eps 3, 4)	**Sean Bobbitt**
Camera Operator	**Stuart Howell**
Focus Puller	**Mary Kyte**
Clapper Loader	**Simon Surtees**
Grips	**Jim Crowther**
	Colin Strachan
Camera Trainee	**Phil Taylor**
Gaffer	**Paul Borg**
Best Boy	**Peter Lamb**
Electricians	**Adam Lee**
	Dave Moss
Generator Operator	**Ron Savory**
Practical Spark	**Tony Hannington**
Sound Mixer	**David Crozier**
	Andrew Sissons
Sound Maintenance	**Jerome McCann**
	John Casali
Sound Assistants	**Ashley Reynolds**
	James Harris

Production Designer	**Linda Stefansdottir**
Art Director	**Astrid Sieben**
Standby Art Director	**Anita Dhillon**
Production Buyer	**Andy Grogan**
Draftsman	**Andrew Hill**
Art Department Assistant	**Vivien Panagos**
Art Department Runner	**Kate Good**
Prop Master	**Merl Homer**
Standby Props	**Johnnie Schinas**
	Lloyd Vincent
Dressing Props	**Nick Turnbull**
	Illugi Eysteinsson
	Charlie Henderson
Prop Storeman	**Jeremy Wilde**
Props Assistant	**Toby Morrison**
Prop Driver	**Gary Morrison**
Prop Maker	**Loan Woolfe**
Construction Manager	**Andy Knight**
Construction / Painter	**Philippe Delestre**
	Martin Hull
Construction	**Jim Crippen**
	Wayne Thompson
	Pete Taylor
Standby Rigger	**John "Buzz" Cooling**
Standby Carpenter	**Graham Wardale**
Standby Painter	**Donna Turner**
Costume Designer	**Andrea Galer**
Assistant Costume Designer	**Charlotte Morris**
Wardrobe Master	**Mark Lord**
Wardrobe Mistress	**Sally Crees**

Make-Up Designer	**Alison Davies**
Make-Up Artists	**Fay De Bremaeker**
	Susie Munachen
Editor (Eps 1, 2, 5, 6)	**Colin Green**
Editor (Eps 3, 4)	**Soren B. Ebbe**
Assistant Editor	**Jim Hampton**
Post-Production Supervisor	**Shelley Powell**
Post-Production Co-ordinator	**Clare Buxton**
Post-Production Scripts	**Ilana Epstein**
Dialogue Editor	**Dan Morgan**
Sound Designers	**Julian Slater**
	Michael Fentum
Foley Editor	**Arthur Graley**
Crowd Artist	**Louis Elman**
Re-Recording Mixers	**Nigel Heath**
	James Feltham
Re-Recording Facilities	**Hackenbacker Audio**
	Post Production
Telecine Colourist	**Chris Beeton**
Titles	**Why Not**
Picture Post-Production	**Pepper**
On-Screen Graphics	**Framestore**
Neg Cutters	**PNC**
Composer	**Jennie Muskett**
Stand-Ins	**Colette Appleby**
	Steve Ricard
Stunt Co-ordinator	**Andy Bradford**
SFX Supervisor	**Tom Harris**

Technical Consultants	**Nick Day**
	Mike Baker
Paramedics	**Brian Baldock**
	Elton Farla
	Geoff Smith
	Capital Paramedic Services
Catering	**Clarkson Catering**
Chef	**Ken Clarkson**
Caterers	**Tim Shaw**
	Jamie Roberts
Unit Publicist	**Emma Longhurst**
Account Director	**Joanne McNally**
Account Assistant	**Lucy Speciale**
Unit Stills Photographers	**John Rogers**
	Joss Barratt
Unit Drivers	**Brian Kelly**
	Robert Hole
Unit Minibus Driver	**Alan Nivern**
Wardrobe Bus Driver	**Rob Bourne**
Make-Up Bus Driver	**Mark "Skippy" Edwards**
Standby Construction Driver	**Simon Delmo**
Standby Props Driver	**Jed Simmons**
Assistant to Stephen Garrett	**Wendy Roby**
Head of Development, Kudos Productions	**Claire Parker**
BBC Production Executive	**Julie Scott**
BBC Legal & Business Affairs Manager	**Lisa Cfas**
BBC Script Editor	**Christopher Aird**

BBC Business Development Manager	**Natalie Wheeler**
BBC Picture Executive	**Lynne Burtenshaw**
BBC Senior Publicist, Drama	**Paul Almond**
BBC Picture Publicity Manager	**Donna Richmond**
BBC Brand Manager, Marketing Department	**Sarah Brandist**
Lead Producer, Interactive Drama & Ent,	
BBC Fictionlab	**Ian Strafford**
Head of BBA Fictionlab	**Richard Fell**
Editor, BBC Fictionlab	**Jamie Cason**
Technical Development Manager,	
BBC Fictionlab	**Piers Beckley**

[S e r i e s T w o]

Line Producer	**Alison Barnett**
Production Co-ordinator	**Dani Gordon**
Assistant Production Co-ordinators	**Evie Bergson**
	Jill Greenwood
Producer's Assistant	**Rory Aitken**
Production Runner	**Darren Vincent**
Director (Eps 1, 2)	**Bharat Nalluri**
Director (Eps 3, 4)	**Rob Bailey**
Director (Eps 5, 6)	**Justin Chadwick**
Director (Eps 7, 8)	**Ciaran Donnelly**
Director (Ep 9)	**Sam Miller**
Writer (Eps 1, 6)	**David Wolstencroft**
Writer (Eps 2, 4, 5, 10)	**Howard Brenton**
Writer (Ep 3)	**Matthew Graham**
Writer (Ep 7)	**Simon Mirren**
Writer (Ep 8)	**Ben Richards**
Writer (Ep 9)	**Steve Bailie**
Script Editors	**Karen Wilson**
	Faith Penhale
Script Clearances	**Sarah Hughes**
Production Accountant	**Nicky Coats**
Assistant Accountant	**Kate Cobbold**
Casting Director	**Gail Stevens**
Casting Associate	**Maureen Duff**
Casting Assistant	**Claire Saunders**

1st Assistant Director (Eps 1, 2, 5, 6, 9, 10)	**Andrew Woodhead**
1st Assistant Director (Eps 3, 4, 7, 8)	**Steve Robinson**
2nd Assistant Director (Eps 1, 2, 5, 6, 9)	**Sasha Mann**
2nd Assistant Director (Eps 3, 4, 7, 8)	**Alex Gibb**
3rd Assistant Directors	**Holly Watson**
	Rebecca Symons
Floor Runner	**Marcello M Crispo**
Script Supervisors	**Jayne Spooner**
	Tess Malone
Location Managers	**Patrick Schweitzer**
	Mark Gladwin
	Nick Wade
Assistant Location Managers	**Katrina Fletcher**
	Emma Reid
Unit Manager	**Greg Blank**
Director of Photography	**Peter Versey**
Director of Photography (Eps 1, 2, 5, 6, 9, 10)	**Sue Gibson**
Director of Photography (Eps 3, 4, 7, 8)	**Adam Suschitzky**
Camera Operator	**Julian Morson**
Focus Puller	**Mary Kyte**
Additional Focus Puller	**Steve Scammell**
Clapper Loader	**Simon Surtees**
Grip	**Jim Crowther**
Additional Grip	**Malcolm Sheehan**
Camera Trainees	**Kylie Plunkett**
	Lorraine Jones
Gaffer	**Paul Borg**
Best Boy	**Peter Lamb**
Electricians	**Tony Hannington**
	Adam Lee
	Paul Kemp

Generator Operator	**Ron Savory**
Sound Recordist	**Rudi Buckle**
Sound Maintenance	**James Bain**
Sound Trainee	**Ricki Hanson**
Production Designer	**Stevie Herbert**
Art Director	**Pilar Foy**
Standby Art Director	**Sara Partis**
Production Buyer	**Sara Grimshaw**
Computer Graphics Designer	**Mark Doman**
Art Department Assistants	**Louise Corcoran**
	James Price
Prop Master	**Ray Holt**
Standby Props	**Ron Sutcliffe**
Standby Props (Eps 5 – 10)	**Mike Booys**
Standby Props (Eps 1 – 4)	**Graeme Wetherston**
Dressing Props	**Malcolm Holt**
	Steven Westley
Construction Manager	**Brian Neighbour**
Chargehand Carpenter	**Dave Pearce**
Chargehand Painter	**Steve Williamson**
Standby Rigger	**Andrew Thompson**
Standby Carpenter	**Laurie Griffiths**
Standby Painter	**Eddie Wolstencroft**
Costume Designer	**Iain Macaulay**
Assistant Costume Designer	**Margie Fortune**
Costume Supervisors	**Mark Sutherland**
	Fiona McCann
Costume Assistants	**Pamela Stewart**
	Helen Bell
Make-Up Designers	**Alison Davies**
	Menir Jones-Lewis

Make-Up Artists	**Fay De Bremaeker**
	Susie Munachen
	Sara Riesel
	Laura McIntosh
Editor (Eps 1, 2, 5, 6, 9, 10)	**Paul Knight**
Editor (Eps 3, 4, 7, 8)	**Barney Pilling**
Assistant Editors	**Jim Hampton**
	Zoe Montagu-Smith
Post-Production Supervisor	**Shelley Powell**
Post-Production Scripts	**Ilana Epstein**
Dialogue Editors	**Dan Morgan**
	Rodney Berling
Sound Designers	**Julian Slater**
	Michael Fentum
Foley Editor	**Arthur Graley**
Crowd Artist	**Louis Elman**
Re-Recording Mixers	**Nigel Heath**
	James Feltham
Re-Recording Facilities	**Hackenbacker Audio**
	Post Production
Telecine Colourist	**Chris Beeton**
Titles	**Why Not**
On-Screen Graphics	**Framestore**
Neg Cutters	**PNC**
Composer	**Jennie Muskett**
Stand-Ins	**Colette Appleby**
	Steve Ricard
	Anna India Cash
	Ceri Hughes
Stunt Co-ordinator	**Andy Bradford**
Stunt Performers	**Tony Lucken**
	Gary Connery
	Stewart Clark

Neil Finnigan
Derek Lea
Ray Nicholas
Stuart Clark
Steve Griffin
George Cottle
Buster Reeves
Colin Skeeping
Jason Hunjan

SFX Supervisor	**Neil Champion**
Technical Consultant	**Mike Baker**
Health & Safety Advisor	**Dave Allen**
Unit Nurse	**Terri Sheed**
Catering	**Woodhall Catering**
Location Café	
Facilities	**HNA Facilities**
	Michael Cohen
	Mark Cohen
Unit Publicist	**Karen Sandford**
Stills Photography	**Amanda Searle**
Picture Publicity	**Donna Richmond**
	Marc Moon
	Jane Record
Unit Drivers	**Steve Gibson**
	Brian Kelly
	David Grose
Minibus Driver	**Mark Rothwell**
Costume Truck	**Gary Davenport**

Make-Up Truck	**Peter Gee**
Camera Truck	**Matthew Firth**
Honeywagon/3-Way	**Mike Shipton**
Production Office/3-Way	**Dave Trewin**
	Andy Dorsett
Assistant to Jane Featherstone	**Lucy Lawson**
Assistant to Stephen Garrett	**Maggi Townley**
Head of Development, Kudos Productions	**Claire Parker**
BBC Production Executive	**Julie Scott**
BBC Legal & Business Affairs Manager	**Lisa Cfas**
BBC Legal and Business	**Valerie Nazereth**
BBC Script Editor	**Chris Aird**
BBC Editorial Policy	**Andrea Wills**
BBC Senior Publicist	**Paul Almond**
BBC Brand Managers	**Sarah Brandist**
	Sue Fall
Insurance	**Lizzie Mann**

[Quotation Index]

Who's Who
Matthew Macfadyen – interviewed for Official BBCi website, 2002.

Episode 101
David Wolstencroft – interviewed by Ian Atkins for [**spooks**] series one DVD.
Matthew Macfadyen & Lisa Faulkner – interviewed for Official BBCi website, 2002.
Hugh Simon – interviewed by the author, May 2003.

Episode 102
Debra Stephenson – interviewed for the BBC Digital Press Kit, 2002.
Lisa Faulkner – interviewed for Official BBCi website, 2002.
Bharat Nalluri – interviewed by Ian Atkins for [**spooks**] series one DVD.
Stephen Garrett – 'Ambushing the audience', *The Observer*, June 2 2002.
BBC comments – BSC Bulletin 56, July 2002.

Episode 103
Keeley Hawes – interviewed by Ian Atkins for [**spooks**] series one DVD.
Jane Featherstone – interviewed for the BBC Digital Press Kit, 2002.

Episode 104
Anthony Head – interviewed by Paul Condon for Live BBCi Web Chat, 9 January 2003.
Esther Hall – interviewed for the BBC Digital Press Kit, 2002.

Episode 105
Hugh Laurie – interviewed for the BBC Digital Press Kit, 2002.
Matthew Macfadyen – interviewed by Ian Atkins for [**spooks**] series one DVD.
Peter Wright – quote from the book *Spycatcher*.

Episode 106
Lorcan Cranitch – interviewed for the BBC Digital Press Kit, 2002.
Peter Firth – interviewed by Ian Atkins for [**spooks**] series one DVD.

Spooks Interactive
Jamie Cason – interviewed by the author, April 2003.

Episode 201
Simon Crawford Collins, David Oyelowo & Natasha Little – interviewed for BBC Digital Press Kit, 2003.
Rory Macgregor – interviewed for Official BBCi website, 2003.
Viewer quotes – BBCi [**s p o o k s**] messageboards.

Episode 202
Gareth Neame – interviewed on *Sunday*, BBC Radio 4, June 8 2003
Jane Featherstone – interviewed for the BBC Digital Press Kit, 2003.
Howard Brenton – interviewed by Jeff Dawson for *Radio Times*, May 31 / June 6 2003.
Nicola Walker – interviewed by the author, June 2003.
Malcolm X – *The Autobiography of Malcolm X*.

Episode 203
Keeley Hawes – interviewed for the BBC Digital Press Kit, 2003.
David Oyelowo, Peter Firth & Matthew Macfadyen – interviewed by Ian Atkins for [**s p o o k s**] series one DVD.

Episode 204
Keeley Hawes & Nicola Walker – interviewed for the BBC Digital Press Kit, 2003.
David Oyelowo & Matthew Macfadyen – interviewed for the BBC Digital Press Kit, 2002.

Episode 205
Matthew Macfadyen – interviewed for the BBC Digital Press Kit, 2003.
Hugh Simon – interviewed by the author, May 2003.
Nicola Walker – interviewed by the author, June 2003.
Peter Firth – interviewed by Ian Atkins for [**s p o o k s**] series one DVD.
Stevie Herbert – interviewed for the BBC Digital Press Kit, 2003.

Episode 206

David Wolstencroft – interviewed by Jeff Dawson for *Radio Times*, May 31 / June 6 2003.

Hugh Simon – interviewed by the author, May 2003.

Natasha Little – interviewed for BBC Digital Press Kit, 2003.

Episode 207

Keeley Hawes & David Oyelowo – interviewed for BBC Digital Press Kit, 2003.

Episode 208

Matthew Macfadyen & Peter Firth – interviewed for BBC Digital Press Kit, 2003.

Jennie Muskett – interviewed by the author, May 2003.

Episode 209

Shauna Macdonald – interviewed for BBC Digital Press Kit, 2003.

Nicola Walker – interviewed by the author, June 2003.

Jenny Agutter – interviewed by Ian Atkins for [**s p o o k s**] series one DVD.

Episode 210

Nicola Walker – interviewed by the author, June 2003.

Peter Firth & Matthew Macfadyen – interviewed for BBC Digital Press Kit, 2003.

Simon Crawford Collins – interviewed by Ian Atkins for [**s p o o k s**] series one DVD.

Abbe Raven – quoted in BBC press release.

[R e f e r e n c e s]

Selected Bibliography

Coogan, Tim Pat, *The IRA* (5th ed.) – Harper Collins, London, UK, 2000.

Rimington, Stella, *Open Secret* (2nd ed.) – Arrow Books, London, UK, 2002.

Smith, Jim & Lavington, Stephen, *Bond Films* – Virgin Books, London, UK, 2002.

Wright, Peter, *SpyCatcher* (1st ed.) – Viking Penguin Inc., New York, USA, 1987.

X, Malcolm & Haley, Alex, *The Autobiography of Malcolm X* – Penguin Books, New York, USA, 1992.

Periodicals

Radio Times, May 31 / June 6 2003 – BBC Worldwide Ltd, London, UK.

The Observer, June 2 2002 – Guardian Newspapers Limited, London, UK.

Heat – Far too many issues to single out as I buy it every week, but all of the ones for May–June 2002 and June 2003 came in very handy. Big thumbs up to Chris Longridge! EMAP Entertainment, London, UK.

Digital Media

BBC Digital Press Discs (2002 / 2003).

[**spooks**] DVD series one – Kudos / Contender, 2003.

Web Resources

Official BBC [**spooks**] site (http://www.bbc.co.uk/spooks) – contains episode summaries for every episode, interviews, behind-the-scenes information, and while the series is running it also hosts message boards for fans to chat with each other.

BBC News (http://news.bbc.co.uk/) – all of the real-life stories referred to in this book can be found by searching the BBC News archives.

h2g2 (http://www.bbc.co.uk/h2g2/) – the unconventional guide to Life, the Universe and Everything, which contains thousands of entries on all manner of existence on Earth. You can also pop into the 'Ask h2g2' forum and receive answers from community-members from across the globe.

MI5 (http://www.mi5.gov.uk) – the official online home of MI5, as referenced in episode 203. Contains info on the tasks the Security Service handles every day, the history of MI5 and details on recruitment (which can also be found at the MI5 recruitment site – http://www.mi5careers.info/).

Government Communications Headquarters (http://www.gchq.gov.uk/) – learn more about GCHQ, the department Ruth desperately wants to avoid returning to.

The CIA (http://www.cia.gov/) – Christine Dale's employers have a rather impressive public-facing site with plenty of useful info on one of the most active security agencies in the world.

La Direction Générale de la Sécurité Extérieure (http://www.dgse.org/) – official website of the French Secret Service.

The Internet Movie Database (http://www.imdb.com) – the essential resource for anyone with an interest in films. They accept updates and additional information from registered users, meaning there's the odd (rare) error from an enthusiastic fan, but it's still the best movie resource out there.

The Broadcasting Standards Commission (http://www.bsc.org.uk/) - the full findings of the BSC on the complaints over episode 102 are available in PDF format from their site (http://www.bsc.org.uk/pdfs/bulletin/bulletin56.pdf).

Also available, the BAFTA Award-Winning

[spooks] **season 1** on DVD and video from

Contender Entertainment Group

[spooks.]

[spooks.]
BBC

[season one]

[season one]

kudos

24
The Unofficial Guide

Jim Sangster
£7.99 / Paperback / Published July 2002
ISBN 1 84357 034 3

'Right now, terrorists are plotting to assassinate a presidential candidate, my wife and daughter are in danger and people that I work with may be involved in both.'

A day that begins with simple family trouble soon becomes the longest day ever for Federal Agent Jack Bauer, after Jack is alerted to a possible assassination attempt on Presidential Candidate David Palmer. As the plot thickens and the web of conspiracy widens, the seconds keep ticking away…

This is the unofficial guide to *24*, the hit espionage thriller starring Emmy Award winner Kiefer Sutherland, where each episode marks another hour of real-time drama. With a detailed breakdown of the events as they unfold – the shocks, the surprises and the many twists and turns – it's the essential companion to the most captivating, 'must-see' drama on TV.

24: Season 2
The Unofficial Guide

Mark Wright
£7.99 / Paperback / Published July 2003
ISBN 1 84357 072 6

24, the most talked-about show of 2002 returns for a second day in the life of Federal Agent Jack Bauer, played by Golden Globe winning actor Kiefer Sutherland. Watching the tragic events of Season One unfold in real-time action, it seemed that things couldn't get any worse. But, tomorrow is always another day…

Set 18 months after the first, award winning season, Jack has left CTU and is still coming to terms with the death of his wife. However, the now President Palmer recalls Jack to help CTU he is the only man who can prevent a terrorist plot to detonate a nuclear bomb in Los Angeles in the next 24 hours. With his daughter Kim missing and unable to trust anyone, the race is on to prevent the beginning of World War III. But time is running out…

24: Season 2: The Unofficial Guide contains everything you need to know about the critically acclaimed second season of the hottest show on TV. With mission briefs, detailed episode breakdowns, profiles of the cast and crew and full reviews for every hour, this is the only guide to take you through the action minute by minute.

Tick, tick, tick…

Andromeda
The High Guard
Handbook

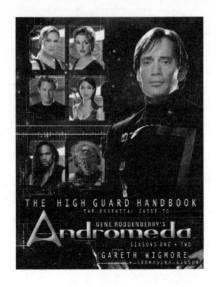

Gareth Wigmore & Thomasina Gibson
£12.99 / Paperback / Published May 2003
ISBN 1 84357 033 5

Set in deep, deep space, Gene Roddenberry's *Andromeda* chronicles the adventures of Captain Dylan Hunt and his motley crew of humans, super-humans, aliens and AI's as they fight to restore peace and posterity to a fractured universe.

Debuting as the highest rated SF show in syndication, the Gemini Award-winning *Andromeda* continues to scale the heights of television excellence all over the globe with superb writing, a supreme case and superlative visual effects.

The High Guard Handbook is an indispensable bible for *Andromeda* fans. Contained within its pages are the most definitive episode guides ever written for the show, giving detailed plot information for each of the episodes in the first two seasons. Peppered with race histories and character biographies, in-depth character guides and exclusive interviews with the cast and crew of the show, this is truly the guide for fans.

ER
The Unofficial Guide

THE UNOFFICIAL GUIDE

Mark Jones
£9.99 / Paperback / Pubished February 2003
ISBN 1 84357 035 1

ER – The Unofficial Guide covers the first eight series of the award winning medical drama that has kept viewers gripped for nearly a decade. This illustrated book is packed full of detail on each episode and charts every character from Carter's early student days to Carol Hathaway and Doug Ross's rocky relationship and Mark Green's tragic illness.

ER – The Unofficial Guide also contains season overviews, colour pictures, cast biographies and special features on the best episodes from each series. An indispensable guide for the true *ER* enthusiast.

Six Feet Under
The Unofficial Guide

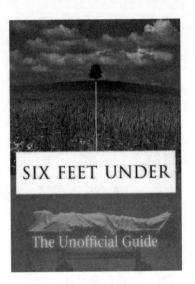

Paul Condon
£7.99 / Paperback / Published October 2002
ISBN 1 84357 037 8

This is the story of the Fishers, a family of Funeral Directors trying to make sense of life and death in the City of Angels. With more sex, swearing and genuine irony than you'd expect from an American TV show, the Golden Globe award-winning *Six Feet Under*, created and co-written by Oscar winner Alan Ball, is one of the most talked about programmes this side of Heaven or Hell.

This unofficial guide to the first two seasons of *Six Feet Under* selects the highlights of each episode and offers a handy route-planner to the Afterlife. Detailing the funniest (and most poignant) moments, cast and crew biographies, soundtrack references, and a complete listing of every corpse to grace the Fisher & Sons slab, *Six Feet Under : The Unofficial Guide* is an indispensable handbook to this original and innovative drama.

The Matrix Unlocked

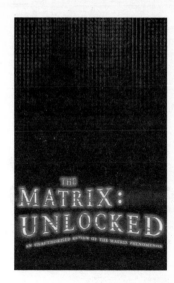

Paul Condon
£7.99 / Paperback / Published July 2003
ISBN 1 84357 093 9

The Matrix	The movie phenomenon
Matrix: Reloaded	The groundbreaking sequel
Matrix: Revolutions	Reveals the final piece of the puzzle
The Matrix: Unlocked	The critical analysis

Take the Blue pill... examine the fiction
What is the Matrix?
Who's in control?
Who can you trust?
What's in a name?
Take a journey into the Matrix universe…

Take the Red pill... examine the facts
Deconstruct the Matrix phenomenon from conception and creation to cast and crew.
Review the place of the Matrix within the science fiction movie genre.
Branding, iconography and manipulating the media, Matrix-style.
Filmographies, biographies, listings.

Covering *The Matrix*, *Matrix: Reloaded* and *Animatrix*, this is the first book written by a fan, for the fans.